SOMETHING IN THE AIR

*American Passion
and Defiance in the 1968 Mexico City
Olympics*

RICHARD HOFFER

University of Nebraska Press
Lincoln

First Nebraska paperback printing: 2011

Originally published by Free Press, a Division of Simon & Schuster Inc.

Library of Congress Cataloging-in-Publication Data
Hoffer, Richard.
Something in the air: American passion and defiance in the 1968 Mexico City Olympics /
Richard Hoffer.
p.   cm.
Originally published: New York: Free Press, 2009.
Includes bibliographical references and index.
ISBN 978-0-8032-3629-5 (pbk.: alk. paper)
1. Olympic Games (19th: 1968: Mexico City, Mexico) 2. Olympics—Participation, American.
I. Title.
GV7221968.H64   2011
796.48—dc22   2010043597

For Carol

CONTENTS

1 **Roads to Glory**   1
Dogs on Ice, a Third-String End, and Robin Hood

2 **1968**   13
Tanks on the Streets, Dead on a Balcony,
and Audie Murphy

3 **Speed City**   21
Pineapple Upside-Down Cake, "Tutti Frutti,"
and Jack Daniels

4 **Countdown to Mexico**   37
Lymphocytes, Zip Guns, and ROTC

5 **Boycott**   51
Hells Angels, a Petrified Pig, and More
Ralph Henry Barbour

6 **A Desperate Innovation**   69
Rolls, Straddles, and an Airborne Seizure

7 **The Trials**   81
Spondylolisthesis, Brush Spikes, and
a Brutal Stomping

8 **Denver**   99
The Anarchists' Convention, a Vote for Nixon, and
a Cold Chill

9 **Mexico City**   103
Thin Air, Fresh Paint, and Shots in the Night

Contents

10 Opening Ceremony   119
Flag Dipping, a Family Feud, and 6,300 Pigeons

11 And They're Off   139
A Grisly Tableau, Pinochle, and a Guided
Missile Launch

12 Protest   153
Licorice Hammers, Tommie Jets, and Black Gloves

13 Harder and Higher   163
The Little Stinker, Beauty and the Beast,
and Hollywood Agents

14 Aftershocks   175
Pimped-Out Socks, a Mutation Performance,
 and Sparks Under His Feet

15 Monday   197
A Grunion Hunt, a Crying Tigerbelle,
and a Jig for Joy

16 Week Two   215
A Cuddlesome Junior, a Ragtag Bunch, and
a Blonde in a Beehive

17 Pappy's Boys   227
Rateros, Various Sarges, and a Lucky Picture of
a Pretty Girl

18 Going Home   235
Boy Scouts, Psychedelic Mileage, and a Black Bra

Acknowledgments   246
Notes on Sources   247
Index   251

What was it like? It was horrible, horrible. It was like those thunderstorms that rolled over the Village. They'd happen late in the afternoon, thunder and lighting, huge thunder-claps, and if you were in the cafeteria you'd dive under the table. It would just scare the hell out of you. But that's what it was like. It was huge. It was frightening. It was exciting. It's a feeling I still get. It was wonderful.

—ED BURKE, *U.S. hammer thrower, on the 1968 Olympics*

Chapter 1

ROADS TO GLORY

Dogs on Ice, a Third-String End, and Robin Hood

GEORGE FOREMAN CURLED under the floorboards, the pipes above groaning and dripping, not at all safe, not anywhere near as safe as he'd like. German shepherds barked in the night, a siren sounded at a closing distance. His knowledge of police detection was extremely up-to-date, coming from the cop shows of the day, as well as Fifth Ward intelligence, passed from curbside gangster to gangster. So he knew what he was in for. On hot, humid nights such as this, Houston police traveled with blocks of ice on the backseat, and the dogs were forever refreshed. Moreover, the canines, already heroic sniffers, now came in a genetically upgraded setup and could smell through water. This he had seen on television, maybe on *The Fugitive*. He couldn't remember. The rain outside, the cracked pavements slick with it, offered Foreman no protection from the man-eaters whatsoever, and he quivered in the crawl-space dampness.

He was small-time, just sixteen, but, up to that point anyway, had tremendous ambition in the hoodlum department. He hardly ever went to school, had no taste for sports, and enjoyed the enforcer's brand of respect. He hoped someday to have a scar on his cheek, and often wore a bandage there until he could acquire his trophy gash. It was 1965, and there was still a juvenile delinquent mystique. Foreman imagined coming back to the neighborhood, having done the inevitable time, say at Huntsville, the kind of guy who "maybe killed a man once." The Fifth Ward would take note of such bona fides as those.

In the meantime, even at this young age, he was not an unappreciated prospect. The Fifth Ward was a hard neighborhood on Houston's north side—small frame cottages with diminishing levels of upkeep, and where violence was a kind of recreation. There were about twelve gangs in operation, each representing the special interests of the young men there. There was a dancing gang, for one thing, reenacting *Hullabaloo* and *Shindig!* in the alleys, and Foreman's far more intimidating Hester House outfit for another. Aside from being on the lookout for the dancing gang, Foreman's bunch occupied themselves with low-level extortion, and quickly earned a local reputation.

"First time I met George Foreman, I was in the seventh grade, hanging around the neighborhood store." This is from Lester Hayes, a future NFL star, whose own gang specialized "in doing mischievous things, pillaging the 7-Eleven, things of that nature." Foreman, older by a few years, approached him for the loan of a nickel, and a bite of a hamburger, which he then consumed in its entirety. "The next time I saw George, the idea of a nickel was null and void. I loaned him a quarter. It seemed to me huge inflation was taking place. Of course, I would have gone home and found a quarter for him if I didn't have one on me. He was a very, very big kid and had a reputation for savage butt kickings. That was his forte. So by the early age of twelve, I had met George Foreman twice and I found both occasions extremely taxing."

Foreman ranged far and wide, at least in the Fifth Ward, extracting his "silver coin toll," as it was known, and administering beatings, often independent of income opportunities. There was no question the money was important, insofar as it could relieve his chronic hunger. He was almost always ravenous, his appetite driven as much by the prospect of scarcity as an actual need for food. His house, absent a male breadwinner, was not one of plenty and, anyway, there was just too much sharing going on. His mother worked at a restaurant for a time and would bring a hamburger home when she could for the six children to share, cut in slivers, and Foreman would nurse his little bite, smell it, kiss it, and glower fiercely at his sisters' remains. But, really, the beatings were the main attraction for him.

It wasn't very long before Foreman and his gang graduated from squeezing little pups like Hayes to rolling citizens of greater means and, of course, more resistance. This wasn't a matter of right or wrong, which Foreman simply could not recognize, but career advancement. Foreman had despaired of anything grander. Once, caught playing hooky in the sixth grade, a cousin said, forget about it, no big deal. He wasn't going to amount to anything anyway. Foreman protested furiously, announced he would, too, amount to something. In a great show of righteousness, he put on his school clothes. He was so angry he very nearly did go to school. But not that particular day, nor many others like it. No, this was the life for him, except for that barking.

The Hester House gang, a workaday bunch, generally used the proceeds from their daytime depredations as a kind of capital investment. They bought cheap wine, emboldened themselves even further, then ranged into the night hunting for larger prey. It became a routine, a job even. Foreman, the biggest and most ferocious among them, that bandage doing something for the imagination if his increasing hulk didn't, would level the victim, hold him down while the others—"the sneaky fellas"—would rifle the victim's pockets, and they'd all take off with their bounty. They could hear the guy screaming behind them, although it never seemed to produce any effect, and soon they'd slow to a walk and count their money. It never once occurred to Foreman that he had committed a criminal act; he was earning a paycheck.

But this time, hiding under one of the Fifth Ward's increasingly decrepit cottages, he suspected he had crossed a line. The mugging had been no more or less violent than usual, screams in the night now a workplace hum for him, but the sirens were a surprise. This, evidently, was against the law! More than that, it was just wrong. The barking dogs argued his worthlessness in a way no adult ever had. Each yelp, their nostrils flared with the scent of George Foreman, was an accusation: *You're no good.*

Foreman was suddenly stung to tears, not so much by the possibility of arrest, which seemed unavoidable now that this new breed of smeller had been unleashed on him, but the sudden recognition that he was embarking on a pointless and, indeed, hurtful life. He prayed then and there, underneath the house, that if ever he got out from under it, he'd never steal again. And if God wasn't sufficient to the task, the dogs being what they were, he covered himself with the dripping sewage from above, slathering it all over himself, a course of confusion, one of last resort for sure, that had been proved somewhat reliable in a cop show of the day.

In time, the sirens moved on and the barking grew faint in the night, and the young Foreman, smeared with slop, uncurled and got on with his new life.

Just because he was from the right side of town (and in little Medford, Oregon, incredibly, there definitely was a right and a wrong side), Dick Fosbury was no less insulated from adolescent angst than the next teenager. He was tall, gangly to the extreme—"a grew-too-fast kid," his coach would say—and not good enough at anything he did to keep him above the hallway fray. Here's how it was at Medford High: Say, Steve Davis (right side of town) spotted Bill Enyart (wrong side), first day of school. He'd grab Enyart by the neck, turn his collar inside out, the source of shame right there on the label, visible for all. "J.C. Penney!" he'd howl. And keep in mind, Enyart was the high school fullback, on his way to becoming Earthquake Enyart, an NFL career down the line. Class distinction offsets brawn, any day. But do you think Davis would recognize Fosbury's shared aristocracy (Fosbury's father was a truck sales manager, his mother a secretary)? If Davis caught Fosbury loitering by his locker, he'd punch him right in the shoulder.

Medford's bucolic charms—peach and pear orchards spreading beyond its modest cityscape (population twenty-five thousand, the interstate still a few years off)—are not a factor during years such as these, not even in these early sixties. A life of privilege, a house on the right side of town, small comfort. Loving parents are great, but not as much use as you'd think when it comes to the ritual humiliation of simply growing up. Did Dick Fosbury have it made? Of course. Was every need fulfilled? Sure. But he was a child of yearning, insufficient achievement, bad skin, his talents such that nobody could possibly take him seriously or dare predict any kind of success for him. He was beginning to understand the curse of the bell curve—he might very well be average. And when his head hit the pillow, no matter how soft the bed, he was as miserable as the next guy.

Nothing was really working out, which might be the shared condition of all thirteen-year-olds, but still seems a singular disappointment if it's not working out for you in particular. Fosbury hoped to play basketball. In fact, being 6'4", he fully expected to. But Medford High was loaded and had six guys who could dunk (Steve Davis, a bigger and better athlete, one of them). Fosbury sat on the bench. His senior year, in 1965, he remained at home when the team, top-ranked in the city, went to the state tournament, so that more promising underclassmen could gain the experience. He played football until his junior year, a third-string end (Davis was the primary receiver), when Enyart came up under him during a blocking drill and knocked his two front teeth out. Enyart was his great pal. In the cold of winter, when the coed physical education classes would be given over to dancing inside the gym, the two would stand together on the court's sideline, trying to remain invisible, which was complicated by their tremendous height. Come ladies' choice, though, Big Lois would pick Fosbury, and that would be quite a scene, the two of them doing the Freddy, their long arms and legs flapping out like hinged two-by-fours. So Enyart felt bad about those teeth.

Fosbury's real love was track. It figures that the arts of locomotion are the first to be explored and, although Fosbury quickly recognized he wasn't going to amount to much in the races, his lankiness was not as big a handicap when it came to the high jump. This was something he could do, sort of. Beginning in the fifth grade, he made that his event, using his height and long legs to get a quarter of an inch a year out of the antique scissors jump, the one where you more or less hurdle the bar sideways, landing feet first. Ladylike, almost. The technique had been considered outdated since 1895 when straddling jumps were introduced. Still, Fosbury got as high as 5'4" in junior high and he'd even won one or two meets a year.

In high school, it was a different story. His varsity coach insisted on the far more acceptable Western roll, which lays the body out and consequently raises the center of gravity above the bar for most people who try it. But Fosbury couldn't get the hang of it. The takeoff foot seemed all wrong. The whole thing was awkward. His first competition as a sophomore was an invitational, a meet of probably twenty teams, perhaps as many as sixty high jumpers involved, and Fosbury failed to clear the opening height of 5'3" on all three chances. He was going backward! If he maintained this level of improvement, he'd be tripping over curbs in no time. Steve Davis, meanwhile, was clearing 6'0", pretty easily.

Maybe there comes a time in every kid's life when he confronts his mediocrity and submits to the tyranny of normalcy. A life without expression. Just another guy, one of a bunch, not a single trait or talent to mark him in a crowd. Maybe. Fosbury, all of fifteen, wasn't there yet. He hadn't been crushed. On a twenty-five-mile bus trip to Grants Pass, for a rotary meet with a dozen schools, Fosbury stared out the window and decided he was going to do whatever it took, make one last jump. If he finished the year at 5'4", the same he jumped in ninth grade, he was done, doomed to a third-string life. That's all that was at stake in his mind.

Fosbury reverted to the scissors for his first jump that day (his coach, sympathetic, had given him a grudging permission) and was relieved to clear his junior high height of 5'4". That wouldn't be enough either, not really. The other jumpers were still warming up, waiting for the bar to be set at an age-appropriate height, while Fosbury continued to noodle around at his junior-high elevations. If they, or anybody else, had been interested, though, they might have recognized an odd transformation taking place right before their eyes, more like a possession, really. Fosbury, his futility undermining all previous instruction and experience, was now arching himself ever so slightly as he scissored the bar, his rear end now coming up, his shoulders going down. He cleared 5'6". He didn't even know what he was doing, his body somehow reacting to a desperation, unrelated to the actual effort. His third round, his body reclined even more, by degrees for sure, and he made 5'8". This was not a world-class height, not even a Steve Davis class height. But there sure was something odd about the jump.

The other jumpers began to gather, coaches looked up from their charts. There was something odd about this, crazy even. For his fourth attempt, Fosbury took a surprisingly leisurely approach to the bar and—My God! He was completely flat on his back now!—cleared 5'10". The coaches began arguing among themselves. Was this even legal? Was it safe? Should this be allowed? What, exactly, had they just seen? This was an event that measured advancement by fractions of an inch, sometimes over the course of a year. Fosbury, conducting his own quiet defiance, had just improved a half foot in one day.

• • •

Madeline Manning did not get off to a fast start, not in life anyway. She was born in the ghetto, brought up in a broken home and, at the age of three, diagnosed with spinal meningitis. She missed a lot of school, didn't do so well when she could attend, and, really, what did it matter? In the early 1950s, the disease was as often fatal as not.

Although treatment offered her a shot at survival, her prospects were not otherwise bright. She was told she'd be a slow learner and was not going to be terribly active in any case. Anemia was a problem, also general nausea. How many times did she duck behind buildings, out of sight of her playmates, to throw up? If sports was sometimes a ticket out of poverty for the black athlete, it was not yet that much of a ticket in the fifties, not much of one for a woman ever, and of no cash value whatsoever for a black woman with spinal meningitis.

Manning was too shy to join anything. The last thing she was going to do, given her condition and her temperament, was play school sports. If it hadn't been for President Kennedy's Council on Youth Fitness, with its physical testing and call for exercise, she might not have kicked up her heels in play. But, when she finally did, tapping into an undiscovered genetic bonanza, the youth coaches were all taken aback. She was fast!

Alex Ferenczy, who ran the Cleveland Division of Recreation Track Club, got her to come out for his team in 1964. At first she was only running sprints. But Ferenczy needed her for the 440-yard dash in one meet and just threw her in. "You got the longest legs," he explained. "Just stretch your legs around the track." She wondered what that meant. She basically ran one 100-yard dash, then added three more. She'd run 59 seconds, flat.

Within a year, Manning became the first woman, albeit a sixteen-year-old one, to ever run 55 seconds in the 440-yard dash. She was becoming quite an attraction on the track circuit and got an invitation to the Toronto Maple Leaf Games to run what was becoming her specialty, the 400 meters. However, the program was switched. While she was in the bathroom, the other girls voted to make it an 800-meter race. Panicked, she called Ferenczy, who told her to relax, don't worry about winning, just use it for training. Maybe, if she wanted to compete, just follow whoever's in front, see what happens.

The pressure off, she settled into a leisurely jog, following a runner from Hungary. It seemed a pretty slow pace to her, but it wasn't as if she'd ever run this distance before. Probably the others knew what they were doing. With a lap and a half to go, though, she heard the Hungarian's coach yell—in perfect English; it would have been much different if he'd encouraged his runner in Hungarian—"Leave her, she's getting tired." *Leave me?* Manning thought. What you mean, leave me? She poured it on and broke the world record in a time of 2:10.2. There was a surprised reaction among the attending press, as they jostled for photos of this new sensation. The next day's sports pages had a picture of Manning, her shoes under her armpits, terrified, racing away to the exits. "Who Is She?" the headline in Toronto's paper read, answering in the subhead, "She's Just a High School Girl."

John Carlos had no excuse for his banditry; he was from a strong, intact family that valued hard work above all, no matter the circumstances. What he had was inspiration. The English fellow in green tights, spreading the wealth. That was his game. He and his partners would break the seals on the freight cars, in the rail yard right by Yankee Stadium, collect their foodstuffs, and race back to Harlem. Carlos had made a deal with the bridge operator at 155th Street, bargaining for time in his flight from cops. "Give me five minutes," he'd plead. The bridge operator, who could swivel the bridge to allow river traffic (and thus deny vehicular traffic, apparently at his whim, or just the requirements of thieves), would say, "Three minutes, that's all I can give you," and accept a portion of the swag for his part in the escape. Three minutes was plenty for Carlos. He was plenty fast. He'd be back in his neighborhood redistributing the nation's wealth, a real Robin Hood, but a black one, before that bridge ever swung back.

It was not like the cops didn't know what was going on. Or who was responsible. They just hadn't caught him in the act yet. That tall, mouthy street kid, quick on his feet. One afternoon, two exasperated detectives showed up at Macombs Dam Park in the Bronx, where Carlos was at play, and forcefully informed him that they were onto him, if they couldn't quite apprehend him. One of them, a huge guy, grabbed Carlos's face in one hand, his fingers wrapping it from ear to ear. "You think you're fast," he told Carlos, "maybe you should run track." Carlos didn't feel he was being presented with a decision, and understood his career in crime had just drawn to a close and, furthermore, that he would be joining the New York Pioneer Club.

For a while it appeared he might be a better thief than athlete. He showed up for his first practice in cordovan shoes and jeans and ran a few 660s and, on his fourth try, passed out. Maybe he would have quit right there, but the laughter from the better-equipped runners (they had track shoes) formed a challenge for him. He persisted and soon was beating anyone who'd ever mocked him. Even so, he was not terribly impressed with the sport, when the highlight was traveling to Buffalo for a meet, eight kids stuffed into an Oldsmobile station wagon. Still, he kind of enjoyed running.

When he was seventeen, in 1962, his coach entered him in a meet in Madison Square Garden, where Carlos made it to the finals, placing high enough to earn a trip to a meet in Trinidad. Carlos's education at Manhattan Vocational and Technical High was stronger in the trades than geography, and he couldn't quite place the country, if that's even what it was. He'd never heard of it, didn't know if it was something you ate or wore. He consulted his father, the neighborhood cobbler, who confessed he couldn't place it either. Together they walked around the corner to the library and found the community globe and spun it around a few times, not seeing Trinidad at first. Finally, his father located it. "There," he said.

Carlos inspected the location but became more confused than ever. "What's all this blue," he asked his father. "Where's the roads?"

•   •   •

Glory germinates unpredictably, and not just on the streets of Houston, in Tennessee cotton fields, or in Oregon suburbs, but also in the warrens of Queens, the wheat fields of Kansas, on the banks of the Charles River. This much we've surely learned, that there's no one source for greatness. And just try to figure who's going to fully blossom, never mind where. Misfits, prodigies, late bloomers. Kids mostly, nobody who could possibly know better, all shielding their dreams from the light of day, guarding their ridiculous ambitions against a reality their parents and teachers might enforce. All of them hanging on to that same frayed thread, the one that dangles all hopes: you just never know.

Chapter 2

1968

Tanks on the Streets, Dead on a Balcony, and Audie Murphy

THE OLYMPIC SUMMER GAMES announce a cultural cease-fire every four years. It's a two-week window of peace, an international armistice, a truce. Simmering world rivalries are rendered harmless, if not quite irrelevant, by the presumed innocence of youth at play, by the comparative silliness of the competitions, by the Games' political pointlessness. It's not possible to keep global scores if the triple jump must do the work of a border skirmish. Totals matter, performances are important. Everything is up for bragging rights, prestige always at risk. But when it comes to the imposition of entire ways of life, which is always the business of powerful countries, nobody confuses a high jump with a moon shot.

The antiquity of the Games, with their strange and curious traditions, helps to give the quadrennial enterprise further remove. The athletes earn medals, they carry torches, they march, they dress in native garb for at least the Opening Ceremony. It's all very quaint. And it is the rare platform where differences can be celebrated, certainly understood, definitely forgiven. Countries that are wrongheaded, possibly even evil, in every other aspect of behavior, are moral equals when it comes to a foot race. Agendas are purified in such simple strivings, and ordinary bitterness dissolves in fair and friendly competition.

The Olympics, in other words, enforce the best parts of childishness, with an emphasis on fun, the joy of sports, the possibility of camaraderie. And everything that is adult, the inevitable corruptions of spirit and the equally inevitable insistence upon conflict, is eliminated. The Olympics are the last refuge of idealism, democratic and welcoming, not so much a brief settlement every four years as a rigidly orchestrated recess. With prizes at the end.

The year 1968, with its long-overdue recess scheduled for October in Mexico City, would test any such notion. The calendar of catastrophes was extensive, and it was sustained and it was transformative and it would have been naïve to think the events of the year would not somehow penetrate the Olympic dream state. Not since World War II had there been so much deadly commotion throughout the world. Not since the Civil War had the United States been so riven.

Although the year began in disaster—Pope Paul VI's call for just a half day more of peace in Vietnam was defiantly rebuked within hours on New Year's Eve, gunfire laying waste to Vietnamese Marines—the disaster did not really start in 1968. The war in Vietnam, begun years before, when the United States had intervened on behalf of its sometimes democratic ally, South Vietnam, was continuing not only to sap resources but also to deplete national morale. A small presence there had grown to more than half a million troops—most of them draftees—in three years under President Lyndon Johnson. Already some nineteen thousand Americans had died and there was no promise of victory, or even withdrawal. Instead, the United States was culling nearly twenty-five thousand kids a month who had other plans for themselves.

It was a platform for protest for a boisterous generation that was desperately looking for one. The generational divide was now exaggerated by all manner of media—music, film, even art—so that it didn't take much to put parent and child at odds. It probably never does, but whereas the fifties had been an era of vague unrest—not even Marlon Brando's Johnny Strabler could put his finger on it ("Whaddya got?" was all he could muster for a source of rebellion)—the sixties had specific drama. A teen in 1968 could afford to take himself very seriously if he was about to be drafted into the deadly jungles of Vietnam.

And the war continued to deteriorate, suggesting more call-ups yet. Just as it was beginning to seem the war was winnable and General William Westmoreland was telling the American people that he was seeing "light at the end of the tunnel," the enemy unleashed January's Tet Offensive, catching the United States and South Vietnam completely off guard. Although the rolling assault was eventually repulsed, the sight of Vietcong guerrillas running rampant inside the U.S. embassy in Saigon (not to mention putting more than a million more South Vietnamese under Communist control) did not encourage anybody watching the newscast back home. This war would take years more. Enthusiasm and support were being replaced by protest, especially as an always agitating youth found its voice.

Demonstration was now part of every college curriculum. College seniors in 1968 had been high school seniors when John F. Kennedy was assassinated. They had long been sensitized to political disappointment, their youthful optimism now shaded by distrust of a bungling and much older generation. Columbia University was the first to go down, students taking over the campus in April. The vague unrest of an earlier decade was now quite particular, and it was being organized into powerful groups: the Students for a Democratic Society (SDS), the Student Nonviolent Coordinating Committee (SNCC), and the National Mobilization Committee to End the War in Vietnam (Mobe). Antidraft riots were now more likely to have at least a parade permit.

This kind of disaffection was not unique to the United States. It couldn't possibly have been a coincidence that students in France were swelling Paris streets at the same time, battling riot troopers, shutting the country down, and nearly toppling the government of Charles de Gaulle. Or that leftist groups in Germany and Italy were likewise rampaging. Youth throughout the world, that baby-boom generation, had never been so rich, so safe, so educated, so self-satisfied. So alert to inequity. Young people around the globe, it seemed, wanted to overthrow the established order.

But the affronts kept coming. In April the civil rights leader Dr. Martin Luther King, Jr., was shot dead on the balcony of a Memphis motel. In June, another charismatic leader with youthful appeal was killed, when Bobby Kennedy was shot after accepting victory in the California presidential primary. Youthful unrest was not an abstraction, their activism no longer an uninformed arrogance. These were injustices by any measure, to any generation. And in the meantime, they continued to be drafted into a war it was obvious that this country could not win.

More than anything else, though, it was the state of race relations that continued to roil America. This, too, predated 1968, at least in its origins. The Civil Rights Act of 1964 and the Voting Rights Act of 1965 may have done much to give America's black population legal standing, but they proved frustrating, maddening, to the extent that they could not provide dignity as well. If you were young, or especially if you were young and black, outrage was the only logical reaction.

From 1964 through 1967, there were riots in more than one hundred cities, the preponderance of them race related. No summer during those years had gone without long and fiery uprisings. Los Angeles was struck in 1965, Newark and Detroit in 1967. Detroit had been on fire for four days as rioters railed against the denial of housing, jobs, and opportunity. By the time National Guardsmen clanked in atop tanks—there were fifteen thousand troops deployed in all—forty-one of the rioters and looters had been killed. This was not in a faraway rice paddy; this was in a first-world U.S. city.

A study that year put some figures to the frustration. The median income for black families was just $4,000, one in three blacks in one of the country's ten worst slums was jobless, the unemployment rate was actually rising and was more than double the rate of whites. Blacks could more reliably use anecdotal evidence to prove the lingering inequality. More than a century after they'd been freed, blacks still could not sit at some lunch counters, use some drinking fountains, go to many schools.

Although they definitely could participate in an unpopular war, dying in it at a disproportionate rate, in fact. Dr. King had not been one to meddle in the country's wartime policies but he could not help himself from doing some especially brutal arithmetic, comparing U.S. defense spending to inner-city funding. It worked out like this: the United States was spending $332,000 for every enemy killed in Vietnam, but just $53 per person in its antipoverty programs.

"We're taking the black young men who had been crippled by our society," he said, "and sending them eight thousand miles away to guarantee liberties in Southeast Asia which they had not found in southwest Georgia and East Harlem. So we have been repeatedly faced with the cruel irony of watching Negro and white boys on TV screens as they kill and die together for a nation that has been unable to seat them together in the same schools."

The war in Vietnam was a kind of accelerant in an increasingly explosive environment. It stepped up the octane, for sure. It also seemed to give a vocabulary to an outrage that had been hard to artic-ulate. Now when Cassius Clay refused induction into the armed ser-vices in 1967—he had earlier explained he had "no quarrel with them Vietcong"—young blacks were able to better express their fury over the hypocrisy of their nation, a country that demanded their service but would not ensure their liberties. The sacrifice of Clay, who would soon become Muhammad Ali, was instructive as well. For his refusal to fight the war he was stripped of his heavyweight title and sent into an exile from which his wits returned, but not all of his boxing gifts.

It was ridiculous, of course, to think that only a year later the single most aggrieved part of this society—young black men—would join in a bit of athletic pageantry without complaint, or worse. Olympic authorities, a cadre of old white men redolent of their privileges, were accustomed to a tremendous level of compliance, of submission even, from the athletes they paraded in front of the world. The athletes were mostly very young, extremely eager, and, according to the normal dynamics of sport, used to doing what they were told. They always ran very fast, chasing the carrot of fame, approval, history. And they did it for free, and they did it agreeably, and they usually did it very well. Until 1968, there had never been a more reliable performer than an Olympic athlete, a U.S. one in particular.

However, this was 1968, and the normal channels of authority were breaking down. Old white men retained the upper hand but were no longer as convincing, given the disappointments with continued obedience. The payoff just wasn't there. Democracy was an abstraction and, no matter the promises or the legislation, was not available to all. There was still a determination among athletes, black and white, to represent their country and their sport, but that determination was now being divided by other loyalties. How, they wondered, could they perform their athletic duties and still honor the demands of their generation, or their race? Be tough, wouldn't it?

In 1968, while the world was looking forward to the proven restorative powers of another Summer Olympics, there was above all a gathering indignity in the United States. Of course, not everyone could see or feel it. Certainly, the old white men in charge of the affair did not and wouldn't have been prepared or willing to accommodate for it, in any case. Would things have been different in Mexico City, during the supposed spiritual sabbatical, if they'd been more tolerant, less arrogant? Would those two weeks, as blessed as they would be in world-class achievement, have been a less terrifying time for the young people there, a less infuriating time for those who watched?

Mel Pender was the kind of miracle this country produces from time to time, proving to all doubters that anything really is possible in America. He joined the army right out of high school, just seventeen, but with a wife and baby to support. He was patriotic, sure, determined to represent his country in the spirit of Audie Murphy, the World War II hero. The slights he suffered as a young black man in Georgia, or even in the army, did not discourage him in the least. Refused service in a Baltimore diner—while wearing his Airborne getup, uniform and jump boots, he just moved on.

He had to love the country, though, for all its flaws. Where else could a twenty-five-year-old man, spotted fooling around in a football game in Okinawa, be plucked from obscurity and turned into a two-time Olympic sprinter, one of the fastest men in the world? After only eighteen months of training, Pender made the 1964 Olympic team. And then, after a tour of duty in Vietnam in 1967—he was an infantryman on river patrol during which his unit did some "crazy things" and he earned a Bronze Star—he returned to make the 1968 team at the age of thirty-one. Where else would this be possible? Thinkable? This truly was a land of opportunity.

And yet, didn't he deserve better than this? Taking his mother to see her doctor, he was directed to a waiting room at the back of the office, furnished with only a small table, one chair. Up front there was a plush reception area, nice couches. But, here, "this is where the black folks had to be." Pender protested. This was absurd. Nobody was more American than he was, had done anything greater for the country's cause, or risked more. He had already represented his nation in one Olympic Games, that great big postcard to the rest of the world, and then he'd gone back into the jungles, fighting hand-to-hand with the supposed enemy. "Boy," he was told, "sit here or don't sit at all."

What if the old white men had known about Captain Mel Pender?

Chapter 3

SPEED CITY

Pineapple Upside-Down Cake, "Tutti Frutti," and Jack Daniels

SPEED CITY WAS MOSTLY A declaration of importance, although it was an actual location as well. It was this country's sprint capital in the 1960s, issuing streams of dash men far disproportionate to its size and resources. By its population San Jose, California, probably should have been called Speed Burg, situated as it was on the outskirts of track Gothams like Cal and USC—but little San Jose State and the amateur clubs that surrounded it had become too vital to world athletics to be thrown any such slight of designation. And, in every sense but having been elected, Coach Lloyd "Bud" Winter was its mayor.

Winter, who had taken over the track-and-field program at San Jose State College in 1944, was not the guy you'd pick to create a powerhouse, local, national, certainly not international. Although he looked the part—doughy, cap askew, stains on his tie if he happened to be wearing one—he had scant pedigree when it came to big-time sports. A high school coaching job in Watsonville, another at a junior college in Salinas. That was it.

He was more than a coach, though. He liked to cook, wrote children's books, fished around the globe, and dabbled in something we might recognize as Transcendental Meditation. His athletes were not surprised if he used a duck call instead of a whistle during practice, or if he showed up in his hunting boots, or wore a coonskin cap. Actually, given how scattered he seemed, there was very little that could surprise them when it came to Coach Bud Winter.

His big thing, maybe the most surprising thing for all that, was relaxation. In 1941, when he had first shown up at San Jose State as an assistant football coach, he had dropped in on a course given by the Stanford professor Dorothy Hazeltine Yates—its title: "Psychology for Aviators and Athletes." As it happened, Winter was about to be as involved with the former as the latter. Joining the war effort that year, he was assigned to a preflight school in Monterey, where he developed a program based on Professor Yates's relaxation techniques. "Using positive affirmation to inspire cool confidence," he later wrote, he was able to put would-be pilots to sleep within two minutes . . . and this was with recorded machine-gun fire for a lullaby.

Once back at San Jose, and now fully in charge of track and field, he was determined to apply these same techniques to sport. Relaxation became his coaching mantra. "Loose as a fish net," he'd tell his boys, over and over.

As mantras go, it was fairly counterintuitive, especially for those quick-timed events that value the sudden release of tension. It was one thing to preach clench-and-release, to hand out zenlike key words, and even to take groups of athletes into darkened rooms and more or less hypnotize them. He'd walk around in the darkness, stopping to lift an arm, and if that arm wasn't completely limp and didn't collapse immediately to the floor, he'd do the routine all over again. But it was another to tell his sprinters not to go all out. "Far more can be achieved with four-fifths effort," he told them.

So it was that Coach Winter would bark, "Take those wrinkles out of your forehead," as his runners steamed down the track. Or, "Drop those shoulders." He understood proper technique and, in fact, was in the vanguard of such niceties as, say, dominant leg movement. His various books on running (*So You Want to Be a Sprinter, So You Want to Be a High Jumper,* all featuring a recurring cast of characters such as Jack Champ, Joe Chump, and Coach Egor Beavor) eventually became required reading for any coach and athlete, and turned Winter into a sought-after speaker in later decades. However, his strange infield advice seemed nonreproducible. "Just let the meat hang on the bones," he'd yell.

But if his track ideas were New Age, his other coaching techniques were old school. He believed, like all coaches of the day, in the absolute stupidity of athletes, or rather in their willing suspension of disbelief in the face of any authority figure. "Boys," he'd tell them, right before a big meet with Cal, "*Sports Illustrated*'s flying in, and if we don't win the mile relay, we won't get the cover." Basically, there wasn't anything he didn't expect them to believe. He rubbed the calves of his runners with a liniment he swore had been purloined at a nearby fairgrounds. "It's racehorse medicine," he'd whisper. And he had an inexhaustible supply of white pills he'd peddle before meets: "Don't tell anybody." Once he produced some "special water" he said he'd been able to smuggle out of France.

Another time he introduced his boys to the daughter of an Indian maharaja before practice. The daughter made a showy gift of some silver medals, believed to have come from the maharaja's own sash. Winter thereafter distributed them, one at a time, to his "Athlete of the Week." And here's the thing: the athlete of the week would wear that piece of tin everywhere, to practice, to class, back at the dorm. . . .

And if they weren't gullible, they were probably hungry. Winter operated on a shoestring budget and had just six scholarships to divide among forty-some athletes, many of them inner-city kids from across the Bay, a lot of them without spending money. Back in 1957, Ray Norton, who was one of Winter's first black recruits to the nearly all-white university, adjusted wonderfully to Winter's sprint program. Norton had been a 10.2 sprinter in high school but, soaked in Winter's doctrine of relaxation (his cheeks jiggled comically as he bore down to the tape), became the world record holder with a 100-meter time of 9.3 seconds. Campus life was another story. The fastest man in the world still had to eat walnuts from a tree in the backyard to feed himself on weekends. He complained to his coach.

Winter was sympathetic, but also inspired. There wasn't much he could do to solve poverty or race relations (a dozen or so university athletes—the Good Brothers, virtually the only blacks on campus—were holed up in segregated housing, a lot of them scrounging food), but he did recognize an opportunity for all parties involved. Soon after, Norton, teased by the others for being Winter's pet, had alerted him to this particular inequity. Winter initiated a rewards system that increased his athletes' performances while at the same time filling them up. If a guy had a good practice, Winter handed him a little token, without the fanfare that might otherwise cause embarrassment, which could be redeemed for a milk shake and a hamburger at Original Joe's.

Winter fine-tuned this system over the seasons until it came to depend almost entirely on the motivational properties of baked goods. There was a hierarchy of cakes—stirred up by his wife, Helen, and his assistant's wife, Betty Bonanno—according to the importance of the achievement. A personal best got you this, a school record that, and so on. As the sixties approached, the world turned, faster and faster, but not so much at San Jose State's red-cinder track. Barely an hour's drive north, in San Francisco, the nation's young were rallying around an assortment of causes and even beginning to marinate themselves in psychotropic substances (reports were sketchy), but Bud Winter's runners were quite happily blasting out of the blocks for a shot at a pineapple upside-down cake. That, by the way, was top cake, baked only on occasion of a world record. Helen and Betty, as it developed, were about to become very familiar with the recipe.

•   •   •

Speed City would become important for more than just its runners. The mix of characters whom Winter assembled, however unwittingly, would have a profound effect on culture, history even, that went well beyond sports. As Winter laid groundwork for some of the greatest achievements in sports, he was also overseeing a tremendous generational transformation. It was partly the times. What coach, what school president, what leader of any stripe wasn't overseeing generational transformation in the sixties? But it was mostly Harry Edwards. Very odd, highly unlikely, that in his recruiting Winter would gather in one place all the combustible ingredients to blow up 1968. His thinking at the time, this Harry Edwards might be worth a few points as a discus thrower. Flamethrower, more like it.

Harry Edwards grew up in East St. Louis, under what might be called formidable circumstances. The family lived on beans and paste, drank boiled drainage-ditch water, and used an outhouse until it simply collapsed upon itself. He pulled his own teeth. His meaningful relatives came and went, seemingly at the whim of the Illinois penitentiary system (sometimes Iowa got involved). Violence and madness was all around him. His mother disappeared when he was eight; the next time he saw her she had eighty-six stitches from a street brawl. He was the first male from his neighborhood to graduate from high school, and the academic diligence that made that possible derived mostly from the availability of school plumbing. By becoming, and remaining, an athlete there, he was able to take hot showers. Otherwise, being a poor student, Edwards would have gone the way of many of the other black, poor kids there. Which is to say, nowhere.

But Edwards stood 6'6" and weighed 220 pounds upon graduation—still growing—and he could do terrific things in a variety of sports. He was, a coach would later observe, "a terrific animal." Edwards was not yet so sensitive to exploitation that he would decline a college education on its account and so found himself a multisport prospect at faraway Fresno City College in 1960. He was there just one quarter, long enough to set a junior college record throwing the discus (and to grow two more inches and add twenty more pounds), when San Jose State located him.

He ended up being a pretty fair basketball player at San Jose State, a very rugged guy in the lane, and was a good enough all-around athlete, certainly a big enough one, that at least two NFL teams would eventually show some interest in him. However, it would be his brief experience on Bud Winter's track team, while less fulfilling athletically, that would transform him and, as we shall see, a lot of 1968.

College was both a surprise and a disappointment to Edwards, as it might be for any black kid in his circumstances. And San Jose State, if it weren't unique among campuses around the country, certainly presented its share of mysteries for Edwards. For one thing, he didn't seem to be able to find a place to sleep there.

His first thirty days at San Jose were spent in the home of a freshman coach. Administrators couldn't find "another negro" to pair with him in a dorm room. For a while after that he was stashed in a fraternity house that had been vacated during renovations.

There were some stinging peculiarities to being a black student there. When Edwards wondered why he couldn't join a fraternity on campus, while his supposed white brothers on the basketball team could, Coach Stu Inman told him he probably wouldn't like fraternity life, anyway. That didn't really answer his question, or solve his problems. Never mind the hurt and shame of exclusion. For an eighteen-year-old kid, racism might not yet be the overarching issue of his generation, but it could be a very serious impediment to a social life. Of the seventy-two black students on campus at that time, most of them were athletes. The harshest math of all was that only six of them were women.

The college was not encouraging any mixing and matching, either. That separation was institutionalized, if not outright decreed. Edwards couldn't join the drama club, for one example, even if he wanted, in case theatrical events transpired that required him to hold hands with a white woman.

Edwards and his buddies did manage to negotiate one roadblock, showing up for the extremely popular Co-Rec dances that were held Wednesday nights. It was the *co* part, as in coed, that drew them. Not the music, which was Top 40, soul hits leached of all their soul by performers like Pat Boone. "Tutti Frutti"? By Pat Boone? They showed up for the ladies, who lowered the color barrier altogether when it came to dancing. Anyone who was nimble enough on his feet could outmaneuver segregation for at least a few hours each week.

Not forever, as it turned out. The sight of black men dancing with white women may not have been actionable, but it was alarming. Organizers changed the format from Top 40 to country-and-western, thinking that might restore racial order. Edwards and his pals were surprised to see their first Virginia reel, but hardly unnerved, certainly not as discouraged as event planners might have hoped. "We can do this," Edwards said. And they could. Enough was enough, and without any hope of introducing a musical theme potent enough to suppress the oncoming crisis of integration (polka?), planners suspended the program altogether.

Edwards was making other discoveries as well, namely that he was kind of smart. He had arrived, as he put it, "unscathed by education." However, here were books, teachers, ideas. Once he had learned how to read, really read, he began devouring books by black writers— James Baldwin, W. E. B. Dubois, Ralph Ellison, Langston Hughes— anyone who might be speaking to him. He was always reading, always. After games on Saturday night, when his teammates drifted off to their campus celebrations, Edwards headed for the library. He was such a regular that, as part of the nightly closing routine, a student would make a run through the fourth-floor stacks to make sure Edwards was clear. He'd been locked in there a few times.

San Jose State was not then accustomed to black athletes leveraging their scholarship opportunities into an actual education. They were almost always quarantined in physical education or, if they were truly confident, nudged toward the academic ghetto in sociology known as *parole and probation*—social work. Edwards argued for a stronger program than that and, after meeting with the department head, was accepted as a full-on sociology major, no parole and probation, but provisionally. Right up to the day he won the Woodrow Wilson Fellowship to attend graduate school at Cornell, Edwards had to carry a blue three-by-five-inch index card, get it signed by his professors, and drop it off at the athletic department every Friday, thereby proving he had somehow remained eligible for another week.

None of this made him angry. Racism was something to be overcome, sure, but it appeared he had the necessary means to do it. He was smart, persuasive, and determined. And he was able to get his way, for the most part. It was hard to find apartments off campus, difficult to conduct a proper social life, needlessly complicated when it came to getting an education equal to white students. None of it, to judge by his progress, was impossible. What did make Harry Edwards angry was Bud Winter.

What was it about those two? Winter had high hopes for him and, for that matter, Edwards himself had dreams of becoming an internationalist in discus under Winter's tutelage. He was stretching himself pretty thin, a full course load and two sports, but it was not unreasonable to think he could top his junior college throw of 180 feet and get into elite territory. He'd done better in practice his sophomore year but never translated his talent into performance, come a competition. One teammate suspected Edwards was not buying into Winter's relaxation techniques. "Maybe he didn't use his key word," the teammate snickered.

Edwards wasn't buying into anything, as far as Winter was concerned. He had become increasingly alert when it came to the foolishness of authority and the abuse of privilege. Often, of course, it was the aggravation of somebody using the advantage of his race, but cruelty has no end of inspiration. Maybe somebody just wants to get ahead.

That's what Edwards suspected of Winter. That sophomore season, Edwards ranging into Olympic distances with his throws and now co-captain of the track team and everything looking up for him, he began to look around a little. He noticed that Winter had stockpiled about eight sprinters, all of them black and all of them from cities back east, and had more or less left them to their own devices. He had split two scholarships among them, meaning nobody had a real place to stay or a real meal to eat. They were cadging dining room tickets off Edwards; that was the first he knew about it. He learned that some of them were sleeping on mats and blocking dummies in a shed by the football stadium, others ganged up in basement rooms off campus. Some didn't even have track shoes.

Edwards arranged to meet Winter in his office to explore the situation on their behalf and was surprised to discover his capacity for spontaneous outrage, his sudden disregard for position. "As captain," he began, "I want to know what the hell you're going to do about these guys, because it's just not right. You should at least give them tickets home, because they're stuck here."

Nobody was more surprised than Winter, though. "Well, what do you want?" he asked Edwards. "What business of this is yours?"

Edwards, just eighteen, raised his bulk and walked over and flipped the lock on Winter's door. "Nobody talks to me like that," he said. "But to bring generation after generation here, and just dump them, that's not right. You are a racist lowlife."

Winter was flustered. "You're through," he said. "You're done. You'll never be on a track team as long as you live." And he got up and carefully sidled by the towering Edwards, unlocked the door, and left. Edwards was by no means done.

• • •

Art Simburg was everything Harry Edwards was not. He was white, affable, nonthreatening, and eager to please, yet he became an important part of the Speed City mix as well. He was a sportswriter for the student newspaper at San Jose State but never once let his journalism duties get in the way of his enthusiasm for the school's track program. He was more fan than reporter, to tell the truth. He was down at the track every day, the chubby guy with the curly black hair, schmoozing with the guys. And he wasn't in search of news so much as family. He adored these guys, loved Bud Winter's crazy scene, and lived off the wild energy they all generated together.

By 1962, when Simburg arrived from Berkeley, Winter's program was already in full swing. Ray Norton, who had made the Olympic team in 1960 as the country's best sprinter (though he finished a shocking last in both the 100-meter and 200-meter events in Rome, and capped the trip off by botching a baton pass in the 4x100 relay—a showing that wasn't very relaxed), had helped announce little San Jose State as the sprint capital—Speed City, indeed. After Norton came Dennis Johnson from Jamaica, who had run five straight 100-yard races at 9.3, as well as several more sprinters like him. It's true, the ranks could be kind of thin at times, with Winter dicing up those few scholarships (one might get room and board while the other would get only tuition) and, as a consequence, too many of the runners had to run too many events at meets. Everybody knew to scatter when Winter had to fill out that fourth leg of the medley relay, the strange little entertainment that ended meets, where some already overused sprinter would be drafted for the heave-inducing anchor mile. "Oh, Bud," Johnson would whine, in a lilting Jamaican accent, seeing Winter approach, "I would be a vegetable." Still, Speed City was about to get a lot faster and Simburg was doing his part.

Tommie Smith arrived in 1963, right out of California's San Joaquin Valley, where he and the rest of his family had picked grapes and chopped cotton. Smith, maybe because of that cotton, had recognized at an early age the value of finishing first. His father, who hated to lose a hand in the fields, said Tommie could run track only as long as he won. "If you run and you get second place," he told him, "you'll have to be back in the field with the rest of us next Saturday." Whether he was motivated or just fast, nobody knew. But Smith won pretty much everything he entered, and he entered nearly everything.

At Lemoore High, in the San Joaquin Valley, he not only played end on the football team but also played basketball. He was, in fact, the team's all-time leading scorer by the time he graduated. It was track, though, where he was creating most of the school's excitement. He ran almost all the races, from the 100-yard to the quarter mile, and all the relays, too. And he never lost. His junior year, he set a long jump record at one of the meets, going 24'2". Simburg was covering the state high school championships for his Berkeley High newspaper when Smith won both the quarter mile and the long jump. He was agog at the silky stride, so smooth he hardly seemed to be trying at all. Later, at San Jose State, he was sure to mention the prospect to Winter.

Smith chose San Jose State when USC, his other suitor, said he'd have to go through junior college first. Anyway, San Jose was closer to Lemoore and 100 yards was 100 yards, wherever you ran it. He couldn't have picked any better, as it turned out. While the status of a black male on campus remained as problematic as it was when Edwards was an undergraduate—there were still no more than twenty blacks at the school, almost all of them athletes—the curriculum for high-kicking runners couldn't have been greater. This was the perfect finishing school for Tommie Smith, the sprinter, at least.

Winter wasn't exactly starting from scratch here, but Smith was, of all his runners, most ideally suited to his strange methods, available for further improvement. The first thing Winter did, once Smith quit his other sports at San Jose and announced his full-time commitment to track, was take him out of the quarter mile, or 400-meter, race at this level. This was not an obvious thing to do; Smith didn't have great early speed and might have prospered in the longer races if he had just learned to run the curves. Winter recognized something special in that stride and knew if Smith bought into his program he'd have another Olympian, greater than all the others. He even improved his start to the point that, when he wrote his next instructional book, *Jet Start*, Smith was the guy on the cover, situated perfectly in the starting blocks.

Just as Winter had turned an ordinary 10.2 sprinter into a 9.3 Olympian, he was wringing seconds out of an already very quick Smith. Smith ran a 9.4 100 yard his sophomore season and matched the 200-meter world record on the straightaway at 20.0. To those who watched Smith run, well, it was just unbelievable. It seemed his knees were now above his competitors' heads. It seemed, moreover, that he was actually accelerating at the end of his races, when others slowed.

With results to show for it, Smith became more than Winter's student; he was practically a disciple. Even the relaxation techniques appealed to him. He began wearing sunglasses on the track, not for the style of it, as most thought, but because they would keep him from squinting. In a leg-bone-connected-to-the-hip-bone kind of way, Smith would explain how squinting eyes would cause a cascade of tension down his body until not even his feet would work properly. The Polaroids cost him $1.98; it took Smith eighteen days to save for them.

Simburg, meanwhile, was an effective and thoroughly industrious witness to all this, chronicling Smith's magnificent come-from-behind spurts in relays, his effortless finishes in the 200 meters, for the *Spartan*. The editorial budget being what it was, though, Simburg had to make his own way to meets. He began selling *Great Books of the Western World* door to door so he'd have money to travel with the team. There was an unexpected payoff to his track itinerary, even beyond the journalism. He met Wyomia Tyus, the great Tigerbelle, at a meet in Oakland and, to the surprise of his friends at San Jose, began an unlikely courtship with the Olympian.

And, by now, the track team members were his friends. He had grown so close to Smith in particular that, when they each got draft notices in 1966 (by then college enrollment no longer assured a student safety from the draft), Winter wrote letters that got them deferments, providing they both join ROTC. "He can't compete without Art," the coach explained about Smith to the draft board.

There was now a question as to whether Winter could recruit without Art. Simburg had been insinuating himself into Winter's program until he was more team manager than reporter, helping some of the guys find apartments, and, going one step further, acting as an unofficial recruiter as well. Simburg was making it his mission to add some depth to the team, to relieve Smith of the burden of running so many races in events. It just killed him to see his friend pull a muscle, the shallowness of Winter's teams forcing Smith into overload. At the 1966 NCAA Championships, Smith had run his sprints, even placed third in the long jump, but strained his leg in the 440-yard relay and was unable to compete in his best event, the 220-yard final. It was almost a crime. So Simburg had his eye on a quarter-mile specialist right in town, over at San Jose City College, somebody who could really take some heat off Smith.

Not that Winter was unaware of Lee Evans, or that anybody was. Evans may have been a brutish runner, at least compared to the grace of Smith, but he was pretty quick around the curves and was among the top-ranked quarter milers in the country. However, it was Simburg, relieved of all NCAA constraints, who was doing the actual lobbying. He went to one of Evans's meets at San Jose City College, watched him run the half mile then saunter across the infield without so much as taking a deep breath to assume his place in the 220 yards immediately afterward. Simburg approached him later and, failing to consider Evans's tremendous ego, said, "Imagine running at San Jose State, imagine the relay team—you running third, Tommie the anchor." It was not the best possible pitch. Evans wondered why in the world he'd be running third.

Evans joined anyway, though he soon began to have second thoughts. It seemed to him that Winter failed to appreciate his talents and was way too protective of Smith and his invincible aura. In fact, Winter was doing everything he could to keep them apart in any quarter-mile races. Let them both keep their auras. Evans might have lived with that if only Winter could remember his name. It got so bad, as far as Evans was concerned, he was thinking of leaving. Following a meeting with the coach, though, the two came to an understanding and Evans agreed to stay. One other thing might have helped cement their relationship: Like Smith and Simburg before him, Evans received his draft notice shortly after he arrived. Winter told him not to worry, but Evans did worry and, sure enough, he was ordered to take a physical and told to prepare for induction. Again, Winter told him not to worry. Evans never heard another thing from the draft board.

There was one other guy out there who everybody agreed ought to be a voting citizen of Speed City. They kept running into this crazy New Yorker, John Carlos, at meets. He was a wild man, dangerous even. Nobody wanted to be on his bad side. Until he came along, track had been a fairly polite sport, and there hadn't been much of a tradition of trash talking while in the blocks. Then Carlos went and told USC's O. J. Simpson, lined up next to him in the Coliseum, that he was going "to go up his ass and out his eyes." Whoa! But he was fast. The first time the San Jose gang saw him, when Carlos was still at East Texas State, was in the Modesto Relays, where he ran a scorching 45.0 leg in a mile relay, in his fifth race of the day. Whoa, again!

The interest went both ways. Like many others in the track world, Carlos had been hearing about Bud Winter, about the loosey-goosey atmosphere at San Jose, and about this tremendous influx of talent, not to mention the growing social consciousness there. The situation intrigued him, especially as how the folks at East Texas had seemed to be reneging on promises. Anyway, it was Texas. He was more of a city kid. Evans talked it up with Carlos and so did Simburg. Smarter this time, Simburg asked Carlos to imagine the relay—Smith third, Carlos the anchor.

Carlos agreed to a more formal recruiting process and so found himself in Bud Winter's living room on Cherrydale Drive one morning. Small talk proceeded, pleasantries exchanged, climates compared. Helen appeared from the kitchen—possibly having made a pineapple upside-down cake for another of Smith's records—to ask if anybody would like a drink, perhaps iced tea. Carlos said he'd like a Jack Daniels. There was enough of a stunned silence that Carlos felt it was necessary to address it. "We're all men here, right?"

Winter laughed. One man's "special water" was another man's Jack Daniels. "Give him what he wants." Carlos signed up that day.

Simburg was thrilled at this assembly of talent, the greatest concentration of elite runners in the world, all together, a big family, doing knee-high drills to Winter's cassette player, laughing, debating the politics of the day, screaming down the red cinder lanes at ridiculous velocities, the coach tootling away on his duck call, telling them, "loose jaws, loose hands."

"Isn't this great?" Simburg asked the coach at one point, so much excitement right at hand, about all anybody could hope for. Winter agreed. "It is great, Art." Pausing, he added, "But I'm afraid we might have to hold our meets at the Napa State Mental Institution."

Chapter 4

COUNTDOWN TO MEXICO

Lymphocytes, Zip Guns, and ROTC

THE OLYMPICS ARE ALWAYS a reliable feel-good story, a clockwork confirmation of national values. Hard work paid off; sports could rehabilitate our troubled youth; risk was rewarded; nobody was ever washed up or too old or too young or too poor or even too rich (and certainly not too black); anything was possible, anything could be overcome. It was a tried and true incubator of miracles, as dependable a source of inspiration and idealism as the United States could muster. At the end of it all, there'd be heroes, guaranteed. And it was possible to mark their arrival on the calendar.

The 1968 Games didn't figure to be any different. The times were different, yes, things a little iffy back home, but amateur athletics was a function of youth, mostly, and could be counted on for a certain level of compliant accomplishment. Those hopelessly unruly kids, in their beads and long hair, might be handing pamphlets out on the streets, or worse, but the athletes were pretty much insulated from politics, discord, drugs, and music. They were clean-cut and comfortably regimented, in uniforms on the field, matching

37

blazers off. Athletes took coaching—orders, that is—and their good behavior was a historical given, as was a high level of achievement. Over the years, there had been escapades, of course, but nothing so frisky as to interfere with their national dedication to bringing home the gold. They were steadfast foot soldiers in the war on, well, any other way of life.

There were hints by 1968, some loud and clear, that these young athletes were no longer sufficiently cocooned by their sports. Rumblings here and there, suggesting a social awareness that could degenerate into activism, but going into the Games early in that tumultuous year these hints were still possible to ignore. Perhaps it was necessary to ignore them. As bad news, and the social rifts that gloomy news created, continued to grow, the Olympics became more and more the last remaining promise of national unity. This was something everybody could get behind, right? Had to be.

The buildup of any important event like that requires rooting interests, actual people. It was one thing to hope for some kind of international conquest, something that the USSR had been delivering with a disheartening regularity (the brutish Soviets had exceeded U.S. medal totals in all three of the previous Summer Olympics, rattling U.S. confidence as much as Sputnik had). But, in the United States, with its comparative emphasis on individualism, idols were needed. The Olympics were not only a national reassurance but a star-making machine as well, churning out faces for Wheaties boxes. Stardom was a kind of reassurance, too.

So it was critical to single out some suitable prospects. Anybody who'd be asked to bear the burden of a country's hopes ought to have a high likelihood of success, naturally, but also had to conform to certain regulations for heroism. In a country that was trying to cope with a variety of revolutions, both small and large, it probably wasn't going to help to present one more fire-breather. That would not have a calming effect. Better to showcase somewhat more conservative and traditional qualities: hard work, stoicism, modesty. A potential gold medal winner who'd be uplifting and unthreatening. Totally inoffensive, but still, someone who could run fast or jump high.

That would be Jim Ryun, by an enormous consensus. He was already known as the Schoolboy Miler and the Kansas Flyer by the time the 1968 Olympics began to loom over the country and he was very much available for poster-boy duty for the Mexico City Games. First, he ran what you'd have to call one of the Games' all-important crossover events, a race that could promote water-cooler talk in all corners of American life. Along with the 100-meter dash, the mile (actually the metric mile) was something everybody could presume expertise, no special knowledge required. Everybody knew what a mile was, and, thanks to the obsessive quest to run it under four minutes, everybody knew roughly how long it should take to finish it.

The four-minute mile—a barrier that had finally been broken by Roger Bannister in 1954—had been an important threshold for a long time, sort of like the speed of sound or the summit of Mt. Everest. It was just something that everybody knew about. Duels at that distance garnished almost all of the attention in track and field and always had. Paavo Nurmi, the Finnish distance runner, had name recognition long after he set the mile record of 4:10.4 in 1923. Names like Glenn Cunningham, Herb Elliott, and Bannister continued to resonate long after their records were eclipsed.

The Olympic version, the 1500-meter race, was actually about 120 yards shorter, meaning a sub-four-minute mile had become difficult to translate. They'd been doing sub-four-minute 1500 meters for more than half a century and without that nominally convenient threshold it was a little more difficult to chart advancement around the water cooler. Still, it was the rough equivalent of the mile and, metric system be damned, it retained its status as an Olympic mainstream event.

Second, there was Ryun himself. He was a middle-distance prodigy, having run his first sub-four-minute mile his junior year in high school, just a year after he took it up. That year, just seventeen years old, he had made the 1964 Olympic team but, sick with a cold in Tokyo, failed to make the final. In the intervening four years, during which he enrolled at the University of Kansas (following his high school coach, Bob Timmons, there), Ryun more than fulfilled his promise as America's next great miler, becoming unbeatable. By 1968 (he had already been *Sports Illustrated* Sportsman of the Year, his earnest face appearing on the year-end 1966 cover), Ryun held world records in the mile and the 1500 meters, an unofficial world record in the half mile, and the American record for the two miles. Going into the Olympics, he hadn't lost in the mile or 1500 meters in more than three years.

There was more to him than that. As the *New Yorker* declared in a summer profile, "The story of Ryun's development into a super-athlete, and an altogether impressive young man, reads like one of those early-twentieth-century novels for sports-minded boys." The profile added, "It serves to remind us that in this confusing age, when growing up is in some ways much tougher than it used to be, there are American kids who actually have the stuff that Ralph Henry Barbour and Owen Johnson claimed for their improbable heroes."

Thankfully for the *New Yorker* (and *Life* and *Look* and *Newsweek* and *Sports Illustrated* and all the other magazines that sent writers to Kansas that summer), Ryun required no invention. He was the real deal, sprung from the Kansas heartland of modest folk. His father worked the night shift at the Boeing plant in Wichita (together they would go out to the backyard and actually look at Sputnik, as if to gather incentive) and his mother sold dresses at Sears. He was hard-working beyond normal understanding, as any middle-distance runner might be. Visitors to Kansas reported that Ryun covered more farmland than most combines—usually fourteen to sixteen miles a day, skipping over golf courses, rural highways, college tracks.

It was further reported that Ryun was so "mentally disciplined and so physically inured to this grueling schedule" that he could maintain a B average at the University of Kansas ("instead of majoring in physical education as most star athletes do, he has been studying for a degree in business administration") and acquire a sufficient proficiency in photography to earn him several awards and a summer job at the *Topeka Capital-Journal.* In addition, he still had the time to conduct a courtship serious enough to result in engagement to "a pretty and lively blonde."

This was the Olympic prototype, driven yet well-rounded, assured yet grounded. Good-looking kid, too. And if Ryun wasn't already the face of these Olympics, he unwittingly added another dimension to the drama. In the spring of his Olympic season, when he would be gearing up for the trials, Ryun began to break down, either physically or mentally, nobody could tell. It was very strange, that was for sure. In April, feeling ill, he dropped out of a race, infuriating both his coach and some previously loyal reporters. "Teammates would have had a lot more admiration for Ryun if he had just taken the baton and given it the old college try," wrote one columnist.

He checked himself into the student infirmary and got a preliminary diagnosis of mononucleosis, but not even his coach was buying it. Timmons thought it was all in Ryun's head. Well, Ryun did have a habit of finding excuses for not doubling in meets: running both the half and the mile. His coaches browbeat him into doubling at the Big Eight championships and, although he won both races, he felt horrible. He went back to Kansas, and the initial diagnosis was confirmed.

There has never, in the history of American pathology, been so famous a case of mononucleosis. The brief backlash gave way to a new awareness of the disease and a fresh wonderment at Ryun's constitution. The press waited out his enforced hiatus—he cooled his callused heels for three full weeks, his fiancée, Anne Snider, the only one left to cheer him—and then descended, one publication at a time, upon the high-altitude training site in Flagstaff, Arizona. There, they each took measure of this invalid, assessing the chances of this feel-good story going forward.

They liked what they were seeing. "There was a lot of ginger in his manner," reported the *New Yorker*'s Herbert Warren Wind from Flagstaff, "and I was relieved to observe this." Ryun had been given a kind of dispensation by the U.S. Olympic Committee, meaning he could miss the Olympic Trials scheduled for Los Angeles that summer and still make the team during high-altitude training in South Lake Tahoe in September. He could make it, that is, if he recovered his health. *Sport* magazine showed up in July and found that his lymphocyte count had come down 47 percent from the 78 percent high in May. Many sportswriters now felt fully qualified to practice medicine, after a summer steeped in the diagnosis and treatment of infectious disease. They were probably more trusted when it came to relaying Ryun's workout regime. After an initial discouragement—the first two days in Flagstaff, the only entry in his journal was "worried"—he was back to running 16 to 18 miles a day. Very good news for America.

And more reassuring than that, as Ryun continued to train in Flagstaff while others were grouping at the South Lake Tahoe location, was a win in the mile at a sea-level meet in August. It wasn't a terribly fast mile—the eighth fastest, almost five seconds off his world record—but it was a nice race for a man who'd been on his back only three months before. An "Olympic Stride," *Sports Illustrated* headlined the result, "Down That Comeback Trail." Great news.

There were other pre-Olympic stories that fit into the traditional template. None of them featured as attractive and wholesome a prospect as Ryun, but they all seemed to validate the American way of doing things, one way or another. Bob Beamon, a former drug-dealing hoodlum out of New York, represented the redemptive qualities of sport, always a popular angle. His wasn't a story that was getting a lot of play—there were some tawdry and troubling aspects to it—but it wasn't unknown, either. Whenever you have somebody so doomed by circumstance that he can reasonably present a switchblade and a .38 Smith & Wesson for a kindergarten show-and-tell—yeah, he did that—then you have the possibility, however remote, for an athletic rebirth.

His story may have been simply too sensational for public consumption. Compared to Jim Ryun's homelife in Kansas, Beamon's upbringing in New York City's black ghetto of South Jamaica was absolutely horrifying. Whereas Ryun lived the *Ozzie & Harriet* show, Beamon watched it on television as if it were so much science fiction. It was amazing. The parents didn't hit the kids, they all ate together, there were flowers in the yard. Every once in a while, Ricky would get in a jam, but Beamon couldn't really relate. Detectives at the 103rd Precinct station knew Beamon by sight, having once pulled him in on suspicion of murder. *Leave It to Beaver* was another of Beamon's favorite shows. Imagine the Beav getting in trouble for stealing something of Wally's. Beamon would just have to laugh.

Beamon had the excuse of so many kids of that neighborhood. His father was in Sing Sing when he was conceived; his mother died eleven months after he was born; he was raised by his grandmother, with a little help from his hard-drinking father, once he was out of prison. He was a problem in school, one time exposing himself to a girl there, other times dancing on the teacher's desk in his floppy, oversized shoes. Clown, the other kids called him. He drank, he shoplifted, he dealt low-grade marijuana. He became war counselor for The Frenchmen, a gang of about fifteen zip-gun-toting kids from the South Jamaica housing projects. Also, he was a poor student, when he wasn't actually being expelled.

If his grandmother hadn't pleaded with the judge after another of his run-ins, he very likely would have been sent upstate, where his career in crime could proceed undeterred. Instead the judge, giving him his last chance, sentenced him to a 600 school, a tier of New York City high schools that was not exactly college prep. Beamon was one of about fifteen kids in class that first day and here is what the fourteen-year-old heard from his new teacher: "My name is Mr. Jones. I am a certified black belt in karate, like all your teachers. We do not play games here. We can crack your skull wide open with a single chop. Order is the name of the game here."

Gradually, though, Beamon began to see himself as more than just an academic inmate. He found he did not have a natural aversion to learning after all and, moreover, discovered he had some innate abilities as an athlete. He was the best basketball player and track man at P.S. 622, no question, but what that meant exactly, he didn't know. Not for a while, anyway. In the spring of 1962, just about to turn sixteen, Beamon saw a poster for the Junior Olympics, a one-hour trip away at Randall's Island. Beamon bummed the sixty cents for bus and subway fare from neighbors, and a pair of spikes when he got there with a couple of other kids he knew from the Police Athletic League, and proceeded to enter the meet unaffiliated. How do kids hold on to ambition like that, what keeps a lifetime of discouragement at bay? What business do they have, nurturing such ridiculous dreams? A mystery. That day, he got his name in the *Daily Mirror* for reasons nobody could have ever predicted: "Beamon Jumps 24'1" in Junior Olympics."

That little headline was his entrée into truly organized sports, as well as comparative high society. He almost immediately enrolled in Jamaica High School, a regular school, not to mention mostly white, which had never before accepted a 600 kid. The school was willing to overlook certain deficiencies in light of his athletic promise. He would become even more familiar with this academic dynamic as time went on. But, for the time being, it was as if he had been added to the cast of *Leave It to Beaver*. It was that strange. Also, on at least one occasion, funnier. Given his first jockstrap for basketball practice, young Beamon put it on backward.

His progress here was storybook, athletically. In 1964 he was the tenth best high school long jumper in the country. In 1965, his last year there, he was ranked second. But, while he had definitely become a better citizen, there were other aspects of his life that weren't hewing to the classic sports feature of the time. His love life was complicated. No fiancée for Beamon; he married not his true love, but the woman who claimed a pregnancy by him. And while he was one of the country's top jumpers, he was one of Jamaica High's lowest-achieving students. A month after his wedding, Beamon graduated 1,093 out of a class of 1,182.

However, that high school had given him opportunity when he had none, dreams when he could afford few. It was there, after the high school had brought in such former Olympians as Donna de Varona, Wilma Rudolph, and Ralph Boston to speak, that he was able to fine-tune his ambition. He'd be an Olympian, too. It was Jamaica High that launched him on to college, first to North Carolina Agricultural and Technical College and then, after a disappointing semester, to the track powerhouse at University of Texas at El Paso (UTEP).

At UTEP, Beamon was a track team unto himself, a possible entrant in as many as seven events, from the 100-yard dash to the triple jump. The failure to list him in the high jump must have been a clerical error; he had cleared 6'5" in practices. It was in the long jump that Beamon, however erratic he was, continued to amaze. Not long after entering UTEP in 1967, he won the national championship with a jump of just under 27 feet. This was remarkable not so much for beating his idol, Ralph Boston, but because he had never even jumped as far as 26 feet before. There was an upside to his inconsistency.

If there was one reason the profile writers couldn't warm up to him, though, it probably had to do with that business with Brigham Young University, something that happened later that summer to cast Beamon more as an activist than an athlete. The idea that athletes were not so grateful for these opportunities—Beamon springing from absolute ignorance into the privileged world of Olympic contenders—that they couldn't swallow a few indignities along the way was not an angle that sold very well, not with magazine editors or readers. An athlete's anger is not easily accommodated in the Olympic feel-good story.

• • •

That was the same problem with the guys at Speed City. These were the fastest people in the world, and pretty conveniently located, too. By 1967, San Jose State's Tommie Smith held world records in the 220-yard dash over the straightaway (19.5) and the curve (20.0) and there was a lot of speculation as to whether that was even his best event. Teammate Lee Evans, who had been recruited there to help Smith set relay marks, was a quarter-mile specialist, a distinction that was largely preserved by coach Bud Winter's efforts to keep the two men apart on the track. The concentration of talent was so extreme that one of the most interesting meets of 1967 was essentially an intramural, a stunt-driven duel between Smith and Evans that could set two world records in just one race.

Not that there weren't some great sprinters in the country at that time. However, Smith, with his silky stride, knees almost to his chin, was serving notice within the track community that he was a species apart from the rest. "By far," said UCLA track coach Jim Bush, "the greatest that ever lived." It did not take an aficionado to appreciate Smith's style. He was not particularly quick out of the blocks, but he ran with such an effortless elegance that he seemed to float down the straightaway. This belied his trademark acceleration—Tommie Jets—as he ran down his opponents in the stretch. Whereas, it has been calculated, the great Bob Hayes reached a top speed of 25 miles per hour, Smith was still on the throttle in the final twenty-five meters, his stride lengthening, his speed now up to 28 miles per hour.

Lee, on the other hand, did not run picture-perfect races, weaving in and out, his arms flailing, his face contorted horribly. He appeared to be in a peculiar kind of agony, the effort a sort of death-throe. His form might have been good enough elsewhere, but compared to Smith, it attracted a lot of unfavorable characterizations. He looked like he was stomping grapes, he looked like he was struggling to get out of a corset, he looked like a drunk on roller skates. And so on.

What was worse, Lee was obviously second fiddle in Coach Winter's Olympic orchestra. Smith, who had arrived first and who was keeping Mrs. Winter busy in the kitchen with his world record times, was Winter's favorite. Lee was an add-on, the world champion in the quarter mile, but still, a backup player on any team that had Tommie Smith. Winter's poor attention to personal detail didn't help either. "What's your name?" he'd say to an increasingly insecure Lee.

In the spring of 1967, Winter yielded to a showdown he'd been long putting off. Not only would Lee and Smith race each other, they'd do it for simultaneous records in the 440 yards and 400 meters, two strings at the finish. It was a scheduled meet, the San Jose State Invitational, the last to be held on the Spartans' cinder track, but for most fans it was nothing more than a shootout with pineapple upside-down cake up for grabs. On a mild spring day, with perhaps four thousand fans, the most ever for a track meet there, competing for the one thousand stadium seats, Lee and Smith reluctantly settled into their blocks. Smith had misgivings about the event, even though it was constructed as a sendoff, a farewell race, with the opportunity for some very newsworthy records. After all, they were teammates, friends.

Still, he took it pretty seriously, climbing the stadium fence the afternoon before Saturday's meet to turn in a secret workout. He had been unnaturally absorbed all week. He even forgot Thursday's ROTC class. But, at the start of the race, he was suddenly ambivalent, even toying with the idea of pulling up lame, preserving good feelings all around. Once the gun sounded, though, Smith realized he did not enjoy the sight of his good friend from behind. Lee held the edge for 220 yards, then Smith, hitting the ignition on the Tommie Jets, caught him in the straightaway and, with a five-yard lead, powered through both tapes—the 400 meters in a world record time of 44.5, the 440 yards in a world record 44.8. "Lee would have won against anybody else," said Winter. "It's just that he ran against somebody who may be superhuman."

The story put Smith on the cover of *Sports Illustrated*—"He Is Built for Chasing Beyondness" was the headline of a story written by Frank Deford—but there was very little follow-up as the Olympic campaign neared. Smith filled many of the demands of the sports feature story, with his rise from child cotton picker to serial world record holder, but his growing involvement in the black movement must have been giving editors pause. On the one hand he was devoted to school and country, on the other he was out in the streets marching, keeping company with radicals like Harry Edwards. Seemed dangerous.

And nobody was going to celebrate the third part of the Speed City triumvirate. John Carlos was a known wild man. It was impossible to know just how much of it was for show, but few were willing to look into it. There were so many underground stories of Carlos competing drunk or high that it made little sense to promote him as a role model of any kind. He had a cavalier approach to sports that was downright off-putting. He could be found at the concession stand between his events, slathering mustard on hot dogs. He might unleash an imaginative string of profanity at any point, or he might just offer to fight. Or pour sand into a gas tank. He was funny, full of charisma, but there was an edge to him. A fellow trackman once looked out the window at four in the morning to see Carlos, not in the act of vandalism as you might suppose, but picking his way through a workout, behind the beam of a flashlight. If he were complicated, there apparently was nobody willing to find out.

These Olympics shouldn't have lacked for stories, but so many of the really good ones were ignored in pursuit of favorable demographics. The Tigerbelles, a vivacious and high-spirited outfit from Tennessee State, should have qualified on personality alone. If that weren't enough for a preview package, they might have drawn some attention for being what was essentially the entire U.S. Olympic team, but coverage was scant to nonexistent. Wyomia Tyus, speedy heir to the great Wilma Rudolph there, was gunning for a second gold medal in the

100 meters, prompting one journalist to write that she might become "the first woman in history" to do so. Well, she would have been the first athlete period, but never mind.

Tennessee State was a kind of Speed City on its own, churning out records and, in the postwar Olympics, winning 22 of the 35 U.S. medals. There were basically just two big-time university programs for women and this was the only one that awarded scholarships. The rest of the female talent was spread out across clubs. So, TSU might have been a place to investigate. Had journalists visited, as *Sports Illustrated* decided to do after Rudolph's triple gold in the 1960 Games, they would have found a fiercely determined and patriarchal coach in Ed Temple and comically woeful facilities: "an oval ribbon of dirt, unmarked and unsurfaced." It was, as reportorial luck would have it, near the pigpen in the school's agricultural facilities.

Such gold was largely unmined. If females were going to get any coverage, and they'd get very little, they would be young and they would be cute. *Life* magazine, choosing carefully, settled on sixteen-year-old swimmer Debbie Meyer, deciding to follow her around in Mexico City. She wishes, said *Life*, "she had more dates."

Tyus was dating plenty, but mainly Art Simburg, the white Jewish kid who'd been making friends of all the black sprinters. This might have been a little too provocative for the mainstream press, but it wasn't like anybody was looking into it, into that or athletic accomplishments. "We could go and win fifteen gold medals and never get the attention we deserved," Tyus complained at the time. "The men are always going to get the glory." Gender equality may have been on its way, but nobody could quite make it out yet.

Better to fly off to Kansas, see what young Jim Ryun was up to. He wouldn't talk a lot and wasn't terribly interesting when he did. However, he was a certified hopeful, with a nice little backstory coming into the Games. "Jim Ryun's Agonizing Year" was the headline in *Newsweek*. Who wouldn't read that?

Chapter 5

BOYCOTT

Hells Angels, a Petrified Pig, and More
Ralph Henry Barbour

THE IDEA OF AN OLYMPIC boycott by black athletes had been around for years. Dick Gregory, comedian-turned-activist (and himself a scholarship athlete), had brought it up as early as 1960. The idea got a little more traction after the Tokyo Games in 1964, when some of the black athletes began comparing notes over treatment there. It wasn't until Tommie Smith made an offhand comment to a Japanese reporter in the fall of 1967 that it really took hold, at least in the press.

Smith was in Tokyo for the World University Games in September when a reporter there asked about the possibility of a boycott by black athletes. The reporter asked, "Were Negroes now equal to the whites in the way they were treated?" Smith was partly amused that he had to travel around the world to field such a question but not so amused he couldn't answer it seriously. Of course not, he said. The reporter followed up, asking about a boycott. "Depending upon the situation," said Smith, "you cannot rule out the possibility." To that point there had been no talk specifically of an Olympic boycott, no organization, not even a particular grievance to rally around. But, given the question, Smith had to admit it was not something to be ruled out, given all the civil-rights disturbances of the time.

Whatever was written in that Tokyo newspaper got quickly translated. By the time Smith got back to San Jose, he was swamped with interview requests. Smith issued a statement through the athletic department, saying he had not meant to make an appeal "to black athletes to boycott the Games," but added, "If a boycott is deemed appropriate, then I believe most of the black athletes will act in unison."

And that might have been that. Anybody who understands sports realizes the chances of organizing a group of athletes, based entirely on race, would be remote. Even in those enlightened times, athletes would divide themselves according to federations and regions and opportunity before they would divide themselves by skin color. A black man would honor his military obligations before any call to boycott. A black man might honor his school, his region, or his family above all. Some might defer employment or endorsement opportunities to promote an unpopular cause. But would enough? As one of the black athletes later said, "Athletics have been mighty good to the Negro." Athletes are groomed by extremely personal agendas; they would not likely be co-opted by any movement that interfered with the instinctual *me first*.

In other words, whatever their politics happened to be, this was going to be a difficult, perhaps even impossible, group to mobilize. If it could ever happen, and it really was a pipe dream, there would need to be an extraordinary combination of provocation, personality, and leadership. And even then, anybody with any common sense, or just a minimum of sensitivity, could easily head the threat off, meeting a few demands here and there.

Yet, as 1968 drew near, a variety of forces were gathering with astonishing speed and they were entirely unopposed by either common sense or sensitivity. Whatever was going to happen in Mexico City later that year was by no means preordained, but a product of a rather unpredictable set of circumstances, each of them interlocking in unforeseen ways. There was an underlying basis to everything that happened, of course, but certainly not an inevitability.

One of those gathering forces was Harry Edwards. Or rather a returning force. Edwards had ignored opportunities to turn pro after graduating from San Jose State in 1964—his father was aghast that he refused an offer from the NFL—to accept a graduate fellowship at Cornell. Edwards's sense of racial injustice was already keen, but weekend bus trips into New York City to hear Malcolm X speak certainly honed it even more sharply. When Edwards returned in 1966 to teach a sociology class at San Jose State, where he found very little had changed since he'd left, he was prepared to take his case to authorities higher than any track coach.

It was back to the original insult of his institute: housing, the lack of it for black athletes. Nothing had improved, as far as Edwards could see. The blacks weren't suffering from a lack of civil rights, but human rights. And, following his little internship on the East Coast, he now knew what to do about it. When he and a colleague there, Ken Noel, failed to get satisfaction on their list of demands, or even to be taken seriously (a dean in a bow tie laughed in their faces), the two called for a cancellation of the school's season-opening football game against the University of Texas at El Paso. Edwards, now borrowing rhetoric from the activists he listened to in New York, promised the university that employed him he would "physically interfere" with the contest if his demands were unmet (he and the black students were prepared to disrupt the game by coming onto the playing field).

By the time Edwards had worked his way up university channels to speak with President Robert Clark, the little protest he and Noel had in mind had spiraled wildly out of control, comically almost. The Hells Angels, the soon-to-be-famous motorcycle gang in Oakland, promised to come down to make sure nobody "interfered" with the game. Hearing that, the Black Panthers promised they would do some interfering with the Hells Angels. California governor Ronald

Reagan, hearing this, promised to send in the National Guard. Any black splinter group worth its salt, hearing that, said they'd be on hand as well.

Clark told Edwards, as if it were the first time he was hearing about it, that the problems of the black students there would definitely be addressed, and he promised to call for a three-day moratorium during which he could implement housing reform and more diverse hiring in the athletic department, and take a look at fraternity admission policies. He was sincerely sympathetic and struck Edwards as a decent and well-meaning man. But, by then, the will-call line at the football stadium ticket booth had grown dangerously long, by both men's measure. "Can you control the Panthers?" asked Clark. No way, said Edwards. "Can you control the Hells Angels?" Edwards asked. Clark said he couldn't even control the National Guard. Both men agreed, no matter the complaint nor the remedy, that this was now beyond them. The game just had to be canceled.

There had never been a game, of any kind or at a college of any size, that had to be canceled on account of race relations. This was coast-to-coast news. Reagan obliged the media by calling for Edwards's dismissal. Reached for comment, Edwards called Reagan a "petrified pig." And just like that, Edwards became a spokesperson for just about anything that had to with education, athletics, and wherever they intersected with the black man. In the next year, he spoke at 105 colleges and universities, appeared in almost every publication of note, including the *New York Times Sunday Magazine* and the *Saturday Evening Post*, and began gathering a very scattered constituency into a tight-knit group.

Edwards quickly realized he was at the forefront of something, and just as quickly seized all the available instruments of persuasion. First thing he did was ditch that Cornell wardrobe. He looked to the Black Panthers for the militant style of the day and was soon wearing berets, guerrilla shirts with a matchbook folded provocatively in a front pocket (he just might burn it down), and other accessories of radicalism. On a man of his size, now grown to 6'8", and 275 pounds, this amounted to some powerful presentation; when Dr. Martin Luther King got his first look at him, he jumped back in shock: "Whoa," he said, "I see why those folks are so scared of you."

And, always a good talker, he fine-tuned his rhetoric so that no right-thinking journalist would dare paraphrase his delivery. Edwards's statements, "Teaching crackers is like kicking through a steel door with Jell-O boots," tended to dictate the narrative. The Edwards message arrived on his terms.

He also, just as quickly, defined his movement. He was not preaching some vague ideology or looking for giant national reforms. He focused on the black athlete and his concerns. And then, investigating the institutions at hand, discovered these concerns went all the way up to the Olympics. In fact, he noticed, the NCAA and Olympic hierarchy were almost identical, certainly interchangeable. Edwards got to thinking. If he could cancel a football game at San Jose State without really trying . . .

On Thanksgiving Day, 1967, Edwards announced the Olympic Games boycott. He had met with sixty black athletes in a Sunday school room of the Second Baptist Church in Los Angeles after a meeting of the Western Region Black Youth Conference. Edwards lectured for thirty minutes, then turned it over to group discussion. Among the group were Tommie Smith and John Carlos and teammate (and fellow Edwards student) Lee Evans, as well as the UCLA basketball star, Lew Alcindor. Evans was typical of the black athletes of the time, torn between what he felt was right and what was necessary. When he sat in Edwards's classroom his notebook was not decorated in slogans but, in large ink lettering, 44.3, the standing world record in the 440, and his goal. Yet he was now leaning toward the boycott, as was Smith and most everybody in the room. When Edwards, at the end of two and a half hours of discussion, asked, "Well, what do you want to do?" shouts of "Boycott!" echoed throughout the little room.

As they filed out that night, though, it was not with a sense of accomplishment but more like a sense of dread. Edwards said it was time. "For years we have participated in the Olympic Games, carrying the U.S. on our backs with our victories, and race relations are worse now than ever," he said. "But it's time for the black people to stand up as men and women and refuse to be utilized as performing animals for a little extra dog food. You see, this may be our last opportunity to settle this mess short of violence." Others were less gung-ho. "All I hope," said Smith, "is that this does some good, that it doesn't create any chaos."

The next day, Edwards was scheduled to speak at the National Conference of the Associated Student Government in San Francisco and it was there that he released the results of the Thanksgiving Day workshop. "Black men and women athletes at the Black Youth Conference," it said, "have unanimously voted to fully endorse and participate in a boycott of the Olympic Games in 1968."

In fact, it was a paltry representation of black athletes and it might not have even been the most interesting protest of the day (back at San Jose State students were in day two of their protest against Dow Chemical Company recruiters; before that was over, Governor Reagan was demanding even more faculty be fired). And it was vague. There was no immediate set of demands. However, *Olympic Games* is a newsworthy phrase, especially when paired with *boycott*, and Edwards's release got immediate attention. It made the front page of the *Chicago Tribune*.

By mid-December, though, Edwards had put together a list of objections and, with Dr. King standing at his side, made them known. His organization, now called the Olympic Project for Human Rights (OPHR), was calling for a boycott of all New York Athletic Club events (a logical move since the club maintained indefensible admission policies). It was also demanding the exclusion of South Africa and Southern Rhodesia from the Olympics, integration of the U.S. Olympic Committee, and, as a bonus, the return of Muhammad Ali's championship crown. Edwards let it be known that they wouldn't mind if Avery Brundage, "a devout anti-Semitic and anti-Negro personality," be replaced as head of the IOC.

Edwards exposed the Olympics' vulnerability to a boycott on several accounts. It was a lily-white organization, starting with Brundage, who owned the Montecito Country Club in California, which, like the NYAC, did not allow Jews or blacks as members. Also, Brundage had been instrumental in keeping the Olympics in Berlin in 1936, when so many were urging a boycott there. Brundage steadfastly refused to allow politics admission to his amateur utopia, saying it was the "one international affair for Negroes, Jews, and Communists." Others, even those who weren't scratching their heads at Brundage's categorization of the human race, wondered if something else wasn't at play, noting that Adolf Hitler had subsequently given Brundage's construction company the contract for the German embassy in Washington, D.C.

Still, as much sense as Edwards's manifesto might have made, the support was scattered, at best. The USOC quickly trotted out Jesse Owens, star of those 1936 Olympics, who said, "I believe you contribute more by entering than by staying out." Certainly his triumphs in front of the Nazi reviewing stand were among the high points in Olympic history, although his subsequent career of racing against horses for money was not. Other former Olympians, such as Rafer Johnson, Bob Hayes, and Ralph Boston, spoke out against it. Although Ali was "with them one thousand percent," former heavyweight champ Joe Louis was not.

A roster of 1968 hopefuls was divided, as well. Sprinter Charlie Greene said, "I'm an American and I'm going to run." Art Walker, the triple jumper, said, "I'd be proud to represent my country." High jumper Ed Caruthers said, "Our participating in the Olympics has given the young Negro kids something to look up to." In fact, a survey by the *Track & Field News* found only one-third of black athletes would boycott. An *Ebony* poll found only one percent agreement. In that poll, the athletes said a boycott went against their individuality, not to mention their earning prospects down the line.

Another person against the boycott, by the way, was Governor Reagan. "I disapprove greatly of what he [Edwards] is trying to accomplish."

At no point did Edwards think an Olympic boycott was actually doable. His was a far-flung congregation, united by an overall concern but fatally divided by self-interest. He had to deal with human nature above all, but if all he had meant to do was provoke debate, he definitely goosed it along with the proposed boycott of the indoor track meet at the New York Athletic Club. Scheduled for mid-February 1968, to celebrate the one-hundredth anniversary of the NYAC, the meet became a real referendum on the black athletes' support of a boycott, or at least a protest. It might be more than a debate after all.

For starters, there were real problems with the NYAC. It had genuine discriminatory practices against blacks and Jews, and the NYAC, an old Irish-dominated club, could hardly deflect attention from them by ticking off its contributions to "Negro youths." Boycotting the NYAC's meet could be done at very little expense to the athlete, and yet the yield in publicity would be quite high. The Olympics might be a soft target but the NYAC track meet was a sitting duck.

Once Edwards announced a boycott, hardly anybody wanted any part of the meet. Public and Catholic school leagues pulled out, entire teams (white athletes joining blacks) from Villanova, Manhattan, and Georgetown. Prominent athletes who didn't yet want to make a stand just found excuses not to attend. Even the seven-man Russian team dropped out.

If this was a preliminary to an Olympic boycott, authorities were rightly frightened. Among the elite athletes, only a few blacks crossed the picket line, among them sprinter Jim Hines, pole vaulter John Thomas, and UTEP long jumper Bob Beamon. With Edwards and

Noel manning the picket lines—"Rather Than Run and Jump for Medals, We Are Standing Up for Humanity. Won't You Join Us?" was Noel's sign—there was no violence, although it had been widely rumored. Altogether, only nine blacks competed, five of them from UTEP. And of those, there was a strong suspicion that the only reason Beamon was there was because he was homesick and wanted to see his girlfriend.

It wasn't much of a meet. However, if someone had set about offering Edwards and the OPHR movement a vehicle for maximum publicity, they could have done much worse. For that matter, they couldn't have timed it any better. The day before the meet, the IOC announced that, after a secret ballot, it had voted to let South Africa, which had been banned from the Olympics since 1963 over its apartheid policies, return. The IOC, meeting in Grenoble, might not have been mindful of the turmoil in New York, but the announcement certainly piggybacked those headlines, providing Edwards with a nice one-two punch. "Where are all the people who say the Olympics should be above racism?" he asked. From an agitator's point of view, the IOC was the gift that kept on giving.

Admittance of South Africa, no matter what changes the country promised in its athletic programs, was a huge validation for anybody with complaints against the Olympics. People ambivalent about an Olympic boycott had to admit the OPHR got at least one thing right. The OPHR was a big winner here. Writing in *Sports Illustrated,* Pete Axthelm said, "When Tommie Smith and Lee Evans joined Edwards in proposing an Olympic boycott last November, their chances of pulling it off seemed extremely remote. In the three months that followed, their cause seemed, if anything, to become even more hopeless. Last weekend this trend was dramatically reversed by separate events four thousand miles apart. A widespread Olympic boycott may still be no more than a distant possibility, but it is certainly possible."

As Edwards said, "Let Whitey run his own Olympics."

It was two months before the IOC, pressured by the possibility of a thirty-nine-nation boycott, rescinded its offer to South Africa. Brundage's stubbornness, or perhaps just his Olympic idealism, was impressive. "In an imperfect world," he explained, "if participation in sports is to be stopped every time the laws of humanity are violated, there will never be any international contests." The black athletes in his own country would not budge him, and the rest of the free world (and Communist Russia, for that matter) almost didn't budge him. It was with great reluctance that he was forced to acknowledge the role of politics in his Games. He'd probably have to acknowledge more yet.

The IOC's capitulation might have taken a lot of steam out of the black athletes' movement if it had only happened much earlier. As it was, the IOC's painfully slow response allowed all kinds of discussion, reaction, and protest. It was shaping a lot of coverage of OPHR. Without that two-month window of racial obstinance, at the very least oblivion, would Edwards's movement have simply expired? But, with the IOC refusing to cave in to what became worldwide popular opinion, other black athletes, and even some white athletes, began to find some resonance in the boycott idea. As Arthur Daley, the *New York Times* columnist, put it, "The temporary return of South Africa also lit a fire under the virtually dead and barely smoldering movement by Harry Edwards to have all American Negroes boycott the Olympics."

That fire began to roar with the assassination of Dr. King in April. Ralph Boston, who had been very pragmatic about the Olympic process (it was a means to an end, his end), immediately changed his mind about the boycott. The murder of Dr. King rolled through the land, igniting riots and discontent. And many blacks took their cue for fresh indignation from white America's failure to understand the importance of the tragedy.

At UTEP, where the black athletes had already obliged their coach by competing in the NYAC meet, they were once more asked to run in the Texas Relays the weekend of Dr. King's murder. They did, but began to think more carefully about their role in this increasingly divided society. The black athletes, including the previously ambivalent Bob Beamon, asked out of their next meet, an Easter week competition with Brigham Young. BYU, with its historical prejudices against blacks, was a tough spot on everybody's schedule that year—but days after Dr. King's death?

UTEP, despite fielding five black starters on their NCAA basketball championship team two years earlier, was notoriously insensitive to its black athletes. Its athletic director welcomed blacks but didn't seem to know what to do with them. He certainly didn't know what to call them. In what was meant to be grudging admiration, he once said, "In general, the nigger athlete is a little hungrier." The school was no more sensitive here, and when eight of the nine black athletes refused the trip to the BYU competition, they all lost their scholarships. Beamon got a call from the bank the very afternoon his scholarship was revoked, wondering if he could pay his bills. Word had traveled fast.

Such response had a way of hardening convictions, and in some cases, creating them. Suddenly, everything was an eye-opener. Ralph Boston was watching the *Today* show later that summer when Joe Garagiola was grilling UCLA's Lew Alcindor. Alcindor was one of about twenty of the country's top players who refused to attend the Olympic Trials (they had very little to lose, compared to the track athletes; the best of them were assured pro contracts). When Garagiola pressed him on the matter, Alcindor said, "Yeah, I live here, but it's not really my country." Said Garagiola: "Well, then, there's only one solution. Maybe you should move." Boston sat bolt upright. Is this really what America believed?

Still, even as converts gathered, the boycott remained a tough sell. Before the so-called Trials in Los Angeles in late June (the USOC, unknown to many athletes, and virtually all fans, would hold the official selection at high altitude in South Lake Tahoe in the fall), Edwards convened twenty-six of the most likely members of an Olympic team and put them to a vote on the boycott. Only twelve were in favor. The idea was doomed.

Nobody except Edwards knew this. He continued to play his hand, cards or not, and was beginning to worry Olympic officials as the summer wore on. USOC president Doug Roby was now desperately relaying assurances to Brundage that he was bringing the situation under control, hiring Stan Wright, a black coach, as assistant and creating a board of consultants to pacify these young black athletes. The board was to be headed by Jesse Owens, hauled out of an ignominious retirement to parrot Olympic platitudes. Even as Edwards's movement faltered among the very black athletes he'd hoped to convert, the movement dying on its own, the largely white establishment was ratcheting up its opposition.

Edwards may have been attracting unexpected adversaries, but he was also gathering some strange allies, even as the call for a protest was petering out. None was stranger than the Harvard crew, an eight-man rowing team—all white—with bad haircuts (bad enough they were called "shaggies"), ironic ties, a tremendous competitive drive, and a sense of adventure. These eight also had a growing social awareness and, whether because of or in spite of their privileged circumstances, were eager to raise a little ruckus on injustice's behalf. Edwards's call for change certainly piqued their interest and, although they were not so arrogant to think they could influence events that had very little effect on them, were still eager to show their support. And so it was that this unlikely band of white brothers came to play an outsized part in that summer's craziness.

On the one hand, there couldn't have been a more obscure group of athletes in America. Rowing is a marginal sport, at best an Ivy League recreation that doesn't attract much attention beyond Harvard alumni. Even during an Olympics, which is a kind of mortuary for antique sports, preserving them long past their natural deaths (fencing? equestrian?), rowing remains as undiscovered as ever. But, on the other hand, rowing enjoyed an abnormally high level of coverage among a very elite audience—the *New York Times* and the *New Yorker* were acting as house organs, devoting long pieces to the sport of crew, and Harvard crew in particular. These guys, in their own way, were actually getting nearly as much attention as Edwards.

Not only did they have access to the prestigious press, guaranteeing them attention in the worst of times, they had some ability. Thanks to a young coach who'd overhauled the program, Harvard had become the team to beat, undefeated at home over five seasons and a growing force internationally, too. The team's ambitions had grown with their record. Ever since little coxswain Paul Hoffman had arrived in 1963, having held off Harvard a year so he'd be a senior for the 1968 Olympics, there'd been little doubt where the team's focus was. On Hoffman's first day of practice, he plastered a poster of Mexico City on the wall of the team's boathouse.

They were troublemakers, full of themselves, interested in the world. In 1967, on a trip to Winnipeg for a big international meet, they found themselves on the same plane as Tennessee State's all-black Tigerbelles, traditionally the best women athletes in America. They were, the Harvard crew was happy to discover, also the liveliest. "Funny, sassy," Hoffman thought. As for the Harvard guys, well, as Hoffman would say, "We weren't looking down at our shoelaces." Harvard could contend when it came to funny and sassy. They didn't lack for ego.

At Winnipeg, the Harvard Club invited all their athletes to a dinner theater one night, one of those perks of belonging to an elite institution. "Could we bring dates?" Hoffman asked. Nobody could see why not. And so the Harvard crew showed up with the Tigerbelles and those women—Wyomia Tyus, Martha Watson, Ellie Montgomery, all of whom had as much personality as speed to burn—simply took over the event. It is an image worth imagining, the Harvard guys cutting the rug with these black women from the South, everybody laughing it up, Winnipeg's Harvard alumni trying to keep their eyeballs in their sockets.

Those guys! A couple of days later there was a picnic for all the athletes there in Winnipeg and USOC president Doug Roby got up to speak. Whatever you do, he told the athletes, make sure you beat the Cubans. The Harvard crew exchanged looks. That wasn't what they were about at all. "These guys," Hoffman said to a teammate, "are just unreconstructed." They all got up and walked out. Also, they won the meet.

The *New Yorker* was intrigued by its backyard juggernaut. Its writer traveled to Long Beach, California, for the Olympic Trials, which were being held in July, and found the guys well-rounded and wholesome. Wrote Roger Angell in the *New Yorker*: "I wanted to learn some of the reasons that could induce young men to give so much of their time to this cryptic, unpublic, and intensely demanding sport. I knew that the members of this group were considered exceptional at Cambridge, and not just as athletes—although they had won thirty-nine letters in twelve different sports in high school—but also for their intelligence and maturity. Of the four graduating seniors, two were headed for the Peace Corps, one was planning a teaching career in chemistry, and the fourth was entering the Harvard Medical School."

The writer found them a delight and despite a count of three separate mustache styles, pronounced them a band of "Ralph Henry Barbour heroes." This would be, by the way, only the second of several recorded references to Barbour's fictional prep-school athletes (*Left Guard Gilbert*, etc.) from the 1800s. Perhaps there were still *New Yorker* readers alive who remembered Barbour and his wholesome characters, enforcing their noble prep-school values, but there couldn't have been many athletes for whom the reference resonated. And if it had, they'd probably have taken offense.

At least one other writer was pleased to learn of their existence. *Pleased* really doesn't seem the word. Jim Murray, traveling from his base at the *Los Angeles Times* for the Trials, was delirious at the opportunity to gaze upon anything Harvard, much less an Olympic contending outfit. "Somehow," he said, "the only race you picture

Harvard winning is the one for the president. And they wouldn't go in the water in any boat that didn't have a chandelier." Murray had a lot of trouble putting Harvard and something as labor-intensive as rowing together. He suspected that the days of prep-school elitism must be nearing an end and that "Ralph Henry Barbour would turn in his adjectives" if he were alive today, which of course he hadn't been for a generation of young men. "The last boat a Harvard man pulled an oar in had George Washington in the prow and it was snowing."

Likely Murray wouldn't have invested as much imagination in the column if Harvard hadn't won the Trials, edging Penn by a mere foot. But Harvard was going to Mexico and what could you do but admire the whole idea, not to mention the Trials themselves. "The finish," wrote Murray, "was as exciting as Dempsey-Firpo."

Harvard wasn't done yet. Along with admission to Harvard comes the guarantee that anything you say is bound to be interesting. They were talkers, nonstop talkers, discussing the draft, race riots, Robert Kennedy, you name it. There is no sport that demands as much solidarity as crew—they are literally and figuratively in the same boat—and respect for differences in politics must be maintained at all times. But, even with differing outlooks on life, they all agreed these were interesting times, and they talked about them constantly.

One of the things they talked about was Harry Edwards. Hoffman and teammate Cleve Livingston, whose parents lived in Sacramento, decided that if they won the Trials they would travel north and seek an appointment with this Harry Edwards, a fact-finding tour. Granted an audience, they spent some time deciding what to wear, settling on summer suits and ties. And then were astonished to greet Edwards himself, rigged out in beret, sunglasses, a dashiki, and "a jumble of fake beads." Hoffman had studied abroad in Africa the summer before; he knew authentic African wear.

They were far more impressed with what Edwards had to say, though, and told him that if they got a consensus from the rest of the team, they wanted on board. They were tremendously conscious of this being a movement about black athletes and did not want to appear as dilettantes, the type of fool Tom Wolfe might mock as "baring their soft white backs the more poignantly to feel the Panthers' vengeful lash, then imploring them not to kill their children." But they were hypersensitive to injustice. Why couldn't they do something?

Edwards said, "Listen, we want anybody who will help." He correctly understood that having the Harvard crew on his side would create a whole new level of publicity. He said he'd come to Cambridge if the crew, somehow, proved its commitment.

Hoffman and Livingston returned to Harvard for summer training and began conducting twelve-hour bull sessions, highly refined debates during which someone might shout, "Define your terms!" Not everybody agreed that a press release backing OPHR was the right thing to do, but after enough talking six of the nine-man team felt comfortable enough about it and another teammate, Curt Canning, drafted a statement. They drove to Coach Parker's house at nine that night and told him what they were up to and asked for the use of the boathouse. Nobody knew where Parker stood on anything, but they knew him for his tolerance above all. He told them, go ahead.

It was a remarkable scene, Edwards in his guerrilla getup, holding sway in the Harvard boathouse. The reporters that the crew had beckoned were rightfully agog. The crew delivered its statement, basically saying they backed OPHR and that they intended to "stimulate an open-ended discussion of the issues between white and black athletes." They didn't mean to "embarrass our country" and promised no specific action or protest but did finish by saying, "Surely the spirit of the Olympic Games requires us, as white participants, to explore all the means at our disposal to further the cause of brotherhood and the claims to equality of our black colleagues."

Robert Lipsyte, the young columnist for the *New York Times*, was all over this, giving them great play in the paper, but it was big news everywhere. "Harvard Crew Backs Edwards" was a typical headline.

Reaction was swift, although it did not come from Harvard. The USOC didn't seem terribly worried about the black athletes and their protest, but if white athletes were going to align themselves and, worse, attract even more attention to the problem, well, something had to be done. The USOC Rowing Committee, at the prodding of a USOC official, wanted to have the Harvard crew sign a "cease and desist" statement, or else get kicked out of the Olympic family. They ended up getting seven of the nine members of Harvard's crew to sign a statement saying they swore off "any demonstration of support for any disadvantaged people in the United States."

Edwards thought it was "beautiful to see some white cats willing to admit they've got a problem," but not all welcomed them to the program. Said Olympic team assistant coach Stan Wright, decidedly less militant than Edwards, "If Negroes want to demonstrate, I don't think they need the Harvard crew."

The Harvard crew plugged along, writing up personalized letters to all the white athletes during high-altitude training in New Mexico. The response, Hoffman thought at the time, was "mighty slim pickings," but they had at least kept the issue alive, fanned those flames even. And had some fun, too.

Whether the boycott would happen or not—some of the athletes, Lee Evans among them, were suggesting it probably wouldn't as early as July—Edwards had certainly prompted a dialogue. *Newsweek* ran a piece by Pete Axthelm that summer called "The Angry Black Athlete." *Sports Illustrated* went to El Paso to do an illuminating story on the plight of the black athlete at UTEP, part of a very influential series of stories called "The Black Athlete—A Shameful Story."

His work done, Edwards announced in late August, at the National Conference on Black Power, that "the proposed boycott of the 1968 Olympic Games by United States Negro athletes is off." By then he was tired, scared, and increasingly paranoid. He no longer ordered from the menu, fearful of being poisoned. He was certain he was being tailed by FBI agents. When Lee Evans told him about the hate mail he was receiving, Edwards laughed, showing him his—violent and ugly. Something had been set in motion, that was for sure, but a reasonable person might wonder at what price.

That summer Edwards's apartment in San Jose was broken into and two decorative machetes were taken off his wall and used to hack his two dogs to pieces. The slaughtered animals were left on his doorstep. In a chilling irony, his landlady looked at the mess, looked at Edwards, and said, "You're too much trouble." And he was once more denied housing, which is pretty much how this whole thing started.

Chapter 6

A Desperate Innovation

Rolls, Straddles, and an Airborne Seizure

THERE HAVE NOT BEEN MANY real breakthroughs in the annals of personal locomotion. Running forward, for example, is still considered the quickest unassisted way from point A to B. Perhaps early man experimented with backward pedaling by way of escape, but the technique probably did not survive even the first saber-toothed tiger. It would have been a brief and unforgettable trial run. All the important means of escaping and chasing—that is to say, of staying alive—were established early on and with a certainty that only life-and-death consequences can provide.

So evolution would seem to confirm common sense, establishing once and forever preferred ways for getting from here to there. This rather obvious reality has frozen sports, which are all just highly stylized versions of getting from here to there, in time, a time long ago. If a cartwheel had been the most efficient way for our forebears to leap a chasm, then today's long jump competition would look much different than it does now. Some movements, tried and tested in the only arenas that counted, are simply beyond improvement. It's obvious.

Consider, then, the Fosbury flop, an upside-down and backward leap over a high bar, an outright—an outrageous!—perversion of all acceptable methods of jumping over obstacles. An absolute departure in form and technique. It was an insult to suggest, after all these eons, that there had been a better way to get over a log all along. With a saber-toothed tiger on your tail? It doesn't seem likely. Perhaps man can afford biases in his relatively recent and harmless pastimes, choosing decorum over utility (it does seem more dainty, probably comfortable, to remain slightly upright during the jump), but it's impossible to entertain the idea that a sure means to longevity, not to mention a gold medal, was ignored for esthetics. Desperation is rewarded over dignity, every time, and almost all our Olympic sports proceed more or less directly from those survival impulses.

It's nearly incomprehensible, in other words, that there would be a new and abrupt development in areas of running and jumping. And if there were to be, it ought to come from a coach, a professor of kinesiology, a biomechanic, somebody with access to higher sciences than an Oregon teenager of middling jumping ability.

And yet, Dick Fosbury was the perfect, maybe only, vehicle for innovation, at least when it came to the high jump. All athletes recognize a performance imperative, a drive to exceed their limits, to explore upper boundaries. It's why they train and tweak. But Fosbury had the additional impetus of being a teenager. There is no swifter, more terrible saber-toothed tiger than the ritual humiliation of adolescence, and he felt that animal's breath on his neck every day, felt it more keenly than his peers. He had picked the one sport that might return the favor of his determination but got embarrassment instead. And it affected him. He couldn't even clear 5' his sophomore year, the opening height in a twenty-team meet. Can you imagine such an affront to your ambitions? "To be the worst," he thought, "was really a shame."

Innovation in sport is exceedingly rare. It usually takes the form of material advances. The development of fiberglass poles transformed the vault into a nearly unrecognizable catapult, making the old standards historically quaint. Most innovation, when it is not dependent on improvements in technology (a better running shoe, the golf cart, the rearview mirror, synthetic surfaces), is the result of rule changes. Basketball became a practical recreation the day they removed the bottom of the peach basket.

Other innovation, sometimes even more powerful, is the result of social change. The integration of Major League Baseball in 1947, when Jackie Robinson joined the Brooklyn Dodgers, is more important to that game than, for example, the institution of the designated hitter.

But true, elemental change, borne out of an individual imperative, is so much more unlikely. The catalogue of tinkering, or invention, that produced substantive departures in form is slim indeed. Candy Cummings's skewball in the 1860s, the progenitor of baseball's curveball? Paul Arizon's jump shot in basketball in the 1950s? Notre Dame's forward pass in 1913? The core movements of athletics, grounded in so much human history, do not easily, or very often, yield to change. Modern sports are somewhat amenable to improvement, as their quirks are understood, but the rewards of experimentation diminish in proportion to the antiquity of the event.

And what could be older than the high jump? If it wasn't an original Olympic event, it nevertheless was a necessary advantage in early man's survival. No pictographs remain, but we can assume that he quickly realized the best way over any barrier (that tiger right behind him) was to lift his knees. He probably wouldn't have explained it this way, but by raising his legs and feet he had also raised his center of mass and was able to clear greater heights. This would have been important if he didn't want to become that tiger's next meal. It wouldn't have taken too much more practice to realize that, by kicking one leg at a time, and by approaching that log at a slight angle, he could raise his center of mass still higher. The technique so resembled a scissoring motion that, well, that's what it was called: the scissors.

As ancient as it was, the high jump did seem to be one event that was at least somewhat agreeable to experimentation. Jumpers found that they could throw themselves over the bar, more or less forward, by tucking their takeoff leg under their body. The eastern cutoff, first seen in 1892, which combined the scissoring motion with a head-first approach, thus gave way to the Western roll in 1912, although its inventor, America's George Horine, could finish no better than third in that Olympics. By 1930, the last great change had occurred, although it was only a change by degrees. Now jumpers, still fling-ing themselves over headfirst, did not tuck their legs anywhere but stretched them horizontally. The face-down technique—like throw-ing your leg over a saddle—became known as the straddle and pro-duced another inch or two in height.

And that, except for the fooling around in run-up speeds and arm movements (the Russians were particularly good at putting all these little elements together, winning gold in 1960 and 1964), was where the event remained by Fosbury's day. All jumpers practiced and used the straddle. It was the only way to go.

Fosbury, who had come to the event by way of the scissors, had not been able to adapt to the preferred straddle. He'd been able to win meets in junior high, using the scissors, but now in high school he was actually regressing with the western roll. He had been humili-ated his sophomore year, unable to clear the opening height in that twenty-team meet, and wasn't really getting the hang of the new technique. He finished the season with only a modest improvement; he had jumped as high as 5'4", about a half foot lower than almost everyone else.

His coach had given him permission to revert to the more com-fortable scissors, reminding him there was very little upside to the outdated technique. At the same time, he realized Fosbury probably couldn't bear any more discouragement. And it wasn't like Fosbury's performances were necessary to team success. There was always Steve Davis, jumping just fine with the straddle.

It was on that bus trip to Grants Pass, the big rotary meet in 1963, that Fosbury decided he'd do whatever it took to get his rear over the bar. He felt it, looking out the bus window on the way to the meet. His mind was pushing his body to meet his goals and he felt certain those two parts of him were somehow going to work something out. If he finished the year stuck at 5'4", he thought, "Game over." Something was going to be done, and it was going to be done now.

And so, trying to reach 5'6" in that meet, he found himself reclining by several degrees, trying to get his hips over the bar. He made the height. And then at 5'8", a height he'd never cleared without knocking the bar off with his dragging rear, he reclined a little further, his hips—his center of mass—now even a little higher. Made it. At 5'10", he was in a back layout position, his shoulders going even further back in reaction to his lifting hips. It was on-site engineering, his body and mind indeed working together, making reflexive adjustments with only one goal, getting over the bar, somehow. In the course of only a handful of jumps, he had raised the bar six inches and, in an act of spontaneity, or maybe rebellion, created a style unto himself.

The authority figures on hand were understandably flustered by what they saw. It might not even be legal. But rifling through rule books, they couldn't find any rule that prohibited it, or allowed for it, for that matter. Who would have seen this coming? But the rules only required the athlete to jump off one foot. After that, it was his business.

There is not normally a lot of creativity in sports. It's a top-down model, ideas and instruction all coming from above, that stifles innovation. Change comes slowly. On the other hand, it's a very pragmatic environment—coaches like to keep their jobs—and performance matters more than orthodoxy. Fosbury's coach at Medford, Dean Benson, was not about to insist that Fosbury give up six inches on account of tradition. The improvement was too sensational to forbid, much less ignore. But he had no idea what Fosbury was doing. He took Fosbury back to his office and together they dug through all the high jumping film they could find, reviewing styles, looking for something that might apply to whatever it was Fosbury was now doing. There wasn't.

The next season, his junior year, Fosbury continued to improve, refining the jump. His arms and legs were still all over the place, but what looked like an airborne seizure was actually a Darwinian activity. Those tics and flailings that served to get him even a quarter inch higher survived added to his growing antigravity arsenal. The rest were gradually pared away. During that next full year of his upside-down layout, Fosbury began to lean with his shoulder, about 45 degrees to the bar, so that now he was very nearly going over backwards as well. Still not setting the world on fire, but improving enough to break the school record of 6'3". By his senior year, his body still searching for a better way, almost on its own, Fosbury had introduced a curved approach, turning his back to the bar, completing the rotation, arching, lifting his hips, and kicking his feet clear in a final motion. He finished second in state, well ahead of Steve Davis, now able to clear 6'5½".

Fosbury was gaining attention, but more as a novelty than the next new thing. In 1964, an alert photographer captured this craziness and the shot went around the world, Des Moines to South Africa. "World's Laziest High Jumper" was the caption in one newspaper. A better caption, appearing under a staff photo in the *Medford Mail-Tribune*, was "Fosbury Flops Over the Bar." A reporter returned to the usage in a game story, saying Fosbury looked like nothing more than a fish flopping into a boat. Fosbury was tickled by the connotation of failure. He was, no matter what he looked like or acted like, a contrarian at heart. The Fosbury flop was born.

You might ask, if this was a far superior method, why hadn't somebody invented it before Fosbury? First, it wasn't a far superior method. It might not have been even the least bit superior. But for a certain kind of jumper, somebody who just couldn't combine all the elements—a fast run-up, exaggerated arm action, or, more important, the straight leg kick at takeoff that seemed to lift the jumper over the bar—Fosbury's new technique might be more rewarding. Fosbury was a bent-leg jumper. Imagine the difference in leg position between dunking a ball (bent-leg) and kicking one (straight). Well, in high jumping, it's all the difference in the world. Enough to frustrate a young junior high school jumper, that's for sure. In Fosbury's upside-down leap, it didn't matter where his legs were, as long as they kicked free at the end.

Fosbury's jump did produce an advantage over the straddle in terms of bar clearance, about two to three inches, but because the jumper's arms and legs are in lower positions than the straddle jumper, his center of mass was probably two inches lower. In other words, Fosbury's new jump offered *him* an advantage, but not necessarily to more traditional jumpers. Neither his jump nor the straddle were inherently superior.

As to why nobody had come across this before Fosbury, well, somebody had. A girl in Canada, Debbie Brill, was doing something similar by 1967. It was called the Brill bend. A boy in Montana was doing exactly the same thing. In 1959. Bruce Quande, an outdoors kind of kid at Flathead County High, had started with the scissors, like Fosbury, and had gradually rolled it over. Just like Fosbury. But Quande was not driven the way Fosbury was—the best part of being on the track team for him was stopping for ice cream on the trip back from meets—and he never made much of it. Nobody did. He placed high in some state meets and went to St. Olaf College in Minnesota, where he jumped his freshman season. He got very little notice for his style, and no attention for his middling heights. He gave it up after one season and returned to school in Montana, where he could indulge his real passions, skiing and fishing. All that documented his precedence was a grainy picture from a 1963 issue of the *Missoulian*, a kid going upside-down over a bar. The editors could produce no accompanying alliteration and there went the naming rights.

Perhaps even others had come upon the flop. However, if there hadn't, there would have been good reason beyond its counterintuitive properties. Completing the jump successfully was only half the battle; the return to earth, and in those days, it was earth, still had to be negotiated. Few would even consider such an experiment in flight knowing they'd have to land on their neck. During Fosbury's sophomore year, the landing pit was only a pile of wood chips and sawdust. It was safe but not comfortable. By his junior year, though, his school had installed a foam pit and the idea of a head plant, while still daunting, was a bit more agreeable.

Still, even with a named jump, Fosbury was mostly unknown and mostly unwanted. Even after finishing second at the state meet his senior year, college coaches were not calling. It wasn't discrimination, just performance. It wasn't until the summer after graduation, when he won National Junior Championships with a jump of 6'7", that even one coach called. Berny Wagner, the new coach at Oregon State, took a chance on Fosbury and got him a small scholarship. That was all Fosbury was looking for anyway, an education, a chance at an engineering career. If his flop could get him a degree, it would have done its job.

Wagner wasn't making a huge endorsement of the flop with his small offer. The cupboard was bare when he got to Oregon State and there was not a high jumper in sight. He knew Fosbury had jumped 6'7", he just didn't know how, or even why. The guy was a mystery. When Wagner first interviewed Fosbury he asked him what his goals were. Fosbury was mystified. Goals? Yeah, 6'9" this year, 6'11" the next, like that. Fosbury had never looked at high jumping like that, only in terms of avoiding embarrassment and competing. Wagner shook his head. "Better than nothing" is what Wagner thought. "Certainly not the future."

Wagner had been a high jumper himself so he took a keen interest in the event. He wasn't hidebound, but he wasn't going to encourage something as crazy as the Fosbury flop. Let's get back to the straddle, Wagner said. "You're the coach," Fosbury said. "You line out a program and I'll follow it." Fosbury never meant to be a radical; he tried to be agreeable.

The straddle wasn't working in college any more than it had in high school, and Fosbury regressed. Wagner had taken a 6'7" jumper and turned him into a 5'6" stumbler. Fosbury was barely making the traveling team. Wagner grew skeptical enough of his project that he suggested Fosbury might like to try the triple jump instead. It puzzled Wagner that Fosbury would persist so mightily when he had so few physical gifts. He had muscle-bound discus throwers who could jump-reach higher than Fosbury. And it wasn't reassuring to know that, while Russian high jump legend Valery Brumel had once won a bet by kicking a basketball rim with his foot (five times in a row), Fosbury had lost a bet in OSU's Theta Chi fraternity when he failed to clear a chair and broke a bone in his hand.

As he had in high school, Fosbury began flopping in meets, even as he used the straddle in practice. It was strictly a face-saving maneuver. What did Wagner care, anyway? He had since acquired a couple of bona-fide straddle jumpers and his investment in Fosbury was small enough not to trouble him further. However, he hadn't entirely washed his hands of him. He kept trotting him out there. And, finally, something did happen. The turning point came the spring of his sophomore season, when Wagner took him to a three-way meet in Fresno. What was it about that meet? The sunshine? Using the flop, Fosbury jumped 6'10", not only an increase of nearly four inches from the season before but a school record. Wagner took him aside after the meet and said, "Okay, that's it. I'm not sure exactly what you're doing but it's working for you. So, stick with it, I guess. This experimentation is over."

Sports can be generous like that, overlooking biases and stereotypes in favor of results. Coaches could resist Fosbury and his flop all they wanted, but his performance would eventually turn them into coconspirators, all of them. Innovation is uncomfortable but when competition is the final arbiter, the best technique, just like the best man, wins. Wagner did not enjoy being challenged but was not so resistant to change that he couldn't get behind the Fosbury flop. Wagner didn't think this was a transforming moment in track but, with wins and losses at stake, hedged his bets all the same. He began teaching some of the others how to do the flop by the end of the season.

Except for the fact that nobody could teach Fosbury how to jump using any of the historical methods, he was extremely coachable. When Wagner told Fosbury he needed more conditioning, Fosbury was running and hopping the eighty-three rows in Parker Stadium. You couldn't appeal to tradition when you dealt with Fosbury, but you could fire his competitive neurons. That was something that was unusual about him, too, that need to win. Setting goals for him turned out to be pointless, as Fosbury simply was not intrigued by benchmarks. In fact he never set a record of any kind—school, state, or national—after his event was won. This is what Wagner noticed: "He jumps against people, not heights."

Fosbury placed fourth in the national championships at the end of his sophomore season, but was still not a world-class high jumper. By result, he was in the top 50, maybe in the top 25, in the United States. He was at least gaining some renown for his style. Meet promoters who first got a look at the flop during those championships began inviting him to their track events: the Oakland Indoor, the San Francisco All-American Games. They didn't really care how high he jumped, just how much hype he could generate. And the press did love it. A *Los Angeles Times* headline: "Beaver Physics Student to Show Unusual Jumping Form Today."

Since the flop was something he just did—he hardly ever practiced it ("There's no use wearing myself out.")—the additional schedule offered yet more opportunity for improvement. With higher grades of competition he was quite literally raising the bar on his event. At a meet in Oakland, he cleared 7' for the first time. *Track & Field News*, the *Rolling Stone* magazine for athletics, finally put him on the cover of its February issue in 1968, as much to herald a format change for the monthly as a sea change for the high jump.

There was still some negativity out there, the guard hating to be changed. Some of the resistance was couched in the language of safety. Here's a letter from a Los Angeles medical director to Fosbury: "For the good of young America, you should stop this ridiculous attack on the bar. Youngsters will be emulating you. And there soon will be a rash of broken necks." Well, it wasn't that dangerous. It just looked weird.

As a junior he became the country's most consistent and outrageous 7'0" jumper, winning the NCAAs that year with a jump of 7'2¼". Up to then, the attention he had been getting was for the character of his jump, not its magnitude. Fosbury had found it amusing to supply feature writers with a variety of origin myths, telling some he'd graphed it all out on paper first, others that he'd stumbled backwards on his takeoff. But now, with these kind of heights, it was getting more serious. "So, Dick," a sportswriter asked him, "any plans on going to the Olympics?" Until then, Fosbury had never registered that ambition. He'd been so mediocre for so long that he never pictured himself in that elite group. And he'd never been to even one international meet. He was going to have his first in an Olympics? Wild! But now that he thought about it . . .

There was one problem. While he was enjoying the success of that extended 1968 season, his grades were slipping. Fosbury was smart. And he was athletic. But he wasn't both at the same time and, favoring the athletic over the academic during this period, got booted out of engineering school. This disaster was somewhat heightened by the fact that he lost his academic deferment along with his major. Instead of wondering if he might go to the Olympics, he was forced to wonder if he'd go to Vietnam. The U.S. Army invited him for a physical in January 1968. Would he be so kind as to run over to Portland and let the doctors have a look-see?

Fosbury panicked. He "didn't want to leave this nice place." Not for Vietnam, not for anywhere. "I wanted to go to the dance on Friday." This was a horrible development. All around him, his peers in a similar predicament were doing whatever they could for a 4-F classification. Friends were getting ready to go to Canada, taking photos of each other in homosexual situations, researching chemical compounds said to scare off even Army docs. Fosbury remembered a neck injury he'd gotten while felling some trees back in Medford (doctors had looked at the vertebrae at the time and declared he'd never jump again) and wondered if X-rays might show sufficient damage to get him out of the draft.

A back-and-forth, involving more X-rays and exams, ate up six extremely frightening months before the Army decided he was a physical wreck, unfit for service, a hazard to his unit. He got the notice at the end of June, about two weeks after he'd won the NCAA Championships, best high jumper in the country.

Chapter 7

THE TRIALS

Spondylolisthesis, Brush Spikes, and a Brutal Stomping

AVERY BRUNDAGE HAD COME back from the Little Olympics in 1966, a fact-finding meet in Mexico City, and proclaimed them safe. "I have seen the runners at high altitude," he announced, "and no one fell down dead." As reassuring as this was, members of the U.S. Olympic Committee decided on a program of altitude acclimation of their own, at least as far as the Trials were concerned, closer to the actual Games. This, too, was a kind of fact-finding meet, not so much to discover whether the Olympics would be a matter of sudden mortality so much as to see what kind of performances could be expected in October.

And so the men were gathered at South Lake Tahoe in early September, thrown into some cabins and trailers, and asked to breathe air at a Mexico City–like elevation of 7,370 feet. It was a glorious tableau, had they been inclined to enjoy the scenery. The actual training site was Echo Summit, the base of a ski run in the Eldorado National Forest. Ponderosa pines not only surrounded the athletes but were among them; the site builders needed approval from the Forest Service to remove every single tree, so that even the new Tartan track infield was studded with timber. Runners disappeared behind parcels of the High Sierra on far turns.

Some of the athletes who showed up thought perhaps they were doing it for scenery, maybe a little tuning up, but certainly not to make the team. As far as they knew, that had happened earlier that summer, when they qualified at the Los Angeles Olympic Trials on the last weekend of June. This was just some horsing around in thin air. According to the rules, as far as anyone understood them, the top ten or twelve from each event in Los Angeles went to the high-altitude camp for further winnowing but the winner had automatically qualified for the Olympic team. The pressure was off, at least. So they thought.

Dick Fosbury had gone 7'1" at the Trials to win the high jump, on a day when neither he nor his competitors were jumping really well, but thrilling the crowd of 23,156 at the Los Angeles Coliseum, and magnitudes more watching the meet on television all the same ("The crowd went wild with joy," *Track & Field News* reported). So, the way he understood it, he was set. The others would fight it out for berths in Echo Summit. But he was set. He had made the Olympic team. He had returned to Oregon, goofed off a bit, then packed his bags and set forth for Lake Tahoe in his Chevy II, no hurry. By the time he got there on a Sunday, the Trials already begun, he wasn't feeling especially springy, but what did it matter. Good to see the guys.

Upon checking in, throwing his bags in his trailer, he learned from a sheaf of materials handed him that his spot was up for grabs after all. The USOC had been getting frantic over the altitude problem and had decided that the sea-level trials at Los Angeles might be a poor predictor of success in Mexico City. In a meeting immediately after the so-called Olympic Trials the committee made a wrenching, and not very public or well-understood, decision to change the selection process, meaning even the winners from Los Angeles would have to qualify anew. "No Moments of Truth," the *Los Angeles Times* revealed, some days after the event. "Trials Lack Drama Because They All Get Another Chance."

Fosbury, not a *Times* reader and thus learning about this decision for the first time, felt a panic rising in him. He wasn't set at all.

In far worse shape was the pole vaulter, Bob Seagren. He also believed he was set, having won the Los Angeles meet at 17'4" in a jump-off against Jon Vaughn. Seagren had not stuck around to read later editions of his hometown newspaper (which, at first, grouped him with other winners "on the United States Olympic team") either, but had flown off to Europe for a meet there. So he too was taken aback when he arrived at South Lake Tahoe and learned he would need to start over.

A lot of the athletes were taking the high road. Bill Bowerman, the Oregon coach who was in charge of Olympic preparations (colleague Payton Jordan of Stanford would step in as the team coach), had anguished over the USOC about-face but was relieved when the 1500-meter winner from Los Angeles, Dave Patrick, told him, "If I can't make the top three [at South Lake Tahoe], I don't deserve to go." Ed Burke, the twenty-eight-year-old hammer thrower, welcomed another face-off and told the *Los Angeles Times*, "Actually, I like the idea of two trials. It quickly weeds out the people of lesser ability."

This was brave talk, especially if you hadn't just been whisked from the Echo Summit infield in an ambulance, only days before the second Olympic Trials, the ones, apparently, that counted.

All Seagren had done was bend over to touch his toes, when he heard a pop "like the Fourth of July." Unlike Fosbury, he'd arrived at South Lake Tahoe in a timely fashion, showing up for an all-comers meet the week before the Trials. He had no particular anxiety about making the Olympic team, the ever-changing selection process notwithstanding, and was prepared to enjoy himself during the altitude camp. But then, that pop, exactly one week before the Trials. And then the pain. He crumpled to the grass, immobile. Ambulance drivers who had far more experience with fallen skiers arrived and transported their first-ever pole vaulter, the country's best chance to extend its dominance in the event, to a nearby hospital.

The others were having a better time of it. South Lake Tahoe had borne the expense of the camp, about $260,000, and produced a thrilling setting, if not a completely organized experience. When Bowerman arrived, according to marathoner Kenny Moore, he was appalled to find a third-rate food service, where "the best shot-putters in the world were getting 800 calories a day." Fearing mutiny, he prodded the USOC into action and conditions quickly improved. This allowed a large contingent of American males to compete favorably and, out on their own, in piney woods far from home, to act just as foolishly as you'd expect.

Some of the athletes arranged for golf outings in their downtime and others conducted trips to nearby casinos, across the Nevada-California state line. They were eager to spend their two-dollar per diem. One of the older guys, a hammer thrower, gathered up a bunch for a gambling run, assuring them he had a system. He didn't. John Carlos attracted a bunch to his scheme, pooling their per diems and running it up to two thousand dollars. It worked like most gambling schemes. They had to hitchhike back up the hill. Bob Beamon, the high jumper, had a learning experience of his own, running twenty dollars into one thousand dollars, then back down to zero in fourteen minutes.

Several more had been asked to take part in a high-altitude experiment that required them to submit daily urine samples. According to the *Track & Field News*, the testing became a new Olympic event. "One miler," *Track & Field News* reported in its Trials update, "set what he claimed as a world record of one and a half gallons. But then the middle distance runner produced two gallons."

There is no telling what Gary Stenlund could have generated, had he been included, but it would have been a competitive, if somewhat suspicious, amount. Stenlund, competing in javelin, was twenty-eight and well on his way to alcoholism. He was drinking his way through the camp, consuming about a case of beer a day, or a gallon of wine, or a fifth of whiskey. Whatever he could arrange. His training regimen. A park ranger did catch him drinking along the lake one night and turned him over to Bowerman. They had a little chat, but nothing more came of it.

Those woods were full of athletes and their coaches. Al Oerter was having a difficult time, trying to make his fourth Olympics, and enlisted the help of Payton Jordan. The two walked under the trees, "breathing the pine scent," and Jordan was able to suggest a couple of changes. Lee Evans was rambling around with a fishing rod, but gave up on the fast-moving streams.

Not all was fun and games, though. The black athletes were still wrestling with the boycott decision. At a meeting during the Los Angeles Trials, thirteen of the twenty-six black athletes said they'd boycott, but two of the dissenters were Jim Hines and Charlie Greene, the best of the 100-meter crop. Harry Edwards announced right before the South Lake Tahoe Trials that the boycott was probably a no-go, but there was still plenty of talk of it at the training camp and not a little bit of lingering resentment between the opposed camps of black athletes.

Others were preoccupied by more mundane matters. The per diem was not much help to the married athletes who brought their families to camp. They and their wives were given a chance at jobs, secured by the U.S. Olympic Committee, and busied themselves in area recreation programs, if they were lucky. Some of the wives found work in nearby casinos, hustling change for slots players.

Still, it was all about making this team. Some would, and a lot more with almost identical credentials wouldn't. Favorites would fall by the wayside, unknowns would rise to the occasion. And who knew just what effect this altitude would have. There would be some athletes, however superior at the Los Angeles Trials, who would indeed be eliminated in the thin air, a preemptive failure that might, if organizers were correct, allow national success later on. In that sense, the USOC had acted wisely, if somewhat unfairly, to base the entire selection on altitude performance. Bob Schul, the 5000-meter gold medalist in the 1964 Games, chugged to a distant last at Echo Summit, "his asthmatic wheezes audible even up in the stands," *Sports Illustrated* reported. He had been a disaster in waiting, found out before he could produce an Olympic humiliation. He ran to the woods and cried. Dave Patrick, who had impressed Bowerman with his gallantry, did not reproduce his first-place finish from the Los Angeles Trials, or even qualify in the 1500 meters. It was a brutal culling, like evolution, the survival of the fittest. But it was absolutely necessary to U.S. chances in Mexico City.

It would be hard, however, to justify the absence of pole-vault favorite Bob Seagren on the basis of a popped back.

Seagren had been playing in pain the entire year, but thought it was nothing more than a muscle pull. He'd been treated with lower-back injections of a Novocain-cortisone cocktail and had managed to keep going. But whatever happened to him that Saturday before the Trials was an entirely new experience. Taken to the hospital, he was quickly diagnosed with spondylolisthesis, a congenital disc slippage that can result in a pinched nerve whenever, it seems, he touches his toes. Or pole vaults. It was serious stuff, and his father was flown up from Los Angeles for the consultation. It was possible, doctors told him, to correct it surgically, but the success rate was only 5 percent. In any case, he'd probably never jump again. Seagren was dumbfounded, first by the news, then by the idea that doctors were willing to cut somebody open with only a one-in-twenty shot of fixing him. In the meantime, he was getting huge doses of Demerol every two hours.

Each day he was in the hospital, however, the pain subsided little by little. On Tuesday, he was feeling more like himself, but doctors refused to release him. On Wednesday, feeling even better, he arranged for his own release, calling a buddy to meet him at the back door of the hospital and drive him back to Echo Summit. He hid out in his trailer the rest of that day.

Nobody had expected him back, not Wednesday, maybe not ever. So, it was a surprise to see him jogging on Thursday morning. A surprise to see him stretching—gingerly—that afternoon. On Friday, Seagren waited until the track cleared in the afternoon, tired of surprising people. With the infield empty, he took his pole, made a little run, planted it, and vaulted (a little) over an imaginary bar and pronounced himself fit. Just a week later he vaulted 17'9" for a world record. "Obviously," reported *Track & Field News*, "no cripple."

The trials were like that. "Triumph and Tragedy at Tahoe," *Sports Illustrated* said. Billy Mills, the distance hero from the Tokyo Games, developed cramps in the 10,000 meters and didn't qualify. He was so popular a figure that teammates petitioned to allow Mills to qualify for the 5,000 meters, but the USOC had stretched its entry systems about as far as it could. A lot of famous names were getting tickets home. Literally. There was a ticket agent on site and as soon as an athlete completed his failure, he was shipped out. Olympic veteran Rink Babka, longtime record holder in the discus, also bailed out of competition there, although teammate Oerter remained.

One of the oddest departures involved Phil Shinnick. He was one of the white athletes there who was a known sympathizer of the black athletes and their efforts to boycott, and he was beginning to wonder if he'd be made to pay a price for it. He'd become sensitive to racial injustices at the University of Washington, where he witnessed the unequal treatment of his black teammates, and gotten involved in one of the issues of the day, redlining in Seattle. He stood on street corners handing out leaflets, protesting discrimination in housing. He continued to get even more involved after that. And, as he did, his paranoia ratcheted up.

He had reason to be skeptical of authority, anyway. As a sophomore at Washington, he'd traveled to the Modesto Relays to help fill out the long jump field. Not much was expected of him; all the attention was focused on a presumed duel between world record holder Igor Ter-Ovanesyan of the Soviet Union and two-time Olympic medalist Ralph Boston. Unfortunately, nobody bothered to turn on the wind gauge for Shinnick's jump. And yet, with the jump of his young life, he cleared 27'4", a quarter-inch better than Ter-Ovanesyan's mark. Everybody there testified to the stillness of the day. "Even a hummingbird's feather would have dropped to the ground without drifting in its descent at the moment young Shinnick made his phenomenal jump," wrote one journalist. "I saw the jump," agreed Boston, "and it was real." Still, it was not allowed because of the wind gauge, and Shinnick fumed at the injustice.

He'd made the 1964 Olympic team and was among the favorites to win but was unable to validate his Modesto performance there, failing even to make the finals on several muddy jumps. And now, he was back in South Lake Tahoe, feeling strong enough to overcome past failures, surmount any obstacles. Actually, he was a shoo-in, having jumped 26'7" in Los Angeles, grouping him with Boston and Bob Beamon. Still, there would be obstacles. Shinnick was a captain in the Air Force now, but hadn't lost his interest in the underdog. When ABC's Jim McKay came around, Shinnick couldn't help expressing his support of the black athletes in an interview. The next day, an Air Force general showed up at the training camp and informed him he was flirting with a court martial or, at the very least, a flight to South Vietnam.

This kind of harassment was to be expected. Something much stranger than that happened during the actual trials, though. Shinnick had noticed that the Olympic coach, Payton Jordan, was off huddling with another jumper, Charlie Mays, kind of a no-no. Shinnick had bested Mays by a quarter inch in the 1964 Trials, and they had not parted friends. And Mays, one of the least militant among the black athletes, was falling apart in these as well, but here he was with Jordan's arm around his shoulder. Shinnick felt that was a knife in his back, and couldn't help wondering if his comments hadn't aroused other authorities besides the military.

No matter, it was the jumps that counted, right? As Shinnick chugged down the runway during his event he passed a clump of trees and was shocked to see Mays emerge from the clearing, running parallel, not four feet from him. Surprised, Shinnick nearly pulled up, and ended by shanking his jump. He only managed a couple of legal jumps after that, none of them good enough, and he was off the team, replaced by Mays. Were Jordan and Mays conspiring against this rabble-rouser? Impossible to say but not, in 1968, entirely out of the question either.

Still, there was more than enough triumph to offset tragedy, and any of the assorted plots being hatched. Lee Evans lowered the world record by nearly a full second, winning the 400-meter dash in 44.1 seconds. On the same day that Seagren was rising from the dead to set a world record, John Carlos set a world record of his own in the 200 meters, beating even Speed City teammate Tommie Smith in a time of 19.7 (Smith, who had a stomachache, finished within his old record, too). *Sports Illustrated,* for one, enjoyed the juxtaposition of record holders that day, "the affluent, handsome-on-handsome Southern California college boy" versus "a goateed, jive-talking slum kid from Harlem."

SI didn't know the half of it. When his coach, Bud Winter, had gone up to him at the start, Carlos was dancing to music coming from a tape recorder. Winter, normally a big fan of relaxation, however it was done, scolded him. Carlos laughed him off. "Never mind," he said. "I'll break the record." Carlos was wearing sunglasses in his event as well, but why gild the lily? In any case, Carlos did break the record, sort of. His insistence on wearing Puma's brush spikes, with the sixty-four soft pins in the sole, cost him the sanction. Everybody knew those spikes would be disallowed, and told him so, but Carlos was going to go for the shoe money above all.

One by one, though, the favorites, most of them, anyway, squeaked in. Jim Ryun, the country's hope in the metric mile, bailed out on his second event, the 800 meters, at the Trials, and his confidence was sorely shaken. Everybody's was. It was widely believed the whole process, with the surprise selection system, had been put in place on his behalf. And now he was struggling just to make the team. "I was kidding myself," he said, after finishing the 800 meters in a jog, dead last. He still wasn't ready at that distance. The 1500 meters was his better event but now, after that dismal race, he had to wonder. "Have I done enough work to even win the 1500?"

Although he was so nervous that he couldn't fall asleep until two-thirty the morning before, Ryun had evidently done enough work. Nobody was close, offering him some encouragement after all. "I feel like a weight that I've been carrying all summer has finally been lifted from my shoulders." On the other hand, Dave Patrick of Villanova, who'd finished first in Los Angeles, let the pack get away from him and couldn't make up ground in the final ten strides. He crossed the line fourth, out of the Olympics, and broke down sobbing.

Perhaps the most dramatic finish, and the least reported, occurred on the final day of the Trials when Dick Fosbury was trying to make the team—again. Fosbury simply could not understand this selection process. Some of the athletes—not very many—held a vote to reinstate the rule that would reinstate the Los Angeles winners, but that was a predictably ridiculous idea. What athlete, except those few event winners, would vote for such a thing? And, whenever the vote was held, it was not held while Fosbury was around. In any case, that idea was crushed.

So, he had to bear down once more. This time around he was jumping erratically, hit and miss, and the competition was all bunching up around him. Fosbury needed all three tries to make 7'2", joining Olympic veteran Ed Caruthers, high schooler Reynaldo Brown, and John Hartfield. But, because of those misses, he was in fourth place. On that same basis, without any misses at all, Hartfield was in first. Since none of them had ever jumped higher than that, it was unlikely the standings would change. Hartfield could not lose, and Fosbury could not qualify.

The bar was lifted to 7'3", which might as well have been 10 feet as far as they were concerned, but the weather was warm and juices were flowing. Caruthers, running ever so slowly, straddled the bar, just ticking it, but making it. Brown likewise touched the bar on his attempt, but also made it. Hartfield missed. Fosbury somehow corkscrewed over the bar cleanly and came up out of the foam pit, grinning madly.

He hadn't made the team yet. Hartfield could still close him out on misses if he made the height, which, as the other three had shown, enjoying the thin air and the bouncy Tartan run-up, was definitely possible. As Hartfield lined up, though, Fosbury's coach had a sudden inspiration. Since that height would have been an Oregon school record, Berny Wagner asked to remeasure, so that it would qualify. Hartfield didn't notice this, absorbed in his own do-or-die drama, and started for the bar, seizing up only when he recognized the congestion of officials under the standards. It clearly shook him up.

With the officials finally cleared, he resumed his takeoff at 7'3" but he had lost all focus at that point and missed his remaining jumps. It was over. Hartfield understood what had just happened—a sure trip to Olympic glory had just been canceled—and he ran off into the woods, disappearing into a thick stand of Ponderosa pines. It was years before Fosbury, back on the team (and with a certified school record!), saw him again.

Not everybody was grouped in South Lake Tahoe. The women were doing their track-and-field training in Los Alamos, New Mexico, another high-altitude site. They got no attention whatsoever, not from the media, not even from the fellows at OPHR. This last example of exclusion stung. Wyomia Tyus, the Tigerbelle sprinter, was especially indignant. It "appalled" her that the men took the women for granted, acting as if they "had no minds of their own." The only visitors to the camp there were Mel Pender, Ralph Boston, and Art Simburg, by then Tyus's fiancée. Pender and Boston were representing Adidas, Simburg Puma. There wasn't much selling to do, though. Boston, a Tennessee State man himself, had the Tigerbelles locked up, including Tyus. Tigerbelle loyalty trumped love and even Simburg understood. He was glad to make the trip, though.

Even when the women traveled to Los Angeles for their trials in late August, there was very little coverage. *Sports Illustrated* did produce a story from the trials—"Dolls on the Move to Mexico" was the title—but it had more to do with the surprise of them being actual females. "A great influx of pretty young things coming into the sport," it quoted a coach as saying. The writer found "a dainty little thing" and a "great many more girls who look great in those warm-up suits, almost as though they were modeling them, for heaven sakes."

The girls—and they were always girls—were given a great shot at Olympic medals, especially Tyus in the 100 meters and Tigerbelle teammate Madeline Manning in the 800, and maybe Margaret Bailes, a sprinter from Oregon, or Barbara Ferrell, a Los Angeles sprinter. However, it was clear that women's athletics were simply one more talent contest in an ongoing beauty pageant. One of the track officials at the Trials observed in the *SI* account: "The girls are finding that there can be a certain glamour in all this. For one thing, running does great things for the legs. It makes them shapelier." Added another: "And they get to meet a lot of boys."

Both the *New York Times* and the *New Yorker* found the travails of the Harvard crew far more interesting than anything the women might be going through. But theirs wasn't the only story missed that summer. Olympic preparations were scattered across the country and the calendar and they took various forms, not all of which could be harnessed by the conventions of young adult novels. None of the boxers, for example, were going to get the Ralph Henry Barbour treatment. Certainly not George Foreman, the team's big heavyweight prospect, whose tale veered closer to Dickens when it came to upbringing and, for that matter, his prospects.

Foreman had been lucky, in a way. He had seen the ads on television. Public service announcements, actually. Jim Brown and Johnny Unitas, thumping something called the Job Corps. Of course, in those days, who didn't want to be like Jim Brown? Or Johnny Unitas, for that matter? It was well known that Unitas had been an athletic discard, had spent one thin dime to call the Baltimore Colts out of the blue, and had gone on to glory in the NFL. "If you're looking for that one last chance," Unitas told the other discards in TV land, "you ought to join the Job Corps."

Foreman had no idea what that was, but it sounded like a pretty good alternative at that point. He had dropped out of school in the ninth grade and, even if he wasn't terrorizing the Fifth Ward anymore, he wasn't moving up any career ladders. He had just been fired at Wald Transfer and Storage, which was too bad, because if he'd only attained permanent status there, he'd have gotten $1.25 an hour and a uniform with his name on the pocket. So maybe the Job Corps, him and Johnny Unitas and Jim Brown.

It was a skill-learning program, part of the War on Poverty, and it was conducted in various outposts of the country. Foreman's first stop was Grants Pass in Oregon and the whole thing, even aside from the tremendous travel this meant, was an amazement. First off, he finally did get a uniform, two pairs of brown slacks and a blazer. Although instead of his name, there was a red, white, and blue "JC" emblem on the pocket. Foreman had never been especially patriotic, the national anthem being a source of irritation to him, signaling nothing so much as the end of the TV programming day, but he was sort of proud of that blazer.

Second, there was all that food. Three meals, every day. Foreman, who had made a fetish of his appetite back in Houston, hoarding small chunks of food against a final hunger, couldn't trust the abundance. Every meal he'd ask his tablemates if they were going to clean their plates. It took him a month to completely fill up.

And, third, there was Carl Hempe, America's Finest Physique, 1939 (medium division). Hempe was the camp motivator, old and retired by 1966, but still able to do a pushup with the biggest kid on his back. This didn't impress Foreman so much, but when Hempe addressed the kids and told them, no matter what everybody on the outside called them, and that was bound to be plenty given their sorry circumstances, they were still Americans, Foreman got a little more wide-eyed than usual. "Nobody can take that away from you," Hempe told them. Foreman was always on the lookout for something he could call his own.

Even so, he wasn't much more than a thug with a particularly high caloric intake and a nice blazer, no matter what Hempe had to say. He was still pushing everyone around, even when he was sent to the next Job Corps camp in Pleasanton, outside Oakland. He was just a big, mean kid, constantly waylaying his camp mates, and was an aggravation to everybody. It was more than an aggravation, actually. It might have been felony assault. There was talk at the Job Corps that Foreman would have to be sent across the street to the Santa Rita State Prison, if he kept this up. In fact, after one of his particularly savage ambushes, the camp director announced Foreman was either going home or to jail, one or the other, but he couldn't stay here.

Charles "Doc" Broadus, who was head of security for the center and who also ran the camp's sports program, was watching *Rawhide* on the gym's television when he heard about this latest Foreman incident. He reacted swiftly. "We do that," he told the director, "we defeat our purpose. We brought him here to make him a marketable item." The director said, fine, he's your baby, then, and told him where to find Foreman. Broadus interrupted Foreman at work—"a stomping and being very brutal about it"—and thought, "Now I've stuck my foot in my mouth."

Broadus put him inside a boxing ring. "Do you really think I can be a boxer?" he asked Broadus. Broadus explained: "Well, you're ugly enough." And, at first, that was about all he could bring to the sport. Foreman quickly discovered that boxing was very different from fighting, and that just about any skinny little kid whom Broadus put in there with him was capable of embarrassing the big fellow. This was a wonderful development for the corpsmen; now everybody was safe, even the other boxers. Foreman persisted, and so did Broadus, and some small progress was made in transferring that fury into, well, a marketable item.

Once Foreman graduated from the Job Corps, with a background in electronics, he moved back to Houston and whatever ground had been made in Pleasanton was lost. There was no immediate work in the electronics-assembly field and he quickly resumed his Fifth Ward ways. When Broadus called the house to see how his big guy was doing, Foreman's mother said, "Just get this man out of Houston, please!" Broadus immediately sent Foreman a one-way ticket to Oakland, got him a job mopping floors and washing pots at the Job Corps there, and resumed Foreman's boxing education during available hours. It seemed better for everybody involved.

The thing about Foreman, and any kid from the Fifth Ward could have saved Broadus that discovery, was he could hit. Broadus worked on various wiles, trying to get him to stick and move, but it was clear that Foreman would advance, if he could at all, on the basis of his power. Foreman would simply close his eyes, tighten up, and let loose. He was, of course, as likely to miss as connect, but who wanted to take that chance? By now there was nobody who could spar with him; somebody would be drafted to "kinda rassle around in the ring" with him. They would bob and weave and duck under the ropes. The work was not meaningful.

Still, Broadus managed to steer him into some amateur tournaments and, in 1968, in only his eleventh amateur bout, Foreman won the San Francisco Golden Gloves tournament. Broadus explained to him that he could probably turn pro, but with these meager credentials and scant experience couldn't expect to make a lot of money, or even win a lot of fights. There was, however, this other amateur tournament and maybe they should be thinking about that. *What*, Foreman wondered, *were the Olympics?*

Broadus got him into the National AAU Tournament in Toledo in April 1968 and Foreman swept through to the championship with four stoppages. His confidence continued to increase, and the idea of fighting in the Olympics grew real. He was even bolstered by an exhibition later in June with ex–heavyweight champ Sonny Liston at the New Oakland Boxing Club. Liston was preparing for a fight with Henry Clark later in the week at San Francisco's Cow Palace and was looking for some rounds. Foreman jumped at the chance, though he refused the five dollars that Liston's manager, Dick Sadler, offered him. By now Foreman knew enough of the Olympics to refuse the money. A story about Jim Thorpe, how the great Indian had lost his amateur standing through similar foolishness, stuck in his mind.

The real point of that exhibition was that he stood up to Liston, more or less. Sadler had warned everybody that "Sonny hurts anything he hits," which was certainly true in those cases he wasn't hitting Cassius Clay. Yet here was this nineteen-year-old kid out of the Job Corps stinging him with a jab. Liston was clearly irritated, enough so that somebody in the crowd felt it necessary to yell, "Don't hurt the kid, champ." Yelled someone else: "He's a kid, don't do it!" Foreman continued to bore in all the same and, then, in the third round, threw what was described in the *Oakland Tribune* as a "crisp right to the button." Furious at the lack of respect, and at the blood that appeared under his eye, Liston delivered an immediate and savage left hook that put the dazed youngster into the ropes, Sadler rushing in to stop the action for the day, lest Liston add manslaughter to his already impressive rap sheet. Foreman was satisfied, though. He had made Liston mad enough to blister him not only with that hook but with a long and inventive string of obscenities. "Sonny just cursed me," thought Foreman happily, clinging to the validation of an ex-champion's anger.

Amateur boxing, which meant Olympic boxing in 1968, was beginning to take notice of this heavy-handed prospect, but couldn't go too crazy over a kid who'd had only eighteen bouts. It was decided that Foreman, who qualified for the Olympic Trials with his National AAU title, would go to Germany for his international season-ing. Foreman knew that this was a critical evaluation and figured if he didn't knock out all of his opponents, the officials would have a chance to second-guess his invitation. He fought accordingly. In the first bout, his alarmed opponent was disqualified for failure to engage. He had all but leapt out of the ring. The second and third, Foreman won by knockout. And that was his international experience.

The Olympic Trials were held that June in Toledo and by now there was almost no chance that Foreman would be stopped. He got through cleanly and was beginning to inspire hyperbole, which is the international language of boxing. "I think," opined Broadus to the *Oakland Tribune* the month before the Olympics, "he'll make the world forget Louis and Clay."

Things were happening very fast. Foreman was just nineteen, only a couple of years removed from the streets of the Fifth Ward, still a beginner in the sport. And now he was being promoted as his country's best chance for an Olympic medal. It was all he could do to keep up with events but it was clear he was trying. When a visitor from *Sports Illustrated* interviewed him at the Olympic training camp in Santa Fe, New Mexico, Foreman was more than up to the task. "Notice me," he advised the writer. "I am a giant. I am six-three, two hundred sixteen pounds, and I cover a lot of ground." He had already covered quite a bit, no question.

Chapter 8

DENVER

*The Anarchists' Convention, a Vote for Nixon,
and a Cold Chill*

THE U.S. OLYMPIANS ALL gathered in Denver, a week before their departure for Mexico City. They were issued uniforms, blazers, and dresses, given instructions, processed, and invited to breathe yet even more thin air. For many of them, this was the first time they'd seen each other. The women eyed the men, the men reciprocated. Olympic functionaries barreled around, looking for troublemakers, protesters, ready to squash the first sign of dissent.

For the black athletes, it was one last chance to assemble. The boycott was dead, but there was still the matter of protest. When Harry Edwards had announced the blacks would participate, he opened the door for individual expression. He offered no guidance there. In fact, from this point on, Edwards would be conspicuous by his absence. He had been persuaded that if he had attended the Games he would in all likelihood be assassinated himself. It was not a far-fetched idea, considering the year's calendar of murder. Moreover, it was explained to him, if he did decide to martyr himself in Mexico City, he would probably take some of the athletes down with him. With Edwards out of the picture, the United States might feel more responsible for the athletes. He went to Canada to enjoy the Olympics there.

So it was now up to each athlete to decide. As Lee Evans, one of Edwards's earliest disciples, said, "We can't go down there without deciding something." That was going to be hard, perhaps even impossible. "It boiled down to a clash," said sprinter Larry James, "between the goal—doing good for all mankind—and the gold—the individual's self-interest." He added, "There was, shall we say, counseling back and forth to sort out the two."

Tommie Smith, who had given birth to the boycott idea a year earlier in that offhand remark in Tokyo, was determined "to make worthwhile this last year." He said, "I hold no hate for people who can't make a gesture, whatever the reason. But I have to preserve the honor of Tommie Smith. I'm an American until I die, and to me that means I have to do something."

Nobody could agree on what. As James suggested, there were competing agendas at play. When somebody suggested the winner mount the podium barefoot, there were widespread guffaws. Shoe money! When somebody said they should race in black socks, somebody else said those made his ankles itch. It was a convention of anarchists. How about black armbands? Hurts my arm. It was a thoroughly exasperating meeting, enough so that sprinter Mel Pender, the Army man with the most to forfeit, finally lost it: "You motherfuckers!" he shouted, quieting the room. "Shut the fuck up!"

Still, there was no agreement, except that everybody would find their own personal gestures, assuming they decided to make one at all. Denver, it was clear, was as far as the movement was going to go. This was no longer a group, with lists of demands, posters, buttons. Any athlete who protested from here on did so on his or her own, and ought to be prepared for the consequences. Each of them recognized they were jumping into a kind of void, beyond which rescue was no longer available. Suddenly, it seemed quite frightening.

After the meeting, some of the athletes busied themselves shopping for black berets, socks, gloves, beads, all the accessories of protest they could imagine. Athletes before them merely had to worry about getting to the podium. How, they wondered, had it gotten to this?

It was a sobering stopover for everybody. George Foreman, the hulking heavyweight, had been somewhat disappointed that, whatever his real politics, he had not been approached by any of the boycott organizers. At the Denver airport, where all the other black athletes were scurrying around, doing their last-minute campaigning, he felt entirely neglected. Nobody said a word to him. They ran back and forth, soliciting everyone but him. "Looking at me like I'm the wind," he thought, furious. The only person who showed the slightest bit of interest in him was an actual political campaigner, somebody working on behalf of Richard Nixon. "We believe you can help us," he told Foreman. If he won the gold, would he come on board the Nixon campaign? Foreman was thrilled to be included in presidential politics, whoever Richard Nixon was, and pledged his support on the spot.

Also at the airport was the Harvard crew, dressed in their polyester Olympic suits, but with OPHR buttons on their lapels. They were happy to have been put on the same plane to Mexico City as the Tigerbelles, their old friends, but otherwise were having their usual problems with authority. Robert Paul, the chief spokesman for the USOC, walked up to 110-pound Paul Hoffman and began poking his finger in the coxswain's chest. He told Hoffman he wouldn't be allowed on the plane without a proper uniform, meaning no funny ties (it was a Harvard thing, wearing the least fashionable ties they could find), and no button.

Hoffman pointed to Tigerbelle Wyomia Tyus, who would be competing in her second Olympics, and told Paul, "See that woman? If you get her to take her button off, I'll take mine off." The one thing Hoffman discovered was that Olympic officials "had this problem" with talking to blacks. They just didn't like doing it. Paul walked off, steaming, and Hoffman kept his button.

Once on the plane, it started to occur to the athletes that they were stepping off into another territory, mysterious, and probably dangerous. Not that it was Mexico. They were headed somewhere much more frightening. When the door closed, so did a part of their lives. Everything they had done before was in a spirit of fun. They had been at play, running and jumping, saying outrageous things, poking a stick at the adults, getting away with murder, really. However, with this trip, they were embarking on a kind of adulthood. They would have to account for their decisions, face real consequences. Whatever happened now was going to matter.

Mel Pender had chills as the plane lifted off. John Carlos was shouting something foolish, like he always was, but this time he was getting no response. Even Carlos settled down. Pender looked around him, at all his jive-talking teammates, all so full of themselves, the Tigerbelles, those crazy kids with the bad haircuts. It was quiet. Nobody was talking, nothing. They just stared straight ahead at the seat backs, scared out of their minds.

Chapter 9

MEXICO CITY

Thin Air, Fresh Paint, and Shots in the Night

THE WATER HEATERS AT Villa Coapa, the spanking new complex created for Olympic visitors, kept popping in the night. If a guest failed to observe water-heater protocol, at least as it was practiced in Mexico (the flame had to be turned on and off as hot water was required), pressure would build and blow out the valve on top, releasing geysers of scalding water. This was more irritating than dangerous, as the water heaters were safely out of the way on an outdoor porch. But, with plumbers understandably stretched thin, an afflicted guest might go days between warm showers.

In the sense that an Olympics is basically a carefully staged culture clash, odd customs and harmless traditions, the real keepsakes of such sports tourism, nobody would have it any other way. Exploding water heaters! Not only did it make for a memorable story, suitable for anecdotal add-ons back home—going off in the evening like mortar fire!—but it proved an apt metaphor for the brief foray into this strange land: no matter the amount of preparation, either by host or guest, there can never be adequate allowance made for international misunderstanding.

Everybody knew a Mexican Olympics would be different. It was going to be warm, colorful, inexpensive, and musical. A fiesta, probably. It was the first ever awarded to a so-called developing nation, the first assigned to a Latin American country, the first in what would almost certainly be a deadly high altitude (according to a medical doomsayer here and there). Some wondered if it might be too different, and if it was going to be at all possible to drink the water, or if there would be plumbing to drink it from.

As an Olympic bidder, Mexico was a decided underdog. The quadrennial event was never meant to be an international marketing campaign, to be broken out in case of poor public relations. The Games tended to go to world capitals like Rome and Tokyo, with trusted infrastructures and established reputations, not to mention the availability of luxury hotels. Just because Mexico wanted to move past its south-of-the-border stereotype would not normally be cause enough to swing support its way. Detroit and Lyons were front-runners, in any case.

Mexico had an unexpected ally in IOC president Avery Brundage who, as usual, was impressed with any foreign policy that was able to ignore the Cold War and its inevitably complicating effect on his Games. "Both Detroit and Lyons were handicapped by NATO actions barring East Germans," he wrote in his diaries, according to historian Eric Zolov. "The peculiar United States foreign policy for the last thirty years, which has lavishly spread hundreds of dollars throughout the world but has left a lack of confidence abroad in the United States, did not help Detroit."

So maybe Mexico City's win at Baden-Baden in 1963 shouldn't have been such a surprise. On the other hand, was Mexico sure it wanted this? The celebration over, Mexico had to face some hard facts: chiefly, it could afford to fund an Olympic buildup only fractionally, compared to past Games. Japan had spent $2.7 billion for railways, roads, and arenas for the 1964 Tokyo Olympics, the so-called Happy Games. Mexico was pledging something like $176 million for a similar preparation. "We are not sure we can guarantee the organization of these Games," admitted a Mexican delegate, returning from Tokyo, "but the weather will be nice."

North of the border, skepticism was even sharper. The U.S. press tried to be generous in its coverage of the forthcoming extravaganza, but familiar characterizations still found their way into print. "It is not true that Mexicans are lazy," reported *Sports Illustrated*, "but they do have great patience in getting things done." Although the same article gave credit to the Mexicans' "inspirational fire when there is a chance to do something bold and fresh," it also included a quote from a "European" that seemed to sum up international expectations: "These people can't do it."

However, they *were* doing it, throwing up four hotels, building a six-lane highway, dredging a canal beside the Floating Gardens of Xochimilco for rowing and canoeing. Famous architects were pressed into service for the construction of several venues. A subway was being built. Murals were being commissioned, others being restored. Even as Mexico moved forward, though, it could not escape its past; every excavation, it seemed, turned up an archeological site. But no matter, work went on. The *New Yorker* sent their man down and he approved of the industry. "The Mexican countryside may not be 'developed' yet, but at least Mexico City has an advanced, sophisticated building trade, whose manpower ranges from many excellent architects, down through master craftsmen, to battalions of easily marshalled raw laborers."

If things were getting done, to the world's surprise, they were at least getting done in their own, highly Mexican way. In the rush to completion, there was scant attention to detail. "Details, nothing more than details," engineers told visiting press, who'd come to monitor progress. "In some cases," reported the *New York Times* as late as September, "the details turned out to be rather important." For example, the *Times* felt there should have been a wooden floor for the basketball court by then.

Athletes would notice this throughout the Games, feeling that things might have been done, but they weren't finished. One of the women divers, hardly trained for such matters, noticed that the dry-wall in her dressing room had yet to be sanded. Hammer thrower Ed Burke leaned up against a wall and realized he was coated with red dust. "They hadn't fired the brick!" There was a feeling, all in all, that organizers had done only what was minimally required, or would be most visible. Robert Lipsyte, the young columnist for the *New York Times*, was traveling into the Olympic Village from the airport when he experienced an epiphany. He saw a one-legged man, hopping, kicking a brown ball against the wall of a shack, and with each bounce, the ball took a little more paint off the wall. Lipsyte understood, in that instant, that the entire city had been whitewashed, however thinly, for visitors' benefit.

No doubt there was a tendency toward pushing the deadline, which did not demolish their reputation as a third-world country any more than their low tolerance for detail work. A coach who was in Mexico City for the run-up to the Games remembers a pre-Olympic meet at the stadium track—which was still incomplete at that point (it was without the approved finish line)—during which a police car, sirens blazing, rolled up to the track right before the 100-meter sprint. The commotion caused his runner to false start.

The Mexicans, no matter their coming-out campaign, still seemed to delight in exasperating their visitors, conducting business on their own terms. Bert Bonanno, one of Bud Winter's disciples at San Jose State, was one of many foreign coaches hired to coach Mexican teams. He enjoyed a gradual indoctrination in Mexican ways, and eventually became an admirer of their work ethic. However, he found that you couldn't really plan your day according to official schedules there. Working as a go-between for the 3M company (which was providing the new Tartan track) and General Jose Flores, head of the Mexican Organizing Committee, Bonanno advised against impatience. They should not expect their seven o'clock meeting to occur anytime before eight. When the officials were kept waiting, as predicted, they ignored Bonanno and just left. Bonanno shrugged.

Bonanno knew how to play the game, and had learned the hard way. Once, when he was petitioning for more money to take his team on an extended trip in the pre-Olympic seasons, he had to wait nearly four hours for the great general to accept him. "What do you want?" Flores finally said, without even looking up. Bonanno worked up the nerve to suggest a sum of $12,000, explaining his team's needs. "Pesos or dollars?" Flores asked, again without looking up. He reached into a drawer, withdrew $14,000 in cash, and told him to beat it.

That was another thing that nobody seemed to get. Cash, and its back-and-forth flow, and how it was best employed. Whatever a successful Olympics would erase for Mexico, it would not be the reputation for piracy conducted in the name of *la mordida*. At least some Olympic officials, like most authorities there, regarded a bribe as a necessary price of business, sort of like a gratuity. Anyone failing to understand this when the Olympics began was in for some frustration.

Take Ed Fox, who was helping to organize the *Track & Field News* Olympic Tour (TAFNOT). As part of his duties, he had arranged for event tickets for his group, which amounted to more than 800 track-and-field fans, TAFNOTers in their language. They were ordered and paid for a year in advance. Yet when Fox arrived in Mexico City, six days before the Opening Ceremony, he found there were no bundles of easily distributed tickets. Actually, there was nothing. When he arrived at the Olympic Coordination Authority, he was made to wait the entire day, then simply dismissed. The next day, more waiting, more chaos, as he jostled with similarly enraged ticket seekers. The day after that, he was admitted to the inner-office sanctums, where he surprised himself by boiling over and slamming the table with his fist. A secretary pointed him to a stack of tickets along the wall and said, "Take what you need."

He needed upward of 6,400 tickets for his group and, more important, he especially needed tickets for the prized Opening Ceremony as well as the October 20 events, the last day of track-and-field competition. They were not forthcoming, and slamming his fist on a table was not going to produce them. He began to understand the chaos was more calculated than he at first imagined. Finally, the day before the Olympics were to begin, a Mexican tour guide who was associated with the group suggested an honorarium of $10,000 for those in charge of tickets. And the TAFNOTers got to see their Olympics.

Besides putting on an actual sporting event, providing for the care and feeding of more than seven thousand athletes from 110 nations and perhaps one hundred thousand visitors, Mexico was obliged to provide a cultural showcase as well. This was partly as international promotion but also to satisfy some of the concerns within its borders, where the Olympics and their tremendous costs were not universally cheered. So, in the Olympic year, in the Cultural Olympiad, there were activities equal to the number of sports, but not always relevant to them. Poetry festivals, folk-arts demonstrations, and sculpture shows were staged. There were also exhibitions on nuclear energy and space travel. And ballet, youth film, Olympic stamps. Both the Mormon Tabernacle Choir and Maurice Chevalier passed through, all in the name of culture. As the *New Yorker* observed, "This is the first Olympiad to feature both Mali and Dalí."

There was art and design galore. Museums were running at full bore; Avery Brundage himself had loaned his collection of Asian art to the Museum of Anthropology. But you didn't have to pay an admission to sense something was going on. The route to the Olympic Village, renamed the Route of Friendship, may have enjoyed only a patina of decoration, as far as housing was concerned, but it did get a major sculpture installation—eighteen abstracts. Nearly every thoroughfare was festooned with the white peace dove, or an "Everything Is Possible in Peace" billboard. Two graphic artists, one from the United States and the other from Great Britain, supplied the MEXICO68 logo, done with a very modern op-art aesthetic. It was everywhere.

Less amenable to good intentions was the oxygen-depleted air everyone would have to breathe. This had been a point of argument ever since the Games were awarded to Mexico. At an altitude of 7,415 feet, an athlete could expect to get, per lungful, less than three-quarters of the oxygen that he or she was used to. This was going to be a problem. The Mexican Organizing Committee had hoped to direct the conversation in a more positive way, sending an acrylic box to international members, inscribed, "It contains air of Mexico City, special for breaking records." It did not forestall early objections and Brundage was forced to bark, "The Olympic Games belong to all the world, not just the part of it at sea level."

One doctor predicted deaths, but most others agreed on less mortal complications. While the air might be special in the sprints, they said, any event contested at distances greater than 800 meters definitely would be compromised by the thin air. Marathoners might not die at the finish line, but they probably wouldn't feel so swell. And there was to be no extraordinary acclimation permitted, that was an Olympic rule. No team could train at high altitude for more than a month in the three months before the Games, and no more than six weeks in the Olympic year. Nor could they show up in Mexico City early. Although these rules would be flouted, and athletes had plenty of opportunity to train at altitude, there was still a lot of concern. Just months before the Games, *Family Weekly*, a Sunday magazine insert that appeared throughout the United States, ran an article titled, "Why the U.S. Will Lose the Summer Olympics." Oxygen-hemoglobin bonding capacity was the answer.

Nearly as invisible, and every bit as troubling, was the growing concentration of spooks in Mexico City. There was a fantastic buildup going on, this being the Cold War, with communists lurking everywhere, Cuba was not *that* far off, campuses filled with Trotskyites, and a pretty big and increasingly suspicious international contingent was growing by the day.

This was becoming Spy City in 1968. And the United States was at least partly to blame for this blossoming community of secret agents. After the Tokyo Games, Mexico had approached U.S. Olympic members and asked about the use of established coaches for its athletes. Mexico had never been an Olympic juggernaut—no country had won fewer medals (one bronze) than Mexico at Tokyo—but this Olympics would have to be different. The country meant to impress on as many fronts as possible and athletic improvement was a priority. The United States didn't immediately cooperate, so Mexico began casting about in other corners of the world for coaching expertise.

Nevertheless, there were a number of U.S. coaches who signed on, one of them Bert Bonanno, the Bud Winter acolyte from San Jose State. Bonanno had left Winter and had been coaching at a California high school when the offer came to become Mexico's track-and-field coach. He immediately relocated to Mexico City. Once there, he recognized some fellow expatriates from the United States, hired hands like him, but also noticed a surprising number of Iron Curtain coaches, some really puzzling characters.

Bonanno hadn't been there very long before the CIA approached him. He was at the track when a man who said he was from the State Department walked up to him and invited him to a meeting at the Reforma Hotel the next morning. Once there, the so-called State Department man admitted he was CIA and that he was asking Bonanno to keep tabs on his foreign colleagues and to report back once a week. Bonanno said, you know, now that you mention it, there are some odd ducks out there. Exactly, he was told.

Bonanno was not practiced in spycraft, and far be it for a Bud Winter acolyte to confuse eccentricity with espionage. But, all the same, he had no trouble producing plenty of material for his weekly briefings. Lots of the coaches, he observed, were fluent in far more languages than their sport required. If this is cause for suspicion, it is the result of an American bias, which associates European bilingualism with the capacity for counterintelligence. But why, indeed, was the Polish coach of the Mexican walking team so fluent in Spanish?

And, for that matter, why did so many of the Iron Curtain coaches bunk in the Olympic Village with the athletes? Why was one of them teaching his Mexican athletes French on the side? And did anybody else think it was strange that one of the foreign coaches was a concert pianist? The boys at the CIA ate it up.

It wasn't all amateur hour, though. The U.S. embassy in Mexico City was its largest, and it was constantly filing cables to Washington in advance of the Olympics. The CIA had a major station there, keeping watch over Cuban and Soviet delegations, filing Situation Reports (Sitreps) regularly, and it was assumed Communist intelligence interests were well represented there, as well. For that matter, not everyone on the U.S. Olympic Committee was on hand to advance the spirit of amateur sport. An assistant Olympic attaché named Philip Agee was actually getting his final CIA posting (he would famously turn on the agency in later years, writing an exposé), and he was meeting with Cuba and KGB there far more often than he was Avery Brundage. "By the summer of '68," said one writer, "Mexico City resembled a spooks' Olympics."

There was plenty to keep them all busy. Aside from banking the embers of paranoia, as was their stock-in-trade, operators there were keeping close tabs on the developing unrest among Mexican students. This was highly important, as it seemed to include all of the major preoccupations of the day: agitating students, creeping Communism, regime change, and international politics in general. And it was occurring in advance of one of the world's most visible extravaganzas. This was one-stop shopping for any spy.

The unrest, which was in a sense just a localized symptom of a worldwide contagion, had begun in July when some students took to the streets to celebrate the tenth anniversary of Fidel Castro's revolution in Cuba. As everywhere else in the world that year, Mexican students were feeling their oats, were looking to flex some ideological muscle, and they were intrigued by the possibility of gathering together to inspire change. Strikes and protests were hardly new to

Mexico but, in 1968, with the government feeling pressure to present an image of prosperity, modernity, and progress—peace above all—to the rest of the world, student reaction was more pronounced than usual. This particular demonstration was not especially organized or even objectionable—it was barely political, degenerating into a street brawl between the students of rival vocational schools—but it was swiftly and vigorously quashed. Two hundred riot police, according to the *New Republic*, were "cracking the heads of all in reach." It was later reported that four students were killed in the disturbance, two hundred injured.

Add a youthful self-absorption to an already politically charged group, and you have a highly flammable community. The youth movement, which had been vague and amorphous, now gathered purpose as an aggrieved and victimized party. This was all apart from the politics of the Olympics, which were still several months off. Demands, which now had the specific context of police brutality and government oppression, were made. Mexico's ruling government, led by President Gustavo Díaz Ordaz, did not so much quell a public disturbance as light a wick.

And so began a summer of roiling protest, nearly fifty rallies in all, gathering steam, galvanizing even more youth, generating even more protest. By August student marches were drawing fifty thousand protesters. On August 13, one hundred fifty thousand took to the streets, and they were beginning to push Díaz's buttons. "Díaz Ordaz, where are you?" read the signs. And, "Díaz Ordaz, get your teeth pulled." They were broadening their protest to include university reform and questioning the tremendous cost of the Olympics. It was clear that the students were gaining intensity as well as numbers. On August 27, they boldly marched in front of the presidential palace and vandalized it with spray paint, insulting the notoriously insecure and not terribly handsome president incidentally. "Come out on the balcony," they chanted, "monkey with a big snout."

These events were of keen interest to ruling parties besides Mexico's, especially with the Olympics scheduled only months away and not so far from one very particular border. U.S. State Department officials in Mexico City were cranking out telegrams as fast as they could type, and so were the fellows at the CIA, but their reporting and analysis were equally flawed. They might have been better off presenting Bert Bonanno's briefings.

"There are not now present in Mexico conditions such as appear to have caused the French crisis," read a June 14 classified telegram from the U.S. embassy to Washington, referring to student demonstrations in Paris that nearly toppled the de Gaulle regime. "And it is most unlikely that such conditions will rapidly develop here to critical proportions, at least until after 1970 when President Díaz Ordaz's terms ends." The report went on to say that student unrest "may break out on a large scale at any time and for any reason" but that the government had shown the ability to "crack down decisively, to date with salutary effects."

The students, meanwhile, had discovered an even hotter button than the president's physical appearance and were now leveraging the Olympics in their regular protests. Students from a group called *Comité Anti-Olímpico de Subversión* visited with Harry Edwards in San Jose to pledge the support of one hundred thousand "young people." They told him, "We are prepared to lose some lives in an initial charge on the stadium, but we will stop the Olympics by any means necessary."

Nobody knew if the students were organized to do any such thing, but Mexican authorities were certainly getting the jitters. Díaz Ordaz used most of his presidential address on September 1 to remind students that he remained fully committed to the Games and would use "all legal means within our reach" to ensure a proper Opening Ceremony. It was not a particularly conciliatory speech. It would have been even less satisfying to protesters if they'd known that Díaz Ordaz had, starting in May, been ordering riot gear from the United States.

Both the State Department and the CIA were trying to gauge the potential for mayhem in October, and whether an Olympics would even happen, but they were also typically preoccupied with rooting out Communist influences. According to the *Washington Post*'s Jefferson Morley, Winston Scott, the CIA's Mexico City station chief, told Washington in an August cable that the riot in front of Díaz's palace represented a "classic example of the Communists' ability to divert a peaceful demonstration into a major riot."

Nobody else in the intelligence community would go so far as to say that. It was the first place to look, sure, but further fact-finding tended not to support the thesis. The problem, according to Morley, who teased this out of a partly declassified history of the Mexico City station, was that Scott was basing an enormous reliance on his good buddy, President Díaz Ordaz. In fact, Scott had set up a "secret spy network code-named LITEMPO" that consisted entirely of Mexican government officials. One of these paid agents was a nephew of Díaz Ordaz, another was Luis Echeverria, head of Díaz Ordaz's "Strategy Committee," which had been formed to react to the student protests.

It was apparent that Díaz Ordaz wanted to put the disturbances at the feet of the Communists and was able to convince Scott of this, at least for a while. It was a bum steer. Scott, however, was forming impressions independent of his LITEMPO misinformation and was relaying his growing misgivings back to Washington. In late September, Scott cabled that the Mexican government was "not seeking compromise solution with students but rather seeking to put an end to all organized student actions before Olympics." Scott had no idea.

On October 2, after a period of relative calm during which the forthcoming Olympics were beginning to overshadow the summer of protest, students gathered at the Plaza de Las Tres Culturas in the Tlatelolco housing project for a modest rally. There were perhaps five thousand students on the plaza, a square of historical importance for its location near Aztec ruins, a colonial church, and the Foreign Ministry: your three cultures of Mexico. It was also important as a meeting place for students from city campuses. It was fifteen miles from the Olympic Village and in the middle of the city's biggest housing development, the long block buildings named after Mexican states. And on this afternoon, beginning at five o'clock, it was encircled with tanks, enclosing the students completely. Soldiers sat on top of the tanks, shining their bayonets, and two helicopters fluttered above.

Student leaders by now had very little new to say and, recognizing the military presence, perhaps a thousand troops, called off plans for a march to the National Polytechnic Institute. It was not an especially alarming show of student gusto. It was not in any way provocative.

However, Díaz Ordaz had been provoked enough—it had been a long and vexing summer—and had ordered a maneuver that would put an end to this foolishness. He would not be embarrassed any longer. With the Olympics just ten days away, and visitors beginning to arrive, it was now time to crush this movement once and for all. So at six that afternoon, the hovering helicopters suddenly flashed green and red flares, army troops sealed the exit plaza, and undercover Battalion Olympia—all wearing a single white glove so they could recognize one another—began circulating among the crowd. From balconies and rooftops, shots poured into the plaza, and people simply fell over.

The haze of history would be slow to lift on this one. To the extent that there was any information at all, it was wrong. Not even that. Immediate reports were a total misdirection. The Mexican government at first said four students were killed. State-owned television said there had been a police incident. The more time and distance involved, the greater the numbers, but nothing to correspond to the carnage. The next day *El Sol de México* said student snipers had fired on the troops, killing a general and wounding eleven soldiers. Firing in defense, the army had killed twenty civilians.

The CIA's Scott had a report filed by midnight. And he, too, had swallowed it whole. Scott wrote Washington, "A classified source said the first shots were fired by the students from the Chihuahua apartments." An American classified source "expressed the opinion this was a premeditated encounter provoked by the students." Yet another source claimed "most of the students present on the speaker's platform were armed, one with a submachine gun . . . troops were only answering the fire from the students."

In fact, according to accounts that would unfold over the years, as documents would continue to be declassified, it was murder. It was an outright massacre. It was genocide. The death toll among students and the neighbors that joined them was not 4 as the government announced, was not 8 as Scott first telegrammed, and it wasn't 20 as the *New York Times* reported at first, or even 39 as it wrote a week later. It may have been as high as 325, thousands more disappearing into prisons, some of them for years.

There could never be an accurate count, no census of the dead. Many of the students went into hiding, some joining guerrilla groups in the hinterlands, so it was difficult to say who had been killed and who had simply fled. Ghastly rumors circulated throughout the city that not all the dead were receiving funerals. Enrique Labadie, who was a sprinter on Bert Bonanno's Mexican team and also a medical student in Mexico City, told his coach that bodies from the massacre were being cremated in hospitals.

As Mexican officials had hoped, the massacre was public enough to have effectively ended the student movement, yet underreported enough that the Olympics would not be stopped on its account. "I was at the ballet last night," said Avery Brundage, "and we heard nothing of the riots." Other visitors were equally clueless. Had anyone known the true scope of the disaster, there surely would have been more outcry, possibly national condemnations, and Brundage would have needed more comment than that to keep his Games going. While *Sports Illustrated* published "Grim Countdown to the Games," taking note of the blood-soaked plaza, it agreed, "The only thing anyone could do was wait and see." There was no question that the Games were going to go on, more or less as planned.

Not even a week after the massacre, the TAFNOTers began arriving, more than eight hundred of them. They found the ride from the airport colorful. Banners in pastel hues hung over thoroughfares and there were white doves of peace everywhere. *Todo es posible en la paz—* on all the billboards. *Bienvenido* had been stenciled on freshly painted shacks along the road. They passed rows of sculptures on the Route of Friendship.

Checking in at Villa Coapa, the TAFNOTers discovered that, while the buildings were done, they were not quite finished. "Certainly there were some problems and inconveniences," one of them observed. Some apartments lacked toilet seats and shower curtains. They marveled at idiosyncrasies of construction. Bedroom doors locked from the outside, for example. Nobody really complained. The Olympics were only days away and whatever problems and inconveniences they encountered would, in later retellings, just add a little color to their yarns. Like those water heaters, going off in the evening, small explosions. They were almost like distant gunfire.

Chapter 10

OPENING CEREMONY

Flag Dipping, a Family Feud,
and 6,300 Pigeons

GARY STENLUND WAS A good man to know at an Olympics. He'd arranged for friends to bring his VW bus down to Mexico City. It was a 1965 camper, a creamy-colored pop-top beauty, perfect for the sort of escapades he had in mind. For that matter, that he'd arranged for friends. When he and Dick Fosbury toured the city, beer cans rattling in the back, it was usually in the company of young women, former swimming gold medalists, as a matter of fact. Stenlund had laid that groundwork back in South Lake Tahoe. He was basically a one-stop party, Stenlund, anticipating all the requirements of fun.

Fosbury was not in Stenlund's league when it came to partying, wasn't really in the same sport even. Stenlund's event was the javelin, but he liked to boast he was a decathlete when it came to the consumption of spirits. He was twenty-eight and had been hitting it hard for ten years, even as he was competing at an elite level. He could drink a case of beer, or a gallon of wine, or a fifth of whiskey. "But not Sterno," he liked to add. And he could throw the javelin 260 feet the next day. Often, anyway. It never seemed a problem for him. When it mattered, he could cut back. The night before finals qualifying at the Olympics he held himself to only four beers; although, as it turned out—seventeenth place!—he might as well have drunk his full schedule.

However, in the days leading up to the Games, with nothing more pressing than the usual imperatives of youth, it was a good time to have wheels and women, and whatever greased either. There was plenty to explore, for sure. And the people were so hospitable, so friendly. You had to take care of business back at the Village, of course, but Mexico City was dedicating itself to the amusement and amazement of its visitors, and you would have been a very poor guest to ignore such an offer.

An event that the guys and gals of Stenlund's camper definitely wanted to see was the arrival of the Olympic torch at the Pyramid of the Moon, thirty miles away in the pre-Columbian ruins of Teotihuacán. This would be a very important part of their itinerary, as well as the flame's. Mexican organizers had used some imagination in the ritual torch relay, choosing the paths of early explorers like Columbus and Cortez. On Saturday, Mexico's "torch girl," a "slim, raven-haired señorita" named Enriqueta Basilio (also known as "a twenty-year-old farmer's daughter," although she might have been even better identified as an 80-meter hurdler), would carry the flame up the steps to the cauldron in the Olympic Stadium and start the Games. The Friday night ceremonies at Teotihuacán, Mexico's first great city, looked very promising, offering considerable more authenticity than was likely to be available for the ticket holders back at the stadium the next day. The Pyramid of the Moon, after all, is located on the Avenue of the Dead.

It was a very lively place, however, when Stenlund and Fosbury and the girls got there. Tens of thousands of Mexicans had gathered at the pyramid for song and native performances (there were fifteen hundred brightly costumed dancers on hand). The four Americans, joined by another Mexican couple they'd picked up along the way, clambered over the pyramids, ate the chicken tacos and bean soup the other visitors offered them, drank the local beer, listened to the mariachis, and settled in for the arrival of the torch. This was not going to be just another stop for the sacred fire, either; Sylvania had rigged the site with nineteen-hundred flash bulbs for one of its "Big Shots," and the instant the runner lit the flame there, the entire pyramid was going to be lit. When the runner bent his torch to the cauldron, it was like a lightning strike.

Stenlund, Fosbury, and the girls were thoroughly seduced by the scene and decided to stay there the night, some of them sleeping in the bus, others scattered at the base of the ancient pyramid, under the stars—incredibly, it occurred to them, the same ones Cortez had looked at centuries before. If this was the Olympics, not bad.

Well, that was part of the Olympics. Their teammates were having similar fun, enjoying the same hospitality. They didn't even need their own car. Hosts would spot a credentialed athlete walking down the boulevard and do a U-turn to pick him up and deliver him wherever he wanted to go. An athlete getting on a city bus was cause for route interruptions as well, the other passengers politely settling in for a detour as the bus driver took care of his new VIP. It couldn't have been more fantastic.

There were many more parts to this Olympics, to any Olympics, than the opportunity for wonderment in a strange land. The Games are, after all, an athletic surrogate for national interests, the veneer of antiquity hiding the clanking political apparatus within. The purity of astonishment, whether it's realized by the pyramids or at the finish line, remains for those who truly throw themselves into the venture, but it's mostly a historical artifact, having less and less to do with the original spirit of the Games as one succeeds another. At Mexico City, you could still enjoy that ever elusive feel, but it was becoming harder and harder, as politics and pettiness began to intrude, as professionalism replaced amateurism, as money began to change it all.

Not even the parade of athletes, the crazy quilting of international fashion that begins every Olympics, was free from this coarsening. In 1968, it was still expected to be a comforting spectacle, the forced march around the track a sign that youth were still amenable to discipline, the agreement of costume likewise a show of reassuring uniformity, the juxtaposition of international communities a satisfying reminder of world peace. This was against all evidence, of course, but the Olympic rites are inviolable and its symbols do not yield their meaning to any real-world experiences and never did.

Even in something as apparently straightforward as a parade, there was one-upmanship at work. It did not take a particularly trained eye to parse the politics in this tradition and, in any case, it was more amusing than it was offensive at this point in history. It was interesting, though, how protest could be couched in even the smallest gesture, seeds of rebellion planted in more innocent times perhaps, producing an uncertain harvest in these.

Harold Connolly was a tremendously popular figure in Olympic circles. He had not only won a gold medal in the hammer throw in 1956, but had conducted one of the great courtships of all time, wooing Czechoslovakian discus champion Olga Fikotova in the Melbourne Village. Their romance was steamy enough to thaw even U.S.-Czech relations, meaning U.S.-Soviet relations, long enough for a fairy tale wedding in Prague in 1957. More than forty thousand showed up for their civil ceremony there, the Iron Curtain parting just a bit for the drama of love.

Almost as important, Connolly remained a perennial contender on the world scene, although he failed to medal in either the Rome or Tokyo Games. In 1968, he was still a medal hopeful and arrived in Mexico City, his fourth Olympic trip, with duties that went beyond the ceremonial. A high school English teacher in Santa Monica (Olga competed as Olga Connolly, and for the United States, in two more Olympics as well), Connolly could still deliver the goods.

With all that in mind, the U.S. Olympic Committee had little trouble settling on Connolly as its flag bearer for the Opening Ceremony. This was an important assignment for a number of reasons. There was the honor of it, of course. It went to someone both beloved and accomplished. Practical considerations loomed as well. It had very recently become something of a strongman contest, the Russians having thrown down the gauntlet in 1960 when their heavyweight lifter, Yuri Vaslov, had done the entire lap, one-handing the flag straight out in front of him. This was an astonishing sight, of course, but also a call to arms for those countries still interested in the idea of world dominance.

U.S. shot putter Parry O'Brien had been chosen to counter this new development in the 1964 Games and he was extremely nervous about it. The Russians were going to be led by another heavyweight lifter, Leonid Zhabotinsky, a 341-pounder who wasn't likely going to have trouble with a flagpole. O'Brien was strong, but lifting a 16-pound ball and tossing it around is not the same as pressing 410 pounds. Zhabotinsky walked his lap, holding the Hammer and Sickle out in front of him as if it were no more bother than a toothpick. O'Brien panicked on the far curve and did a quick switch from one hand to the other. Everybody saw.

But that's not what was bothering Connolly. There was the matter of the dip. Ever since 1908 (with several exceptions) the flag bearer represented American independence or, some might argue, arrogance, and was supposed to act in partial opposition of the Olympic spirit. The American flag was not to be dipped, must never be dipped, in front of the host country's reviewing stand.

Everybody else dipped, and always had. It was considered a sign of respect, or at least good manners. However, starting in the London Games, when U.S. shot putter Ralph Rose held his flag defiantly aloft in front of King Edward VII, supposedly saying, "This flag dips for no earthly king" (unfortunately, this quote didn't turn up until many years after he'd died), it had been America's maddening tradition to flout this international nicety. The rest of the world was expected to shrug it off.

Connolly wasn't so sure about this particular honor. O'Brien said he had to do it, one-handed or not. "You'll never regret it," he told Connolly. "You'll get your picture on the front page of every newspaper in the world." That was probably true enough. But the idea of not dipping bothered Connolly. At thirty-seven, he was much older than most of the other athletes, had been more places, seen more things, experienced national imperialism, at least secondhand. He and his wife were keenly aware of world politics, not just the part that affected Olga's occupied homeland. He might have seemed stodgy to his younger teammates but, in fact, he was among the most radical of them, alert to hypocrisy, whether it be gender, political, racial. The idea of not dipping the flag struck him as "ridiculous." How could this country insist on a protest-free Olympics at home while, at the same time, abuse this worldwide platform to make a big show of its own superiority. "They were," Connolly decided, "full of shit."

The committee went ballistic at his refusal to carry the flag and, mulling it over, decided to award the honor to Janice Romary, a fencer in her sixth Olympics. It was an ingenious move, at once looking forward (a woman!) and backward (an old woman!). It also assured the status quo, although organizers must have been starting to understand just how precarious that status quo was becoming.

Of all the rivalries that animated the 1968 Olympics, the least reported, and yet without a doubt the strangest, was the Dassler family feud. It may also have been one of the most important, not so much because it landed poor Art Simburg in a Mexican hoosegow and put Wyomia Tyus in a tizzy but because it began the slow erosion of the Olympic ideal, that quaint notion of amateurism. If the Dassler brothers, in their familial wrangling, didn't usher in an age of professionalism, they certainly opened the door.

Brothers Adolf and Rudolf were unlikely agents of change, for sure. Unlikely brothers, for that matter. Adolf—Adi, the quiet one—had begun a small shoe business after World War I, collecting industrial debris from postwar Germany to set up shop in the Bavarian town of Herzogenaurach. Devoting most of his line to the needs of sportsmen, Adi finally hit the jackpot in 1936, when he managed to get a pair of his Gebruder Dassler spikes on the feet of Jesse Owens. Owens wore them on the way to four gold medals at those Berlin Games and Dassler shoes, with the two leather stripes on the sides, immediately became favored footwear for athletes, at least in Germany. And the company, with Rudolf, the loud one, joining his brother, was becoming a player.

However, World War II, during which Rudolf was called to serve Germany while Adolf was allowed to stay home to run the shoe plant, exacerbated an already iffy relationship. The two had always been contrasting personalities—Adolf the introspective shop mechanic, Rudolf the gung-ho salesman—and it didn't help that they lived together, with equally contentious wives, in the same house. It also didn't help when the war split them apart. Rudolf was convinced that his brother had conspired with Nazi party officials to have him drafted and could never be convinced otherwise. With one war over, another picked up momentum. "As people," Adolf once said, "we are not compatible."

When it became clear by 1948 that they could not work together, they split the company in half, Adolf remaining on one side of the Aurach River, the watery divide of Herzogenaurach, Rudolf setting up a factory on the other banks. This created a civic tension in the town, as well, as scores of employees were now forced to take sides, some with Adolf's newly formed Adidas company, others with Rudolf's Puma. It was said that townspeople walked the streets with their heads down, the better to check out their neighbors' footwear, and thus identify their family allegiance.

It also fostered a fierce competition, with the brothers applying stripes (now three for Adidas), bolt-on cleats, screw-in studs, and all other manner of design innovation, some of them no doubt frivolous. Adidas offered a "vulcanized nylon sole without a leather middle layer," while Puma countered with a "living nylon shoe with air conditioning." Other, more substantial improvements probably did make the athletes faster. There is no question it made the Dasslers richer. While Puma maintained a foothold, so to speak, in soccer boots, Adidas was doing better on the track scene. In any case, both prospered for the next twenty years, a second generation of Dasslers taking over their fathers' companies, not only maintaining the rivalry but stepping it up considerably.

The Olympics were still insisting upon their not-for-profit ideal in 1968, at least as it involved the actual athletes. The movement's hierarchy sometimes benefited outrageously from the Games but there was to be no taint of professionalism in the lower ranks. Amateur status was rigidly enforced. Neither Adidas nor Puma had any interest, at first anyway, in interfering with that particular hypocrisy. Horst, Adolf's eldest son, had seen his brand benefit by Olympic exposure; all he had to do was give the spikes away, thirty thousand pairs in one Olympic year. This was uncontested by organizers, on the ground that spikes, an expensive necessity for the athletes, were technical equipment. You can give them technical equipment, at least. Beginning in 1956 at Melbourne, Horst managed to give away a lot of technical equipment, to as many as seventy eventual medal winners. Including sprinter Bobby Morrow, who ended up—striped shoes and all—on the cover of *Life* magazine. Orders for Adidas shoes picked up.

So now athletes could expect free shoes from both Adidas and Puma (whose shipment of shoes at Melbourne, according to Barbara Smit's account in *Sneaker Wars*, had at first been blocked at the docks). At least one athlete wondered if he could expect more than that by 1960, when the Games went to Rome. According to that same book, German sprinter Armin Hary played Adidas and Puma against each other, getting a "thick brown envelope" from Puma when Adidas refused to give him cash and a shoe distributorship in the United

States for wearing its shoes. Adidas, knowing nothing of the arrangement, was surprised to see their previously loyal runner win the 100-meter gold medal in Puma spikes. Then again, the Puma folks were pretty surprised when Armin, never one to overlook an angle, took the podium in Adidas shoes.

By 1964, free shoes were no longer enough. The top athletes, guys like U.S. sprinter Bob Hayes, were now seen as valuable, if fleeting, shoe ads and were highly sought after. Hayes in particular was part of a bidding war, Horst winning him over from Puma. Athletes were delighted to see the shoe reps skulking about, surreptitiously slipping envelopes here and there, hard cash, often in the hundreds.

But now in Mexico City, the demands of global commerce being what they were, it was all but out in the open. Adidas, after having dominated the 1964 Games, had somehow secured an agreement of exclusivity from Mexico's Olympic committee, in flagrant disregard of Olympic rules, and was able to erect a hospitality complex right in the athletes' village. And what hospitality! Athletes could drop by, give Adidas their shoe sizes and uniform measurements, and leave with brand-new outfits. Adidas was just following through on a campaign that aimed to put its shoes on all the elite athletes in the world. Without the ability to enforce signed contracts—there was still the fading patina of amateurism on the Games, no such "professionalism" was permitted—it was still as unpredictable as in Armin Hary's day. You couldn't be quite sure what the runner would be wearing when he hit the tape or mounted the podium. But payments rumored as high as ten thousand dollars did buy some loyalty.

Adidas was well ahead in this particular footrace. And yet Puma, almost without intending to, got back in the running. It seems that John Carlos, back in his Harlem days, had been recruited by Beconta, which happened to be Puma's U.S. distributor. When he arrived in Speed City, he informed his teammates of Beconta's particular generosity and the whole bunch of them would travel several miles from San Jose to a Beconta warehouse in South San Francisco and pick up new gear. Not only did Speed City become part of the Puma team but their Boswell, schoolmate Art Simburg, got a job representing Puma at meets around the country.

It was an underdog role for Simburg, who had to face off against a better-funded, better-connected, and far more ruthless Adidas force. Simburg couldn't even get Wyomia Tyus, now his fiancée, into Puma. Olympian Ralph Boston was representing Adidas around the country, and he had long since sewed up the Tigerbelles, from his alma mater at Tennessee State, who were still very loyal to Adidas. Over dinner one night at the women's training camp in New Mexico, Boston and Simburg agreed to carve up the field—the three Olympic Tigerbelles to Adidas, Barbara Ferrell and Jarvis Scott to Puma—so they wouldn't have to waste any of their entertainment budget on pointless court-ships.

Simburg was up against more than team loyalties, though. All he was supposed to do was travel the track circuit and win as many hearts and minds as he could with his allotment of two thousand pairs of shoes. The idea was to get them on the feet of the top ten guys in each event, or at least get them in their gym bags. Even that proved diffi-cult. Simburg would show up and discover his hotel reservations had been canceled. How did that happen? Simburg was pretty sure how but, instead of being furious, was more likely to be admiring. "Adidas was always on top of everything," he thought.

In Mexico City, Adidas had gotten more aggressive, if anything. Its agreement with the Mexico Olympic Committee, which allowed for the manufacture of some of the shoes in Mexico, also allowed for the free import of additional shoes from Germany. Puma would be taxed at ten dollars per pair.

Armin Dassler, Horst's cousin, tried to escape the tax by masking the Puma shipment as Adidas shoes, but Mexican officials had been tipped to the scheme and impounded the whole lot. With less than a week before the Games were to begin, Puma could not outfit its own athletes, never mind recruit more.

Puma was desperate and sent Simburg around the Village with a petition, asking the teams to demand that the shoes be allowed into the country. While doing this, Simburg was suddenly surrounded by Mexican security agents who snatched him and took him to an immigration station. Simburg, like everyone else there, had heard about the student massacre just weeks before and, moreover, had heard stories of people just disappearing in the system, never to be heard from again. As far as he knew, nobody knew what had become of him. He had simply vanished.

In fact, he was in a holding cell with six or eight others, a raffish collection that the authorities had been sweeping off the streets in the Games' run-up. A guy who had tried to sell the spare tire off a Hertz rental. Some kids who had the poor sense to wear hippie garb at a torch lighting ceremony in Vera Cruz. Simburg, eating beans and bread and enjoying one hour a day in an exercise yard, had ample reason to despair. Explaining his importance to these Games simply did not translate. The guards would laugh. "Puma very busy," they would tell him. "Well," thought Simburg, "they are kind of disarrayed." Tyus was frantic. Puma, disarrayed or not, was concerned. Simburg was worried, among other things, that he wouldn't see any of the Olympics, much less contribute.

After three days, during which time Simburg was able to wonder who tipped authorities off to his activities, the State Department managed to locate him and have him released. Moreover, Puma arranged for groups of British athletes to circumvent customs and retrieve a lot of the shoes out of the impound. "Good news," Simburg was told by a Puma rep upon his freedom. Simburg had plenty to celebrate, but now this: "The English are bringing in the shoes!"

Once the Puma inventory was established, the shoe race resumed, with athletes lining up at both Armin's and Horst's hotel doors, traveler's checks to be had behind them. It had become fairly blatant, in fact. Athletes had been negotiating with the shoemakers for airfare for wives, for outright pay, you name it. A few remained skittish about the legality of the arrangements; reports of payoffs were brought to IOC chairman Avery Brundage, who said anybody caught might forfeit their medals, but otherwise declined to investigate. One anonymous runner said he woke up and discovered $500 in his shoes. What could he do against such serendipity? Not many others were as discreet. Athletes were jockeying for payoffs, as much for pride now as the actual money, although that was nice, too. There was a new measuring stick and it was in dollars. Maybe you were worth only $50, maybe you deserved a retainer more appropriate to your abilities, say, $500 or $1,000. It was a new day in Olympic sports, brought on by the hypocrisy of amateurism, the eye-opening times, and, for sure, the Dassler brothers' hatred for each other.

In any case: The Village was abuzz when an American athlete tried to cash a Puma check for $6,400. Apparently he hadn't been the first that day and the bank turned him away. It was out of cash.

To the extent that an Olympics is basically a forum of international one-upmanship, only some of which is dedicated to athletics, there should be little surprise at the innovation of advantage. By 1968, pharmacists around the world were identifying athletic performance as the next frontier, developing and administering strange compounds. If they weren't yet affecting outcomes, they were certainly heightening levels of global paranoia, not that the Olympic movement required another layer of that.

The Americans were becoming increasingly wary of the Russians and whatever they might be doing to enhance their chances for Cold War glory, particularly the use of steroids and other drugs. It did not require a high degree of skepticism to believe that whatever they were doing might be extreme. The Press sisters, Irina and Tamara, had disappeared from competition in 1966, the first year athletes at the European Track and Field Championships had to undergo gender testing. Russian officials said the two sisters, who had won five

Olympic gold medals in events ranging from the 100-meter dash to the discus, and had set twenty-six world records between them, had abruptly retired to care for their ailing mother in the Ukraine. Both of them?

The Americans were far more certain of Russia's men, at least those who competed as such, particularly in events that had anything to do with heavy lifting and throwing. The weight lifters were coming home from international competitions with all sorts of tales, and had been since 1954, when Russia had started sweeping in those events. U.S. doctors were pretty sure the Russians were using some form of testosterone, presumed useful in the building of muscle, and set about building synthetic versions of it. By 1958, the FDA had approved a steroid called Dianabol, and just about any athlete interested in its advantages could get a little pink tablet.

Jay Silvester, the discus thrower, was at Cal Poly Pomona in 1964, training for the Tokyo Games, and was feeling a little rundown. A team physician, Dr. H. Kay Dooley, offered him a small bottle of Dianabol and suggested, "Take these, they might help you." Silvester didn't think they had any effect. But he didn't forget about them, by any means. By 1968, the athletes and doctors had learned that the dosages suggested by the manufacturer were conservative by half. Hal Connolly, a hammer thrower, discovered you could get results with "double, or triple doses." He "played around with them" following his disappointing finish in the 1964 Games, when he could not recover from injury in time to repeat his 1960 gold medal performance, but, like Silvester, wasn't immediately convinced of their benefits.

For the 1968 Games, though, just about everybody was fully aware of the muscle-producing effects of those pink pills or, more likely, a well-administered syringe. Some athletes talked openly about them, others furtively. But they all talked about them. And used them. Silvester found their use "rampant." It might have helped that Dr. Dooley had become one of the high-altitude camp physicians at South Lake Tahoe and was a big believer in the rewards of pharmacological training. "I did not give steroids at Tahoe," he told *Sports Illustrated*, "but I did not inquire what the boys were doing on their own." He added, "I don't think it's possible for a weight man to compete internationally without using anabolic steroids." So, presumably, he was available for consultation.

Steroids were not illegal in 1968, or even felt to be dangerous. Whether steroid use was unfair or not was another story. The IOC did institute drug testing in 1967 but it seemed its officials were more interested in enforcing good habits than in leveling the playing field. Anybody with heroin, amphetamines, alcohol, or cocaine in their system was risking expulsion. Dianabol? You were good to go. The question no longer was whether the Russians used steroids to unfair advantage, but whether they were using better steroids. "We are usually a long way behind the Russians in drug use," a weight lifter complained.

The Olympics were like that, a confusion of agendas, some less noble than others, all dolled up as an international reassurance, an "all's well" that's sounded every four years. Certainly the Opening Ceremony, a tightly scripted pageant that seemed to date directly from its Greek origins, was an important way to reinforce this notion of stability. The familiar symbols and traditions, all the rites of international cooperation, were layered with some modern ambitions—no country would vie to be host without the opportunity for self-promotion—but it was mostly a celebration of a status quo.

On the other hand, as everybody had to admit, there was increasing emphasis on the celebration, to the point of entertainment one-upmanship. This escalation of spectacle every four years produced high expectations, and Mexico City, having paid through the nose for this platform of boosterism, intended to deliver. The host had put the following in place for Saturday's extravaganza: a 340-piece band, forty thousand balloons, two four-gun batteries of 105mm howitzers, forty trumpet players in addition to that band, another musical group playing native instruments, helium-filled Olympic rings, and sixty-three hundred pigeons (which are sort of like doves) hidden in 150 baskets in the stadium infield.

They had also arrayed a disconcerting number of armed troops around the stadium. For the first time at an Olympics, security was an issue, although it was quickly clear that the guests were not meant to be the subject of any particular scrutiny. The military struck a relaxed pose, outfitted with both machine guns and peace dove insignias, and were casual about their duties. For one thing, the students' strike committee had confirmed earlier announcements that the Games would proceed undisturbed (not that it was possible to find much news of those outbreaks; several English-language journalists hired by the Mexican government in public-relations roles were told to respond to questions on the matter with "There are no riots"). For another, what possible harm could these gringos represent? It was no trick at all to penetrate supposedly secure barriers; visitors roamed through the Olympic Village almost at will, unchallenged and unchecked. The Tigerbelle Madeline Manning was particularly surprised when prospective apartment buyers were going through her Village quarters, as if it were an open house.

The police presence, in other words, was strictly a show of potential enforcement. By Saturday, ten days after the so-called disturbances (all that remained of the event were red splotches on the square and, all around the city, the desecration of the peace symbol, the white doves now with bleeding hearts colored in), there was hardly anything to fear but gate-crashers. Kids scaling the outside walls of the Olympic Stadium, even if they did reach the tops of the fortress, which were studded with spikes and jagged glass, got a knuckle bashing from cops with nightsticks. Ed Fox from the *Track & Field News* group watched in horror: "Visions of kids falling hundreds of feet into the alligator-infested moat below . . . or worse."

If there was a moat around the stadium, it had more to do with traffic control than children. All roads were blocked to a radius of one mile or more, closed to everybody but officials, taxis, and buses. However, there was vehicular chaos as even sanctioned traffic exceeded the event's parking capacity. Cars and buses were simply abandoned as close to the destination as seemed convenient to credential holders. There was double and triple parking, to the point that the avenues ringing the stadium became auxiliary lots.

Those who did gain access sat among a hundred thousand others, twenty thousand beyond capacity according to estimates, in Olympic Stadium, at first wondering if the dark clouds hiding the sun promised more rain or just welcome shade. The actual program was scheduled to begin at one that afternoon and, according to officials, was going to last exactly two hours, eight minutes, and fifteen seconds. While the precision struck visitors as bold, if not outright comic given their recent experiences, it was clear that organizers intended to use these Games to obliterate their reputation for poor time management along with other equally south-of-the-border stereotypes. Indeed, the whole shebang had a glorious, unexpected, and even whimsical meticulousness. Preliminary to the ceremony, and not meant to be counted against the 2:08.15, were orchestrated rope-skipping and choreographed lawn-mowing. This last, scores of workers marching their huge machines across the infield in perfect lockstep, had the crowd roaring.

Before the organizers could deploy all their remaining instruments of excitement, the parade of athletes took place. This, for the first dozen nations anyway, is a lump-in-the-throat moment, contingents of otherwise unfriendly tribes marching in, one after another, and quite happily at that. There is only one moment, and it's only once every four years, that the family-of-man notion does not seem wholly preposterous. This was it. In came the Australians, then the Bulgarians in their blue shirts, tossing roses into the crowd. Here came the Czechoslovakian delegation, getting the cheer of the day

("Czech-o, Czech-o"), a surprising show of solidarity, while their oppressors, the Soviets, were scolded with barely polite clapping. On down the alphabetical line, each nation's politics approved or condemned by crowd reaction. Not to mention its haberdashery. The U.S. bunch, the biggest of the 111 nations with 484 athletes, got very faint applause, fainter even than Russia's, either for the offense of the men's red polyester blazers (the women were more smartly attired in extremely brief dresses, white with red-and-black chevrons) or flag-bearer Janice Romary's refusal to dip. There could have been other reasons, too. The three-man Liechtenstein team, meanwhile, got a rousing welcome from the crowd, but probably more for their sombreros than any supposed neutrality.

The parade, with its sartorial emphasis on diversity, is always a journalistic crowd-pleaser, if nothing else. There is a long tradition of press-box stupefaction as columnists weigh in on its magnificence, its meaning, its majesty. It is a wonder they can type, their eyes are so misted with tears. The *New York Times*'s Arthur Daley reported on the variety of garb before him, including Australian miniskirts ("Fortunately, they had the nifty legs for it"), Bermudan shorts, African robes, and proclaimed it "an exquisite spectacle" and "an emotional experience as well." Daley decided that "none can remain unmoved by it. Even those who have witnessed other Opening Ceremonies find themselves responding to the heart-clutching impact of the glorious show."

Not everyone was so pleased with the procession, though. Soviet weight lifter Leonid Zhabotinsky, as he had four years earlier, did the entire lap with the Soviet banner unbraced in his left hand. It was a big hit with the crowd, but the U.S. weight men seethed at the cheap parlor trick, imagining the Dianabol required for the feat. Zhabotinsky also refused to dip before the Tribune of Honor, stealing even more of their thunder. It was pretty infuriating.

However, politics was mostly absent. U.S. sprinter John Carlos, almost alone among his teammates, had refused to join the fun. "I didn't care to march," was all he said. According to the *New Yorker*, "there was inevitable speculation about how its Negroes might behave" and "some United States officials were obviously edgy about this." The U.S. delegation couldn't have been more proper in its procession. All in all, the athletes seemed above the fray, any fray. When asked about the international friction produced when Czechs and Soviets rubbed elbows, Czechoslovakia gymnast Vera Caslavska explained all too reasonably, "No athlete is responsible for the activities of his government."

Once the athletes were settled in the infield there was a pregnant pause before a final emotional moment. "The tug at heartstrings was constant," Arthur Daley wrote, "but the supreme wrench comes with the arrival of the Olympic Flame." Here came Norma Enriqueta Basilio, the farmer's daughter, the first woman ever to assume such a role, scrambling up ninety steps, holding the torch aloft before touching it to the fuse. If that didn't announce the start of the Games, or the howitzers, or the various bands, then the pigeons did, flying away as one hundred thousand people held newspapers over their heads.

It was quite a show and nobody cared to criticize organizers for going over schedule (the *New Yorker* timed it at thirty-three minutes and four seconds beyond the original timetable, close enough, they decided). There was, really, nothing at all to criticize. If the Opening Ceremony does anything, it creates a mood of possibilities, establishes an optimism, encourages brotherhood. This had done all that, even in such difficult times as 1968, with blood in nearby plazas, revolt over the borders. For these not-so-few hours, Olympics trumped all.

There was, however, at least one vanload of people who were unable to experience this wonderful glow. Try as he might, Stenlund could not get his group back to Mexico City in time for the ceremony. Who knew there'd be this much traffic, or that people would have gotten so frustrated they'd simply leave their cars right in the middle of streets? Then again, the bunch had their own ceremonies, out under the stars with a lot of their hosts, the antiquity of the ruins a better reminder of history than any Olympic proclamation. Stenlund tried, beeping his little horn and maneuvering as best he could, but it was no use. He and Fosbury, and the girls for that matter, just tootled on as far as they could, laughing all the way.

Chapter 11

AND THEY'RE OFF

A Grisly Tableau, Pinochle, and a Guided Missile Launch

J IM MURRAY, THE *Los Angeles Times* columnist, was excited at the carnage. Six of the runners in the 10,000 meter race simply failed to finish—one dropping out after two laps—and three of those ending up unconscious. The presumed favorite in the event, Australia's Ron Clarke, keeled over at the finish and required oxygen, a phalanx of physicians and trainers (one of them covering his face, crying) and nearly ten minutes to wake up. Even then, he wasn't right. Murray had no reason to expect such an easy column, but he certainly wasn't going to refuse delivery. "There are people in the morgue who look better than Ron Clarke did at the finish line," Murray wrote, delighted at the grisly tableau, "and have a stronger heartbeat, too."

Aside from the opportunity for Murray's mordant observations, the Olympic opener was not a welcome one. The optimism of Saturday's Opening Ceremony was yielding to an awful reality by Sunday. The Games were on, and it was quite possible they shouldn't have been on in Mexico City after all. The warnings about Mexico's thin air, its scant oxygen unable to break down sugars with sea-level efficiency, seemed to be coming true. This was, apparently, more dangerous than even the biggest skeptics had suggested. Ron Clarke, a holder of seventeen world records, and an Olympic veteran, nearly dead!

Everybody knew going in this would be different. The word around the Village was that the rowers were having trouble in the mile-and-a-half altitude during their acclimations as well; eighty collapses in the first two days, it was reported. Almost every country that could afford to had managed some kind of high-altitude training to prepare but, with this disaster, it looked like even that wasn't going to save these kids. "It was a cardiologist's delight," Murray continued. "Nearly an undertaker's."

Clarke had been a bronze medalist in 1964 and, while he had higher hopes for his other event, the 5000 meters, was certainly a favorite. Although it did occur to observers that runners from higher elevations, the Kenyans for example, might have an advantage in Mexico City. Kip Keino of that country was a definite possibility to medal, although he would really be pushing it, as he intended to run the 5000 meters and 1500 as well.

The race began ominously, "As if," Murray wrote, "it would wind up in the critical ward of County Hospital." The first runner was carried away after keeling over in the third lap, which was not an encouraging sight for the other runners, who still had twenty-two laps to go. With six laps left, two more were carried away. It wasn't as if anybody was trying to burn it up, either. The pace at the halfway mark was fifteen minutes, slower than any such split since the 1924 Games. At eight thousand nine hundred meters, about five and a half miles, Keino dropped out. He was suffering stomach cramps, having only recently endured a gallbladder infection, but obviously wasn't quite himself, either. He stumbled into the infield and then, not realizing he had disqualified himself, tried to resume his course on the track.

And on they plodded, all of them amassing incredible amounts of oxygen debt. Runners at shorter distances burn up ready glycogen and can repay the debt later at their leisure. Long-distance racers must use oxygen from the air they're breathing during the race to break down the sugar, financing the debt as they go. Runners in events longer than eight hundred meters run more slowly in oxygen-thin air and, not only that, if they push themselves past a certain comfort zone, can shortchange the brain when it comes to oxygen levels in the blood. At ten thousand meters, this was definitely the challenge, estimating the amount of consciousness left, against the distance remaining.

With 800 meters to the finish, about a half mile, there were only four runners from the thirty-six-man field left. One of them, Naftali Temu, was, like Keino, from Kenya; the other, Mamo Wolde, was from a similarly elevated Ethiopia (and would compete in the marathon later in the week). The others were Mohamed Gammoudi of Tunisia, who had trained for a year in the Pyrenees, and Clarke. Clarke faded after another 200 meters. With one lap to go it became a race between Temu and Wolde, who moved ahead and created a five-yard lead. And then Temu, a twenty-three-year-old Kisii tribesman, caught Wolde barely fifty yards from the finish and went on to win by four yards.

Clarke, meanwhile, was experiencing a constellation of symptoms as he tried to finish, none of them good. With six laps to go, hoping to move it into another gear, his legs had begun refusing communication. Then his arms started to go dead as well. His heart was trying to burst from his chest. His vision was starting to blur, but he could see Temu charging ahead of him to the gold. He stamped on, although "the straightaway looked two miles long." And then, well, he didn't really know what had happened.

The winning time of 29:27.4 was absurdly poor. Not since 1948 had anyone run so slowly in the Olympics and won gold. This was a monumental regression. A kind of advance, on the other hand. This was the first time that Africans had won all three medals in any event. The sight of them running around after the race, darting up the stadium ramps to accept the congratulations of fans, put them in stark contrast to the lolling human wreckage below them, husks of men struggling for air. "They could have blown up balloons after finishing," Murray decided.

Clarke, once he regained his wits, immediately sought absolution of all the fallen runners he had mocked before. "I apologize to them all," he said. Although maybe he hadn't regained all his wits. A series of electrocardiograms reassured team officials he'd live (and could probably participate in the 5000 meters four days later). More telling was a run-in Sunday night when he bumped into British miler John Boulter in the Olympic Village. "Good show, Dave," he said, thinking he was congratulating Dave Hemery for a good result in a 400-meter hurdle heat. Yikes!

The first week of the Olympics, with its familiar events and names, reminds some people of a track-and-field competition. It is nothing of the sort. It has been so pumped full of importance—whether by political considerations, a sudden and bewildering international attention, or just the do-or-die implications of its quadrennial cycle— that it becomes a different beast altogether. From the athletes' point of view, it is not just an inflated spectacle, an experience heightened by orders of magnitude, a contest of increased expectations. They could deal with an escalation of pressure, if that's all it were; that's how they advanced to this level in the first place, gradually acquiring an immunity to stress. The Olympics are different in kind, not degree. They're totally unrecognizable. It is a shock for many of the athletes to realize just how unprepared they are.

Jay Silvester had been this way before, having made the 1964 Olympic team as a discus thrower, so he should have known better. He should not have been shocked. Well, he did know better, and he wasn't shocked. He understood, as dominant as he was in this event, that his ability and determination simply did not translate into this sort of everlasting glory. The Olympics were not his cup of tea, and probably never would be. It was disappointing all the same, every time.

For him, the whole point of the discus, the heaving of a four-and-a-half-pound plate, was seeing it fly. He played all sports, going to

Utah State on a football scholarship, but was mostly intrigued by the discus, as ancient an event as there was. He'd handled his first one in the eighth grade when a friend brought one over to his family's farm. They played in the pasture, sailing it as far they could. It would just go.

Not that he wasn't a competitor, as well. He was hardly so much an admirer of awesome parabolas of flight that distance didn't matter. He was, after all, the world record holder, having just recently thrown 224'5". It was his fourth since first breaking American Rink Babka's mark in 1961. Man-to-man, he was nearly impossible to beat. Coming into the Olympics, he'd been national champion four times and, as far as his competition with Al Oerter, the 1964 gold medalist, he'd beaten him more often than not. That much was in the books. The Olympics were always another story for Silvester. His problem was compounded further because the Olympics were always another story for Oerter, too.

Oerter was a mystery to Silvester, no matter how much time they spent together in training or even in competition. Silvester didn't get him. It didn't seem Oerter particularly cared about throwing long. He could, that was for sure. They'd be working out, and Oerter would boom one 220 feet and beyond. It struck Silvester that Oerter wasn't impressed by distance, that he might not even like the discus that much to begin with. He didn't seem to tax himself like the others, didn't really explore the boundaries of his abilities. He was an under-achiever, except in the Olympics. In the same way that a track-and-field meet is transformed by its Olympic designation, so somehow was Oerter. There was something about him, come the Olympics. Hammer thrower Hal Connolly, who roomed with him in Tokyo, was always impressed, maybe even a little scared, at the sight of Oerter before his event. He just sat on the edge of his bed, his hands shaking uncontrollably. Then, once he got on the field, another transformation took place. "He was just frozen." He refused to talk to his competitors. He didn't even acknowledge them.

In 1956, Oerter had been rated sixth in the world, yet he launched the three longest tosses of the event (his first throw broke the Olympic record and established a personal best for him) and won gold in Melbourne. The favorite, teammate Fortune Gordien, who had held the world record, finished five feet out of it.

In 1960, Oerter was once more the dark horse, making the Olympic team behind Babka. Like Gordien, Babka held the world record at the time of the Rome Games. What's more, Babka had beaten him in the Olympic Trials. Oerter beat Babka by nearly four feet for another Olympic record and another personal best. Oerter might have been the favorite at the Tokyo Games—he'd been trading the world record back and forth with Russian Vladimir Trusenov and had already become the first to throw more than two hundred feet in a 1962 meet—except for a series of injuries, and heightened competition. Czechoslovakia's Ludvik Danek, the new world record holder, would have been tough to beat under any circumstances. Danek had won forty-five straight meets and was a huge favorite. Oerter was hurting. In addition to a chronic cervical disc injury, which required him to wear a neck brace, Oerter was also dealing with a rib injury, suffered just six days before the Olympics, when he slipped in a wet ring. Doctors warned Oerter against competing for six weeks—weeks, not days—lest the torn cartilage in his lower rib cage lead to internal bleeding.

Oerter refused, of course, but realized he couldn't conduct a full program. He was in enough pain, even though he was wrapped in tape and shot full of Novocain and wearing his big foam-rubber horse collar, that he couldn't imagine persisting beyond his first all-or-nothing heave. "If I don't do it on the first throw," he said, "I won't be able to do it at all." He didn't, but he could. Going into his fifth excruciating throw, Danek was in first place, with a toss seven feet farther than Oerter's. Oerter whirled, let loose, and immediately doubled over in pain, not even looking for where the discus landed. It was two feet past Danek's, and Oerter had his third gold medal and third Olympic record.

In other words, when it came to Oerter and his Olympic prospects, you had to be wary. Even though he was now thirty-two, even though he was injured anew (he pulled a thigh muscle a week before the event), even though he'd had just one good season out of the previous four—he was scary. "When you throw against Oerter," Silvester had said once before, "you don't expect to win. You just hope." Silvester held the world record, had beaten Oerter in the Trials, and was improving his distances in amounts that no longer seemed possible for Oerter, yet it was foolish to be confident when Oerter and the Olympics coincided.

Silvester knew he was in trouble when he got to Mexico City, but this time it had nothing to do with Oerter. Hardly any of the athletes were enjoying their shared housing, but Silvester was more upset about it than most. He needed quiet and he needed peace and here he was, crowded into a room with five other guys, black guys with their loud music playing. Silvester was in a dither. In Tokyo, the athletes had been housed in an American military barracks and he'd enjoyed a room that had been built for pilots. It was virtually soundproof. Now he had these roommates, a gang of 800-meter guys, Olympic novices, all excited, and extremely loud. It seemed to Silvester that they believed they "were in Disneyland." He knew this wasn't going to be a vacation. It never was, not with Oerter out there.

He pleaded with coaches to move him to different quarters, but head coach Payton Jordan said that would look like segregation. They weren't inclined to address his problems anyway; that's not what Olympic coaches do. So Silvester curled up on the military cot that he'd dragged into the kitchen, listened to the music from other rooms of his apartment, even the outside noises, reverberating in the tiny canyons those concrete apartments made. He was getting more and more fried by the night.

Oerter, meanwhile, was breezing through the experience with an otherworldly nonchalance. Ed Burke, one of his roommates, used to play pinochle with him by the hour. Burke never won a game but they played anyway. One time Oerter had suddenly slapped his cards to the table, saying, "You know, I could have thrown twice today." Burke, startled, asked whatever did that mean? Oerter picked his cards up and said, "It's just a feeling, it just happens sometimes when it all comes together."

Oerter's seemingly casual approach was tremendously offputting to Silvester, who met everything with enormous earnestness. When Oerter told reporters that he didn't care for the discus one way or another—"I use it as an invitation to visit foreign countries," he said—Silvester was dumbfounded. He never regarded Oerter as a friend but still looked up to him. That same week in Mexico, flushed with encouragement from home, Silvester had shown Oerter a good-luck telegram. "It's signed by almost everybody in my hometown of Orem," he said. "All four hundred of them." Oerter could be a deflating presence, or else just an expert competitor. "Can't be much of a town," he said.

The first Olympic finals had been Sunday and it sounded a menacing note, a good portion of the field failing to even finish in the thin air. Monday, the first full day of finals, dawned warm and sunny, and without a killing distance event on the schedule, promised much better.

Even Silvester had reason to be optimistic. In qualifying the day before, he'd set an Olympic record with a distance of 207'10", a full 16'6" short of his world record, but inches better than anything Oerter had ever done. It wasn't as good as he wanted, but the rules at Mexico City prevented him an additional allotment of throws once he met the qualifying distance. So it was at least good enough. Jim Murray had playfully predicted that Silvester would throw far enough that "it would have to be measured by bringing the curvature of the earth into the computation."

By Monday, Silvester was less confident than Murray. He was on edge, feeling weak, more anxious than he'd ever been. He was nervous. "Everything's so important," he thought. Still, he was ready, probably ready enough. And then, as the sky suddenly filled with low-hanging clouds way out by the curvature of the earth, the storm hit.

The discus ring, without much drainage, quickly filled with water and turned the dirt circle into slippery muck. It was like ice in there, and there would be no telling where a discus, or its thrower, might end up. The officials asked the athletes if they'd prefer to postpone the event until the skies cleared and the ring dried, and they all agreed, as much for safety's sake as anything. Silvester retired to a nearby building, a "very cold room," stripped out of his wet clothes, took a training table and covered himself with a warm blanket. It felt to him like he "just melted right through" that table. It was his first peace and quiet in days.

Oerter had remained outside, pacing back and forth beneath a tarp, refusing a rubdown or any other invitation to relaxation. And when the competition resumed an hour later, he was about where he'd been. Silvester, back at the ring, discovered he was even more drained than before the rain. "No excitement, no fire," he thought.

In the third round, Oerter stunned everyone when he flew the discus 212'6", a full five feet farther than he'd ever thrown in his life. It was not particularly a threat to Silvester's inventory of covered distances, whose record after all, was twelve feet beyond that. On this day, it was going to be more than enough. When Silvester finally came back, Murray wrote, he "was as wild off the tee as a 20-handicapper with a built-in slice." In fact, he fouled three times and—drained, tired, nervous, or just outfoxed—could throw no farther than 202'8", a shocking fifth-place finish. Murray had the last word, as usual. "He could have thrown a saucer farther with a cup in it."

If there were a cup in it, and if it were filled with tea, it wouldn't have been Silvester's, would it?

Group photos of the sprinters, especially, but not necessarily, when in street clothes, tended to look like album covers. A slightly raucous soul group, maybe. They were the stars of any meet, their fast-twitch fibers ensuring an instant gratification no other event could deliver. The guys in the field events toiled in the trenches, doing blue-collar work with scrap iron. Plus, they were usually older, maybe not as trim. And the long-distance men, who had patience for that? They looked skeletal and promised just as much fun. Sprinters, they were rock stars, coiffed and aloof, all style, leering at the camera, their shades cocked provocatively. There wasn't a bigger star among them than Jimmy Hines.

There were a lot of good dash men that year: Charlie Greene, Ronnie Ray Smith, and Hines had all cracked the 100-meter world record earlier in the summer, running 9.9s, taking a tenth off the mark. Mel Pender, with his shocking starts, was a factor as well. All of them had flash to go. There was something about Hines, and he certainly knew it if you didn't. In every photograph, whenever somebody managed to gather them for a sort of team picture, there's Hines hanging back, a foot from the others, always maintaining separation. If there's a lead singer in this group, it's Hines.

However the 100-meter race is about the most unpredictable race there is. There are a lot of moving parts in any race, but when it's this short, they all have to be working perfectly. If a runner drops a gear here, he's out. Within those ten seconds, there is no allotment for recovery of technique, no time to make up for a bad start, no overcoming a bad decision. A 100-meter race is a guided-missile launch, all the important work done back in engineering. The runner's just along for the ride, holding on for dear life. "We're a different breed of cat," Greene explained. "We don't need a lot of time or space or air. One gulp and it's all over."

After such languorous competitions as the 10K, lap after lap of that, and the discus and shot put, with their interminable inching away of marks, all of them taking most of the day and requiring vast amounts of concentration, the 100-meter dash restores all the Olympic excitement you'd ever need. The coolest guys in the world, not to mention the quickest, would perform a slightly controlled explosion, artifacts of their energy thrown off into the stands to create even more buzz. And it would take, in this case, less than ten seconds. At the end, as they all tried to pull back, flaps up, we'd have the World's Fastest Human.

What else we'd have was anybody's best guess. Politically, this was an extremely unpredictable group and nobody knew how, or even if, the U.S. sprinters would protest or show any form of sympathy or support for their button-wearing brothers. Hines, behind those sunglasses, was a complete cipher. When he and Greene were told that Avery Brundage would more than likely present their medals if they happened to make the podium, they suddenly clammed up and drew their faces tight. The message was clear. On the other hand, Hines had had nothing to do with the movement to stymie the Olympics. He had obeyed the NYAC boycott but only, he said, because he'd been threatened if he crossed lines. His role model was not Harry Edwards or Dr. Martin Luther King, Jr., but "Bullet" Bob Hayes, who'd traded his Fastest Man credentials from the 1964 Games for an NFL contract and who, by the way, remained opposed to the boycott as well.

Like Hines, Greene was an early opponent of the boycott. He thought it would be unpatriotic. "I'm an American, and I'm going to run," he had said. Greene was not a radical by any means. He was an ROTC lieutenant at Nebraska and favored a heightening of activity in Vietnam, not a withdrawal. "Those Orientals won't give up till the last one of 'em is dead." He appeared more interested in girls than political and social change.

Pender, who had actually been to Vietnam, and who'd seen dead "Orientals," maybe even made some of them that way, was the activist among them. Racism within the military, in which he'd served without much question, had pricked his social conscience and he'd become a vocal leader of the OPHR group. He was older, he had seen things—he had a Bronze Star, for goodness' sake—and he was listened to. Pender knew there was nothing he could do come the Games; as a loyal Army man he would never do anything to dishonor the uniform. It was out of the question, no matter how he felt, no matter how much he worked on behalf of the OPHR. Just in case, though, an Army colonel representing the military in Mexico City had met with him before the Games and began to explain there could not be, would not be, any demonstration on his part. "Mel," he said, "you could really ruin your career. You could be court-martialed, you could even go to Fort Leavenworth." Furthermore, the colonel told him, "I understand you're supposed to go to flight school in February. When you get back, you'll be ready to go." He left that hanging.

It seemed that every event would have an overlay of tension beyond the actual competition. How much weight could a simple footrace support? The Olympics had always been a delivery system of world politics, as nations used the competitions to put their best foot forward, but now it was getting even more complicated, as factions within nations were struggling for, and sometimes even against, social progress.

The race would have been exciting enough, in any case. "There is no hush," wrote *Track & Field News*'s man in Mexico City, "quite like that which settles over the Olympic Stadium (any Olympic Stadium) just before the men's 100-meter dash." In that silence on Monday, eight men settled into their blocks, although most eyes were on Hines and Greene. Greene had beaten Hines in eight of the last twelve finals. Hines, who was now wearing gold shoes, had beaten Greene in each of the two Olympic Trials. "They were," *Sports Illustrated* had written, combining the two men's attributes, "the fastest four-legged sprinters ever sent to the Olympics." Greene did not intend to compete in tandem, though, and he was all confidence, no matter the recent finishes. "My start'll be sweet and superb," he predicted. "I'll be running like razors."

And here's how it went, the brief silence of the stadium yielding to a sustained roar, the runners off their marks:

It was Pender whose start was sweetest. There was nobody out of the blocks like him. Pender, even at thirty years old, is a startling burst and he owns the first 40 meters. He believes he is on his way to a world record. However, Hines is coming to speed and so is Greene and they both catch Pender at 50 meters, passing him. Greene is trying to make his move but is cramping, faltering, unable to shift gears. Hines shifts. He passes Pender, who is thoroughly mystified ("I have a stride and a half on everybody," he thinks), and wins by a meter, in the world record time of 9.95 seconds. Greene, briefly considering pulling up, powers on but is beat to the finish by Jamaica's Lennox Miller. Pender finishes sixth.

And that was all the drama the 100-meter race was going to produce, although it was plenty. Neither Hines nor Greene behaved in an out-of-the-ordinary way on the podium, accepting their medals as tradition required. Of course, Brundage had been careful to absent himself, deciding to enjoy the sailing events in Acapulco that afternoon, and the two got to shake the inoffensive hand of Lord David Burghley, a British official.

A press conference later Monday was similarly anticlimactic. Although it was jammed and oppressively hot—an interpreter nearly fainted and had to be carried out—it was not heated. When Hines was asked what he thought of Harry Edwards and the black athletes' protest, he replied, "No comment." What he most wanted to say was that he expected to be wearing shoulder pads, not track shoes, very soon. "I'll be talking to the Miami Dolphins," he said, "and hopefully I'll be wearing one of their uniforms two weeks from now."

He was asked if he thought he could get a $200,000 bonus from the Dolphins and he laughed. "I certainly am going to try to get as much as I can." In that respect, he intended to follow the example of Bob Hayes, previous Fastest Human, who was making a lot of money with the Dallas Cowboys. "Bobby has always been my idol," he said. "I hope to follow in his footsteps."

Chapter 12

PROTEST

Licorice Hammers, Tommie Jets, and Black Gloves

THE BOYCOTT HAD FIZZLED, the movement had failed for lack of solidarity, and all that was left was the possibility of individual protest. And that possibility seemed to be fizzling as well, event by event, as the black athletes accepted their medals without demonstration. There was still enough residue of reaction that Avery Brundage planned to make himself scarce whenever a U.S. black athlete was on the podium, but not enough, apparently, to justify a summer's hullabaloo. There was a lot of good behavior when complaint had been promised.

Of course, it was hardly over. It was still early in the week and there was Wednesday's 200-meter event. The movement's founding fathers, Speed City's Tommie Smith and John Carlos, not only promised a blazing race—a one-two punch, the drama being only in the order—but some kind of protest. If not Wednesday, when? If not them, who? "Will Negroes Snub Brundage?" wondered one headline. Not that Brundage would be around to see.

Smith had originated the whole idea with his comments about a boycott while in Japan. Throughout the long summer he had been among the most devoted to the cause, along with teammates Carlos and Lee Evans. It might have been hard to predict such involvement, given his personality. "Write me a rule," he used to say, "and I'll follow it." He was quiet, devout, and industrious. He actually enjoyed his time in ROTC. Hardly a militant. A reluctant crusader if there'd ever been one. However, during his time at San Jose State, as he became more and more aware of the black athletes' plight, he began to wonder why he couldn't make as much a difference off the track as on.

In 1965, his sophomore year, Smith couldn't help noticing the swirl of student activity, both in the Bay Area and at his own school. Harry Edwards, who'd already impressed him with his activism and who later became the first black professor he ever had, was spreading word about a march. It was in support of black freedom, especially for those in the South, and it was going to involve a sixty-mile protest, from San Jose to downtown San Francisco. Smith was interested, but there was a problem, something more than an inconvenience for a scholarship athlete. His coach, Bud Winter, had been prepping Smith for a double world record in mid-March, a shattering of both the 200-meter and 220-yard dash on the same straightaway. Same day as the march.

Smith decided to do both, accommodating both activism and athletics, catching up with the demonstrators as soon as he could. Early Saturday afternoon, with finishing tapes set at 200 meters and 220 yards (about three yards further), Smith settled into the blocks. As the team workhorse, he'd already won the 100-yard dash and had also helped San Jose State to victory in the 4x100-yard relay (he'd run in the mile relay later). He felt strong and started fast, maybe even too fast, but without troublesome curves, a relative weakness for him, Smith just tore down that straightaway, his stride actually lengthening, top speed going up. When he was able to stop and look back, he saw the timers puzzling over their stopwatches. They had reason to give the time a second look; it was 20 flat, matching world records for both distances.

Smith managed to get a shower, but then he was immediately on his way. His friend, Art Simburg, got his Volkswagen into gear and drove Smith halfway up the Bay to catch up with the marchers, about one hundred of them, for a night in a high school gymnasium. The next day he hiked the remaining forty miles, hassled all the way, bottles and epithets flying, and they all got TV time when they arrived in San Francisco. It probably didn't hurt that a world-class sprinter was in their throng.

Carlos was a different case. As the certified life of the party, he was always hard to take seriously. "Tommie wants to change the world," a journalist thought, "and Carlos wants to get laid." He was a little better traveled than Smith, a bit more worldly. He was a city kid, sure, right out of Harlem, but more than that, he'd already experienced firsthand the exploitation of the black athlete while he was in the South.

He'd been miserable at East Texas State, almost from the minute he got there. Surprised, for sure. The first thing he'd seen, as he stepped into the Dallas–Fort Worth airport, was a sign for a "white" restroom. Huh? Once on campus, he was equally surprised to discover his name had gone from "John" to "Boy." He'd run into racism in New York, but to him it was more a sign of ignorance than anything else. Here, it was actually systemized.

While Smith was undergoing his own transformation at San Jose State, Carlos was experiencing his. Of course, given his personality, it would be a little louder. Balking at his coach's instructions his freshman year in 1966, Carlos decided to show him up, turning a sprint into a jog. The coach was furious and picked up a hammer from a construction site near the stands and came toward Carlos. Carlos said, "Coach, that hammer better be licorice, because you're about to eat it." The confrontation, which soon cooled, was hardly typical of his time there, but it wasn't surprising either. The chemistry was such between Carlos and authorities—virtually any authorities—that some New York athletes were brought in specifically to watchdog him, to maintain him.

Nobody watchdogs John Carlos, he thought. When his team won the conference that season, coaches tried to present the athletes with championship rings. Carlos realized the gem was not commensurate with what football players got. "This here's just a flake, coach." And he demanded proper stones. After much groaning, the runners did get them.

He wasn't long for East Texas State, anybody could see that. His indignation, however, building as it was, remained vague, and he had no idea how or even where to work it out. Leave it to Harry Edwards to help articulate anger. Reaching out to him back in New York (they'd met several years earlier and had kept in touch), Edwards invited "Quick Cat," as he called him, to a meeting at the Americana Hotel. That was how Carlos met Martin Luther King, Jr. Carlos, for once, found somebody worth listening to. At the end of the meeting, when King called for questions, Carlos piped up and said he'd heard that somebody had written him, promising a bullet with his name on it if he returned to Memphis. Why would he go back? "I've got to stand up for those who won't stand," said Dr. King, "and I've got to stand up for those who can't." Carlos was, if only briefly, speechless. Finally, he had a slogan.

Now he had a place to go. Following Edwards to San Jose was a logical next step, as much to satisfy his fascination with the competition there (he'd been keeping track of Speed City all along) as to learn more about this boycott. When he'd first heard of it back in Texas—the first reports came in an issue of *Track & Field News*—he thought, *They're talking it and I'm living it.* Really, there wasn't much question where he was going to end up.

Smith and Carlos were paired entirely by that circumstance, certainly not by personality. They were teammates and competitors and, as a consequence, were always together. But they were not friends. That they happened to believe so strongly in Harry Edwards's project, maybe even for different reasons, certainly added to the relationship but it would always be an odd, perhaps even uncomfortable, one.

Still, there was no question that they were going to do something on the awards podium and that they would do it together. They felt the burden of the entire movement, the responsibility for making sense of this strange summer, the need to express their dignity. And by now they felt it alone.

There was, foremost though, the matter of racing well. No amount of personal conviction was going to matter if they didn't first get to the podium. While Smith and Carlos were clearly the best in the field—Smith owned the 200 meters, setting record after record, until Carlos beat him in the Trials, using those illegal shoes—the Olympics are often a platform for surprise. That is, things happen. On Wednesday, something happened.

In the heats earlier in the week, Smith and Australian Peter Norman had been passing the Olympic record back and forth. Smith tied the record of 20.3 in the first round; Norman, who had never run faster than 20.5, ran 20.2 to break it in his heat; and then Smith came back in his to tie it. This was inspired running. In Wednesday's two semifinals, both Smith and Carlos won their races in new Olympic records of 20.1.

In that race, Smith had pulled up too quickly at the finish and he felt a sudden and sharp pain in his groin. *I've been shot*, he thought. He'd been getting enough hate mail, mock airline tickets to Africa, and death threats that it was a reasonable explanation. He quickly realized he'd pulled an adductor muscle. Which, really, was just as bad. The big race, the stage from which he could at last make his show of defiance, his plea for justice, was less than two hours away. And here he was, couldn't even take his own shoe off.

Coaches and trainers quickly hustled him to a nearby room under the stadium and placed him on a table. Smith said, "I'm gonna be here for a while, maybe forever." It was a little panicky. Art Simburg, his great admirer, made his way there, desperate to see him. This was a disaster. How many times had he seen Smith pull up at San Jose State? He could have cried. When he got there, Stan Wright, the no-nonsense assistant coach, tried to wave him away, misunderstanding his visit. "You can't bother these guys about shoe stuff now." They packed ice along Smith's groin and were able to stop the swelling, and they left him there for forty-five minutes until—of course!—Bud Winter appeared, wearing a fisherman's vest and a novelty hat.

Winter was at the Games as a fan, hobnobbing with all his foreign friends and just having a great time. He made a big game of testing security, holding up matchbooks at the gate as if they were credentials, and waving all his friends in behind him. That was always great sport for him. When it came to his Speed City boys, he was always there. "Let's go, Tom-Tom," he said, and with less than an hour to go walked him up a flight of steps to the practice field.

It was getting dark as Smith began to jog, knees high. It actually felt okay. Maybe the quick icing had reduced the damage. Encouraged, he decided to save everything for the race and, with twenty-five minutes to go, shut it down and tried to relax.

It was going to be hard to relax under these conditions. Because the U.S. team was so strong, Smith had felt he could afford to concentrate on just this one event. He certainly could have competed in the 400 meters—he held the world record there, after all, and wouldn't he have made a nice leg on the relay team. He thought he'd be better off without that workload, without running race after race, all those heats, for an entire week. Yet here he was, broken down all the same, but this time without the possibility of coming back in a later event. He did not have a Plan B when it came to climbing onto that podium.

Smith settled into his blocks, carefully. Alone among the eight runners, he did not rip off a practice start or two. He was determined to husband every bit of energy, to keep that thigh, tightly taped now, as calm as possible. Both Smith and Carlos had drawn good lane assignments. The three middle ones are considered the best and Smith was in lane three, Carlos in lane four. This meant, because of slightly staggered starts in the curved race, Smith would have Carlos in sight from the start. So conditions, if not ideal, were acceptable.

It was just a matter of waiting for the starter's pistol, which would compress everything that was ever meaningful in his life into the next twenty seconds.

Smith got off to a good start, that thigh muscle holding up out of the curve, at least. Carlos was about 3 meters ahead as he attacked the straightaway, but the Tommie Jets were lighting up. He went by him with 80 meters left, the crowd cheering the pass and Carlos checking him out a couple of times, as if surprised at the company. Smith was so far ahead in the last 10 meters, and so relieved, that he threw his arms up in victory, nearly jogging at the finish, a huge smile on his face. It was another world record for him, a time of 19.83 seconds. Incredibly, Peter Norman had snuck by the head-swiveling Carlos at the end to get silver, but at least the two Speed City men had medaled together.

Smith and Carlos had already assembled their artifacts of protest, their tokens of defiance, backstage. The two of them had worn their OPHR buttons, of course, and, having gotten permission from their coach, they had raced in black dress socks (there was no other kind when it came to black; Smith paid eighty-nine cents for his pair). That was only part of the show they'd planned for the victory stand. Smith's wife, Denise, had bought a pair of black leather gloves in Mexico City, the idea at first being they would insulate their hands from the racist touch of Brundage. Carlos had gotten a string of beads for himself and Smith added a black scarf. But, really, that was about all the planning they'd done. There was no script for the medal presentation, no choreography of revolt. It was only in the twenty minutes they spent together, between the race and awards ceremony, that the two finally discussed what they'd do. Smith kept the right glove, giving Carlos the left.

Norman, meanwhile, had begun to pester Smith. What could he do to protest? This was crazy, Smith thought. He didn't really have time for this. A white Australian? He was going to protest? Crazy.

Sitting together in the stands that day, waiting for the ceremony among eighty thousand others, were the two wives, Denise Smith and

Kim Carlos, along with *Newsweek* journalist Pete Axthelm and his new buddy—you guessed it—Harvard coxswain Paul Hoffman. Axthelm, who had begun coverage of the 1968 Olympics at *Sports Illustrated*, had by now become the sports editor of *Newsweek*. He wasn't necessarily sympathetic to the leaders of the black athletes, but he certainly wasn't as suspicious of them as many of the older hands in press row. And he definitely was interested in them, writing often about the boycott efforts, meeting regularly with Harry Edwards, Smith, Carlos, and Evans, and now sitting with their wives. It was Axthelm's impression his sympathies were getting under everyone's skin at the USOC, as if he were a co-conspirator. His credentials were held up at first, which was strange, and when he finally got them, according to Hoffman, a USOC spokesman spat out, "Hope you have something better to write about than niggers."

Hoffman, who'd been sitting with Axthelm in the press section at a lot of the track-and-field events, decided to wander down to the railing, where the athletes would pass by on their way to the field. As he loitered, Norman walked by and noticed that Hoffman was wearing an OPHR button. "Hey, mate," he said, "you got another one of those?" Hoffman was as suspicious of Norman, whose country might have been even more racist than the United States, as Smith had been. "You gonna wear it?" Norman nodded, took the button, pinned it to his own uniform, and continued to the infield.

Smith and Carlos marched out together, forming a strange procession. Smith was praying, Carlos listening for gunfire. They were in their black stocking feet, a single shoe clutched behind their backs. And they were each carrying one black glove as well. Something was up, that was for sure. But what? In Canada, hiding out from assassins, Harry Edwards leaned in to his television. Bert Bonanno, sitting alongside Bud Winter in the stands, was shooting some film with a Bell & Howell movie camera. Lee Evans got as close as he could. So did Mel Pender. What were these guys going to do?

The two placed their shoes on the platform—this was a slight departure from their purely political program, but Puma had to get its due—and stooped to accept their medals. As the first strains sounded, Smith and Carlos bowed their heads and shot their gloved fists skyward, Smith's ramrod straight, Carlos's cocked. Carlos's beads, representing the lynchings of southern blacks, hung before him, his open jacket, unzipped in a kind of solidarity with the working man, flapped loose. Their outstretched arms, in an unintentional symmetry, formed a V. "Oh, shit," said Evans softly. "No, they aren't," said Pender, suddenly envious of their bravery. Edwards leaned back, the perfection of it beyond his imagining. In the stands, the color drained from the old coach's face and Bonanno put down the camera. Smith and Carlos did not sing along with the national anthem.

Carlos felt the hatred pour down on him. It seemed to him they were shouting the national anthem, "screaming" it at them. Not everybody understood what they were seeing and not everybody there reacted. But many others recognized anger in the pose—the balled fist! It was worse, according to the *Los Angeles Times*, "a Nazi-like salute." And the bowed heads were seen, at the very least, as an insult to their country. Said *New York Times* columnist Arthur Daley: "They stood on the podium with heads bowed in defiant refusal to look at the American flag while it was being raised." After the first shocked silence, the *Los Angeles Times* reported, "the stadium rocked with boos and catcalls and some of the spectators made thumbs-down gestures as they would a Mexican matador preparing for the kill."

Clearly, there was some explaining to do. Smith was not one to do much of it, usually ceding all public relations duties to Carlos. However, here is what he said to Howard Cosell of ABC afterward: "It was not a gesture of hate," he said, "it was a gesture of frustration. This was going to be a silent gesture that everyone in the world would hear."

Carlos was doing some talking, too, though it seemed he was speaking more out of a personal hurt than a need to set the record straight, especially in the immediacy of the event. The boos had rattled him, distracted him from his purpose. "Print it the way I say it," he told the press afterward, "or don't print it at all." He went on: "We feel that white people think we're just animals to do the job. We saw white people in the stands putting thumbs down at us. We want to let them know we are not roaches, ants, or rats. If we do the job well we get a pat on the back or some peanuts. And someone says 'good boy.' I've heard 'boy, boy, boy' all through the Olympics. I'd like to tell white people in America and all over the world that if they don't care for the things black people do, then they shouldn't sit in the stands and watch them perform."

Nothing either would say was really registering. They had, in almost total spontaneity, created a scene of discontent that was so powerful that words would always fail it. People would interpret it as they had to, seeing anger, black power, or just bad manners. It was an insult to a country, it was a call to arms, it was a dangerous defiance. Some others saw desperation, a plea, a final frustration. Smith and Carlos tried to explain their symbols of protest, their furious pose, but the words piled up uselessly against the image they'd created. It was beyond words.

Chapter 13

HARDER AND HIGHER

The Little Stinker, Beauty and the Beast, and Hollywood Agents

THE U.S. BOXING TEAM WAS a quasi-military unit, to the point that many of its members and coaches were actually addressed by rank. Henry "Pappy" Gault, first-ever black coach for a boxing team, had been in two branches and had served the Marines at Iwo Jima. He was Sarge. His assistant was Ray Rogers, another Marine, also a Sarge. Six of the eleven members to qualify for the squad represented one of the armed forces. Some of them were Sarges, too.

So, this was not a group of athletes that the Olympic Project for Human Rights was interested in targeting. For many of the boxers, even though they were all either black or Hispanic, the opportunity to boycott or even protest was severely limited, possibly by law. Nobody knew for sure.

Moreover, they probably were just not interested. OPHR leaders had decided, fairly or not, that the boxers were not an educated bunch, that they were incurious, and that they were satisfied with the status quo, which, in the case of their particular sport, tended to reward the best and most agreeable of them with professional careers. The comments they heard from the boxers seemed to justify the tactic. "That's for college kids," said George Foreman, asked for his thoughts on the proposed boycott earlier that summer.

For all his comments, Foreman was not so much unenlightened as he was practical. Nobody guessed it at the time, but Foreman was not nearly as straightforward a patriot as he was characterized. He was more confused and conflicted, as it happened, than his far more vocal brothers. Maybe he didn't take any of Harry Edwards's classes, but he had not come to these Games without social baggage. He had been around.

At his first Job Corps stop in Oregon, he had met some corpsmen returning from a march in Mississippi. That was intriguing. A so-called hippie in the corps there had introduced him to the music of Bob Dylan. "Sounds like he's crying" was Foreman's initial critique. But repeated listening seemed to open his mind somewhat. Soon, starting from scratch on the way to a GED, he graduated from the soft porn available to entry-level readers there ("He touched her leg . . . she breathed heavily") to the *Autobiography of Malcolm X*. He was not unaware, or even uninterested.

However, he was not ready to be involved. He understood that this was his time, and it was going to be exceedingly brief. Lew Alcindor, who did not come out for the basketball team, was debating Joe Garagiola on television, but to no possible detriment to his career. *Nothing to lose*, thought Foreman. *He'll be on TV again. I have only one year to be on TV.*

Anyway, Gault had made it very clear, in an appropriately salty language, that he would not tolerate any foolishness. The bowdlerized version of his stance appeared in the *New York Times*. "None of my fighters have been involved in any of this demonstration stuff," he said. Moreover, he said, he'd told his fighters, "If anybody had any plans to demonstrate, he'd better tell me before he did it or else get the hell out of Mexico fast."

For all his tough talk, Gault was beloved by his fighters, who all adjusted their politics according to his presence. A few of the boxers were college kids and a few of them were more sympathetic to the protest than Gault (or the fellows at OPHR) ever suspected. But they had come together as a family during boot-camp conditions of training—sixteen-hour days in mile-high Santa Fe—and none of them felt it was necessary to disagree with their forty-six-year-old father figure, no matter what their politics. Patriotism was the order of the day.

If outsiders failed to get it, couldn't quite understand this political cohesion, woe to them. Paul Hoffman—Hoffman!—had become friendly with featherweight Albert Robinson, a Navy man. They had marched together during the Opening Ceremony. But when Hoffman showed up at the boxing venue, more in the spirit of a fellow supporter than an organizer, Gault took note. Furious at what he took to be proselytizing, Gault confronted Hoffman in the mailroom of one of the Olympic midrises and threw him, all 110 pounds of him, against the wall, warning him away from his boxers. "Stop intimidating my athletes!" Hoffman was stunned.

The boxers had their hands full, anyway. U.S. boxing, which had been dominant around the world since the beginning of time, was in comparative decline. The Soviet Union had shown unexpected muscle in the 1964 Games, as had Poland, which had taken the team title in Tokyo. In fact, Poland was coming to Mexico City with three of its 1964 gold medalists and the Soviet Union, which had placed seven finalists in those Games, was showing up with several medalists as well. The United States—which always promoted its gold medalists onto the pros (heavyweight Joe Frazier was the only boxing gold medalist for the United States in 1964 and was well on his way to fame and fortune)—had none returning.

Chief among U.S. prospects was Harlan Marbley, competing in the new light-flyweight division, and Robinson, the featherweight. Marbley was well schooled in the international style of boxing, having been the All-Army, All-European, and Pan-Am champion. He had an amateur record of 189–5 and was satisfying some additional requirements of a sports star. He had a tattoo of a skunk on his left arm—"That's me," he'd tell the writers, "the little stinker"—and a flamboyant wardrobe. Teammates thought he should have more than the twelve pair of shoes to go with his twenty-four medallions, though. Robinson, who himself had a record of 123–19, speculated he'd have more but "he ain't heavy enough to wear them out."

Others with extensive experience included Marine Sergeant Arthur Redden, who had a 65–5 record as a light heavyweight; Army Sergeant James Wallington, who was 76–2 as a light welterweight; and welterweight Armando Muniz, another Army man and former UCLA student, who was 34–3. The other college student, Ronnie Harris from Kent State, had been successful on the national level and had a record of 56–4.

Yet, as it is almost every Olympics, the heavyweight entry was getting most of the attention. Foreman's twenty-one bouts in less than two years was scant preparation for these Games. Everybody knew by now, though, that he could hit. "Really hit," emphasized Gault. The coach had found Foreman enough of a handful during camp that he had threatened to send him home, but like any reasonable coach whose reputation hinges on the success of his athletes, he found cause to forgive the big man. "I'm not making any predictions," said Gault, "but we have won the Olympic heavyweight title three out of the last four times. We usually produce good ones."

Foreman had been hurt by how little attention he was drawing, both from the media and his own U.S. teammates, who had excluded him from all their boycott talks. Once in Mexico City, though, he was drawing crowds more to his satisfaction. The writers were finding him an important resource. Foreman had been experimenting with doggerel, as was then the fashion of the day, and tried this out on the grateful scribes: "Many a man has fell and stumbled, when he met big George in that square jungle." They all wrote this down. He was becoming a go-to guy for the off-day feature. A wire-service story about his superstitions—"I spit on my thumb when I see a load of hay," he explained—appeared in nearly every newspaper in the

United States. He was just nineteen, but was quickly adjusting to the demands of fame.

He was, all in all, having the time of his life. The Olympic Village buffet was in particular a delight, especially for a man who was free to explore upper-weight limits. The camaraderie was also unexpected fun. He was rooming with Robinson, and the sight of the 218-pound Foreman and his 126-pound pal made for a comical juxtaposition. Those first days in the Village, well, there had never been anything like it. One day, Bob Beamon showed up for lunch at the buffet, which was Foreman's turf, carrying his tray and wearing his gold medal. Everybody just gathered around and said, "I want one of those, now!" Foreman examined the sight. "It stood off like something falling from the sky," he thought.

They were simply exhilarating, those first days. Once, he arranged to walk through the Village in the company of Iris Davis, one of the U.S. sprinters, and a comely one at that. It was another comical juxtaposition, compounded further when he dared to put his hand on her shoulder. And for three minutes of their stroll, beauty and the beast, she allowed it. "Put your arm back down," she finally said. No matter. His arm had been up there, a full three minutes, and anybody in this international community of youth could have seen it for themselves.

Boxingwise, nobody was sure what to make of him. His first bout, during the first week of a two-week boxing tournament, with Poland's Lucjan Trela, went the three-round distance and impressed no one. Foreman couldn't breathe, the high altitude causing his lungs to burn. And he was slipping all over the ring. And Gault was shouting from ringside. Here's what Foreman heard: "Use your jab. Jab that blankety-blank." This so-called Olympic story might not have legs, after all. It wasn't even a unanimous decision, the Hungarian judge scoring it for the Pole. Foreman, who believed he had scored a knock-down blow in the third round (the ref ruled it a slip), explained afterward that his opponent was too short and he lost power by punching down. "Otherwise," Foreman said, "he'd be sleeping right now."

The desperation of the excuse—too short to be knocked out?—was a kind of alarm. Good stories evaporate all the time, once the difficulties of actual competition are introduced. Foreman had been great copy, right up until the bell.

Foreman was having reason to doubt the whole experience, notwithstanding the uncooperative stature of his opponents. The very day that Trela had dared stand up to him, the two U.S. sprinters had demonstrated, fists high, on the podium. Foreman, like the rest of the boxers, had been largely unaware of the protest. It was not important news at their venue, the hijinks of some college kids. Foreman hadn't even registered the fact that Tommie Smith's and John Carlos's fists were gloved.

However, two days later, when the two were suspended, Foreman became very much engaged. He didn't know Smith, except that he was a U.S. teammate. Carlos, well, he was about the coolest guy in Mexico. Everybody knew that. Foreman happened to be out and about that Friday when the two were marched from the Village, a flotsam of reporters in their wake. The two sprinters, disenfranchised by their country, had vacant looks on their once-expressive faces, it seemed to Foreman. They were in shock. He was suddenly and unexpectedly furious. Whatever the issues were, and he wasn't certain what they were, they were beside the point. His teammates, kids just like him as near as he could figure, were now cast out from this great party, where you could walk with beautiful women, eat as much as you wanted, and bask in the attention of adults.

He started an uproar and announced he was through with boxing. "We're a team," he told Doc Broadus, his trainer back in Oakland, who had made the trip. "We all got to stand together." Broadus calmed him down, saying he had a specific conversation with John Carlos about this very matter and that Carlos had told him that Foreman needed to box and he needed to win. The unlikelihood of such a conversation didn't register with Foreman and he agreed to do Carlos's bidding, though he could no longer do it cheerfully. "Everything's changed," he told Broadus. He felt a gloom creep over the Village, nobody smiling so much anymore. He'd box. "But the fun's gone."

Bob Seagren finally had to tell *Life* magazine to leave him alone. It had been fun for a few days, a photographer and writer following him around, setting him up with "the daughter of a wealthy local businessman," taking him to clubs and other sights. He'd enjoyed it at first, especially as he had nothing else to do the first week in Mexico City and was famously susceptible to boredom. So the pace of the photo shoot had been welcome but, by Monday, his event just two days off, he had to start attending to the work at hand.

And it was going to be work. He was the best in the world but he was erratic, sometimes failing to clear even 14'. This tended to make his appearances more exciting than was absolutely necessary. Ordinarily this wasn't an enormous problem, as he could usually uncork a world record vault before the evening was over. An early failure just served to provide entertainment value to an already fascinating event. However, with an international field this big—there were fourteen other finalists who'd start the day with him Wednesday, all of whom could clear 14', no problem—every miss was going to be important.

They'd all filed into the infield about noon, their long poles ensuring an exaggerated separation, prepared for a full day of competition. With this many entrants, the event could easily take as many as eight hours to conclude. A big issue for vaulters, consequently, is remaining interested. Seagren, bored sitting around, began to investigate an alternate pair of shoes in his bag, his roommate's shoes, actually. Jeff Vanderstock, who was also a USC teammate of his, had failed to medal the day before when, in the space of only two strides, he went from second to fourth in the 400-meter hurdles. As he packed to go home, he suggested Seagren try his shoes, the Pumas with the Velcro straps, to see if he liked them. Same size, after all. And, he laughed, he wasn't going to be needing them. Seagren toyed with them while he waited, tried them on, and decided they made him feel "like you were running on your toes." On that basis, he changed his equipment before the most important meet of his life.

Equipment is obviously crucial to a vaulter. For other athletes, the pole represents an irritating obstacle: you have to get over it (high jump) or get rid of it (javelin). But modern vaulters rely entirely on the bending property of the pole, an ever-changing technology of flex, to conduct their sport. It's not that the athlete is incidental to performance but consider this: Seagren, who actually bridged two eras, increased his height by two feet the minute he changed from bamboo to fiberglass. The ability to bend the pole made all that difference. You don't teach that or train that. You invent it.

In fact, because the event was more a product of innovation than technique, nobody really knew how to coach it anymore. Seagren's coach at USC, Vern Wolfe, had once been a vaulter, but his experience with stiff, wooden poles was now irrelevant to a contest that had essentially become a trebuchet, a kind of catapult. The guys with the real know-how were the manufacturers, fellows from Cata-Pole, Pacer, and Silaflex, who worked with the vaulters to fine-tune this translation of energy—from head-on to up-and-over. They were always hanging around the infield, especially Seagren's in Los Angeles (home base for the manufacturers), filming, talking to coaches and vaulters. The emphasis was on innovation, not instruction. This is all to say, Seagren was basically self-taught.

Indeed, the event enforces a particular independence, all around. The pole, roughly twice an athlete's height, may be the welcome source of his performance but it is, on the other hand, an irksome travel companion, requiring an ability to adapt and improvise. The poles do not unwind like pool cues, after all, and thus must be lugged in their fearsome entirety from airport to hotel, where they do not fit in rooms. Seagren was not alone in his fraternity, helplessly hailing taxis, 16 feet of fiberglass on his shoulder. A vaulter is not only a passenger in this event, he is his own Sherpa.

Oddly, given how equipment-dependent it is, there are few rules governing the sport. A pole can be any length, any girth, and of any material. All the same, an Olympic official began hassling Seagren about his pole as soon as he began his warm-ups. He objected to Seagren's taping job, where two thicknesses of adhesive are wound to provide a hand grip. This resulted in some bickering. There was even more when the same official accused Seagren of spray-painting a marker across the runway, illegally indicating a takeoff point. A West German vaulter had done that.

All in all, not a promising start. But Seagren remained unconcerned as the rest of the field opened competition. He had waited almost three hours, and five passes, before he finally joined them at a height of 16'6¾", a middling height for him but a silver medal height in the previous Olympics. He made it easily but was beginning to wonder if he'd misjudged the competition. With the bar at 16'8¾", the gold-medal height from 1964, there were still eleven men remaining.

At 17', there were still nine others left and the competition was proceeding fitfully, misses here and there for everybody, but the bar going up quarter inch by quarter inch (actually, in international increments of five centimeters) with everybody keeping pace. Seagren, who was not doubting his own abilities by any means, was, nevertheless, getting alarmed by those of his competitors. Had he been totally wrong? The West German, Claus Schiprowski, had only cleared 17' once in his life and here he soared 17' and a fraction to equal it. And then he cleared 17'¾" and then 17'2". Normally, a vaulter has no more than one personal best in him, the self-satisfaction of performance quashing ambition. So, this was unusual, and a little disturbing.

With the bar set at 17'6¾"—announced as 5.35 meters— Seagren decided to pass again. He knew the metric system after seasons abroad but it was still easy for an American to become confused. It just didn't sound that high to him, 5.35. Besides, he figured his competition would start falling by the wayside. They didn't. All four remaining vaulters cleared the bar, dropping him to fifth place. If he did not clear the bar again, at a near-record height, he had no chance for a medal.

Well, this was somewhat unnerving. The bar was reset at 17'8½", not that far under his world record from the Trials. All five of them missed on their first attempts. Seagren cleared it on his second try and, as he'd hoped, the others began misfiring. Christos Papanico-laou, who was representing Greece but who trained with Bud Winter at Speed City, missed twice more, as did John Pennel, the U.S. vaulter who had long jockeyed with Seagren for records. They were out. East Germany's Wolfgang Nordwig made it to join Seagren. Then Klaus Schiprowski made it, too. Schiprowski! He had now recorded five personal bests in one day and there was no way to know if he was done.

The bar was reset at 17'10½", or 5.45 meters, and the three groomed their poles, walked back and forth, and muttered to themselves in the growing darkness. It was nearly eight. Then, the competition was halted—nobody knew why—over some disturbance at the medals podium. There was booing and whistling. Again, none of the vaulters knew what was going on, even what event was being celebrated. Eventually, the stands quieted, some eighty thousand people settled back in their seats, and the contest resumed.

Seagren was leading the event, although it would have been hard for anyone in those seats to know it. By passing at 17'6¾", whether out of strategy or confusion, he had reduced the opportunity for misses that his opponents, both Nordwig and Schiprowski, had made at that very height. Now at 17'10½", he had to vault first in the three-man rotation, a disadvantage, psychologically at least. If he missed all three tries—and he did—he would have to sit there and watch, knowing there was no longer anything he could do to protect a victory. If Nordwig or Schiprowski—and who knew about that guy—made a final attempt, he would not get gold.

They didn't clear any of their three tries either and so Seagren won, not quite as expected, but with a daring that was much appreciated. "Gambling Seagren Takes Pole Vault" was the headline in the *Los Angeles Times*. "Bob Seagren, taking chances that would put a Mississippi riverboat gambler to shame," proclaimed the article, "preserved the United States' unbroken string of Olympic victories in the pole vault here Wednesday, but just barely."

Although Seagren failed to see that much gamble in his mid-event ploy (he thought it was simply prudent, a way to save energy) he played along. By the time *Life* magazine came out a week later, the Olympic photo essay having been crowded from the cover by a picture from Jackie Kennedy's wedding to Aristotle Onassis, Seagren was taking credit for Olympic bravado. "It was like playing roulette," he told that week's biographer. "The ball happened to stop at my number."

Seagren had indeed been fearless that week, but it may have had little to do with his gold-medal performance. Three days after the event, while he was packing up to go home with his family, his roommate Jeff Vanderstock told him, "Wait, we have to get our reward first." Reward? They trekked over to Armin Dassler's hotel, where the president of Puma was entertaining visitors. Dassler was not being well represented in the Olympics, so the sight of a Puma-wearing gold medalist like Seagren was a welcome sight. After some pleasantries, the two retired behind closed doors in the suite and Dassler asked, "Okay, what was our deal?" There had been no deal, of course; Seagren had avoided the whole shoe circus, feeling he had pressure aplenty without a major company counting on him, too. The riverboat gambler, if that's what he was, wouldn't fold this hand. Seagren pulled a price from the air—actually, it was whispered in the Village that medals were paid off "1–2–5," as in thousands, so he had something to go on. Dassler was startled by the amount, all the same, and peered skeptically over his Ben Franklin bifocals. It was as if he suddenly recognized the scam. Seagren wondered, *Too much? Too little?*

But he remained poker-faced and Dassler, whether admiring his gold medal or his brazenness, slapped him on the back and paid up.

And that was Bob Seagren's Olympics. He left on Friday, just as everything was boiling over in the Olympic Village, the press showing up, picking off whomever they could, for whatever comment they had. Seagren missed all that. Back home in Pomona, there were scores of messages for him, some even from Hollywood agents.

Chapter 14

AFTERSHOCKS

Pimped-Out Socks, a Mutation Performance,
and Sparks Under His Feet

OMMIE SMITH AND JOHN Carlos were on their way down the elevator at the Hotel El Diplomático, where they were staying with their families. That's when they first learned of their suspension. The door opened to the lobby, and there was one of the Olympic officials, Jesse Hawthorne, who was the athletic director at East Texas State during Carlos's contentious stay. Hawthorne measured his former problem child for a second. "John Carlos," he said, shaking his head, "always causing trouble." And pushed by him into the elevator.

The lobby was filled with newsmen, as if to emphasize the growing consolidation of the reaction. At first, it had been confused and scattered. Not everybody had seen their protest and few were sure of what to make of it. Robert Lipsyte, the columnist for the *New York Times*, wasn't sure what he was seeing from the press box. "After all we'd come through this year," he thought, "and this is it? This is the mildest, most civil demonstration of the year. What's it even mean?"

Some newspapers did not immediately gauge the impact of the gesture and led their coverage of Wednesday's events with Bob Seagren's so-called heartstopper victory in the pole vault. The *New York Times* did not feature the two runners' protest on the first page, but further inside the sports section. The *Chicago Tribune* seemed to miss it entirely. "Smith and Seagren Win Gold Medals" was the banner headline; the story below it allowed that there had also been a "somewhat discordant note" on the podium but overall was more impressed with Smith's "climaxing stirring performance."

The sight of the two on the victory stand at least registered with the *Los Angeles Times*'s Jim Murray, who apologized for the clumsiness of his column that day, saying he was typing with "my black glove." Yet it didn't feel important enough to him to move him off his obviously preconceived topic: Dick Fosbury's odd style in the next day's high jump.

Even the runners' hometown newspaper, which was presumably aware of the possibility for protest, glossed over the post-race image. "Tommie in Record 200 Win" was the headline in the *San Jose Mercury News*. Although there was a long story on the race, the paper covered the victory salute with *Washington Post* wire copy.

This was odd, considering the initial crowd reaction and, for that matter, Carlos's post-race diatribe. But ABC-TV, and certainly Howard Cosell, guessed its importance. Cosell was an extremely polarizing figure, alone among the white establishment in tolerating Muhammad Ali's radicalism, and was not the network's choice to represent its Olympic presence. Producer Roone Arledge insisted he be there, for the very reasons the network wanted him home. Black athletes would talk to him, and here would be the payoff.

Cosell tried to interview Smith immediately after the demonstration, to give meaning to those gestures, but he couldn't find either Smith or Carlos. Only when he learned the next day that they were staying at the El Diplomático could he make his case. Smith didn't want to do an interview, telling Cosell, "You'd think I committed murder." But Cosell managed to persuade Smith to come to the ABC studio, where he gave his only substantial interview on the subject, at least the one that most people in the United States saw.

It was there that Smith decoded the symbols of protest. "The right glove that I wore on my right hand signified the power within black America. The left glove my teammate John Carlos wore on his left hand made an arc with my right hand and his left hand, also to signify black unity. The scarf that was worn around my neck signified blackness. John Carlos and me wore socks, black socks, without shoes, to also signify our poverty."

Smith and Carlos also talked with the BBC at their hotel that same Thursday, agreeing to the unbelievable offer of one thousand dollars apiece for the interview. This amounted to an unexpected, but very welcome, first-place prize. While they were waiting for the crew to show up at their hotel, Smith got yet another phone call, but this party was presumably less interested in their version of events. It was the USOC and they were demanding the two of them return to the Village and meet with them. Smith knew there was nothing to gain from that and told them he wasn't coming; his race was over, his legs hurt, he was finished. They asked to speak to Carlos, who was staying in an adjacent room, connected by a door. Smith handed the phone over and listened to Carlos's side of the conversation, which was basically "motherfuck" this and "motherfuck" that. It appeared he wasn't going, either.

It wouldn't have been a pleasant meeting, had they agreed to go. IOC president Avery Brundage may not have been at the victory stand—he didn't want to shake their hands either—but he had been kept informed. The day of the protest, he wrote in his journal that "the athletes had deliberately violated" the spirit of a politics-free Games and that he had spoken with Douglas Roby of the USOC and was assured of a speedy report.

It wasn't that speedy, with the USOC convening a series of meetings that, according to different reports, lasted either four or ten hours on Thursday, the day after the 200-meter race. The USOC's resulting statement offered a formal apology to the IOC, "for the discourtesy displayed by two men who departed from tradition during a victory ceremony." It did not include any sanctions against Smith and Carlos, called "immature," but warned against more "black power acts" by teammates.

This did not satisfy Brundage, who threatened Roby with removal of the entire U.S. delegation. This was outrageous, of course, but it did signal to the USOC that their original statement had perhaps not gone far enough. They met again Thursday night and made another announcement Friday morning, this time declaring that Smith and Carlos had been kicked off the team and had been ordered to "remove themselves from the Olympic Village."

The committee was having a hard time getting any news of this to Smith and Carlos. The USOC sent Jesse Owens to the Village to meet with any other would-be protestors, as well as give Smith and Carlos their walking papers. He didn't find Smith and Carlos there— still back at the hotel—but did run into a buzz saw when he met with a group of athletes, almost all of them having come together in support of their ousted teammates. Owens badly misread the situation and even tried to oust Hal Connolly, one of the white athletes there in support, saying, "You don't even need to be here. I'm talking to my black brothers." Connolly was more their brother at this point than Owens and the former Olympic great was shouted down.

The bigger misreading was the IOC's, who had pressured the USOC into ordering the suspensions. They had now turned an interesting sideshow into the main event. The press, which had been only mildly interested to this point, was now fully absorbed in the drama, obliged to offer commentary and insight. Some, like syndicated columnist Red Smith, recognized what was happening. "By throwing a fit over the incident," he wrote, "the badgers multiplied the impact of the protest a hundredfold." *Time* also detected poor impulse control on the part of those "badgers," the functionaries with insignias on their Olympic jackets, and said, "The IOC bullheadedly proceeded to make a bad scene worse." Almost everyone else with a press credential reacted more predictably. The *Chicago Tribune* was compensating for any initial listlessness in its coverage with a second-day editorial that called the demonstration "an embarrassment visited upon the country." Brent Musburger, reporting for the *Chicago American*, compared the two athletes to "dark-skinned storm troopers."

Smith's and Carlos's gesture had now grown to define the Olympics. For *Sports Illustrated*, they were now the Problem Games. *Time* magazine, its observations of overreaction notwithstanding, felt the two had given the Olympic motto a new translation: Angrier, Nastier, Uglier. All across America, as the event was recast as a selfish movement, there was a sense that a once-innocent platform of play had been ruined by the insult of two young black men.

For the two young black men, it hardly mattered for the moment. The USOC could dial Smith's room all it wanted but it wasn't going to get a meeting, and it wasn't going to get its medal back. When Smith and Carlos walked into the lobby of the Hotel El Diplomático Friday morning, into that scrum of newly inspired newsmen, they felt pretty much beyond the Olympic law. Learning they'd been expelled was a shock, of course, but not really a problem. As Carlos reminded them, they'd run their race and pocketed their medals. What about being forced out of Mexico, one of the press wondered. Carlos withdrew his visa from his back pocket and, scanning its provisions, informed them that was simply not possible. It turned out it was (the two were flown out three days later) but, again, what did it matter at this point?

Of a larger concern was not what to do about Smith and Carlos but what to do about the rest of the U.S. athletes. The USOC's Roby had felt the IOC rebuke sharply, especially the criticism that it was "not controlling its athletes and that racial dissension might spread to other delegations." Their man Owens was unable to keep the kids in line. Owens had told the athletes to beware of "pimped" out socks, either in competition or on the podium, explaining they cut off circulation. Not really hearing it. The officials, moreover, had made martyrs of Smith and Carlos and managed to direct at least one nation's attention from even the normal affairs of state to yet more turbulence. News of Smith's and Carlos's suspension, and the forty-eight-hour ultimatum to get out of town, nearly crowded coverage of Jackie Kennedy's upcoming wedding to Greek shipping magnate Aristotle Onassis off the front page. The USOC was sitting on a lit powder keg, in other words. But instead of attempting to defuse it, the committee began striking matches.

In fact, there was no growing movement to turn the Olympics into a manifesto, everybody still agreeing to do their own thing, as before. However, as the media began assessing the situation within the Olympic Village, it was also becoming clear that there was more support for Smith and Carlos than the obvious racial divisions would have led them to believe. Of course, the black athletes were lining up behind Smith and Carlos. "It is unfair, it is ridiculous," said Art Walker, the triple jumper. He correctly pointed out that the Olympics have never been free of politics, not as long as the United States had been refusing to dip its flag at the Opening Ceremonies. Sprinter Ron Freeman warned, "I think there will be a lot of guys going home."

More troublesome to Red Smith's "badgers" was the support of some of the white athletes, some of whom were more adept at finding voice in the mostly white media. When asked if he thought some of the black athletes might be sent home, Harold Connolly said, "Some white ones, too." Decathlete Tom Waddell, another white athlete who seemed to be spiraling out of USOC control, said he "was disappointed more Negro athletes backed down." When the *Washington Post* wondered if he thought the action had discredited the flag, he shot back, "I think they have been discredited by the flag more often than they have discredited it." As Waddell was an Army medic, this kind of talk had repercussions beyond the usual media scorn. It earned him the threat of a court martial—this came on the second day of his own competition—which required the literary efforts of Harvard coxswain Paul Hoffman to fend off. "A non-retraction retraction," Hoffman's specialty.

As for Hoffman, there was hell to pay here, too. Roby had not forgot his part in the protest and recognized in Hoffman the kind of athletic small-fry he should be able to bring in line, maybe even make an example of. Hoffman and his Harvard teammates were having their problems, anyway. The crew, a gold-medal favorite and as smooth a team that ever rowed, was suddenly having problems with equipment. Two rigging bolts.

Worse, everybody was getting sick. Worse yet, the altitude was just killing Art Evans, their stroke, the most important man in the shell. Well, it was killing everybody. The first day on the water, all those rowers carried off in medical boats. But Evans! The crew knew he was going to be a problem in Mexico; he had been a problem at high-altitude training in Gunnison, Colorado. Harry Parker was reluctant to replace him because he had been so important to their rowing rhythm. They could be down five seconds in the last 500 meters and Evans would dig them out in a fury. Now, there was just no choice. Evans had basically collapsed in the last 200 meters of one of the heats—he was all but unconscious when they lifted him out—and Parker was forced to implement a series of changes.

Hoffman, who had engineered his life for just this opportunity, couldn't believe what was happening to this charmed group. "It was as if God decided he'd finally had quite enough of us." The crew would have one more chance to qualify for the finals, in the do-or-die repechage on Friday. Everybody knew this was important, because Harvard had sent down a dean, Fred Glimp, to cheer them on. In the repechage, Dean Glimp could be seen on a bicycle, pedaling unsteadily along the 2000-meter course, following the Harvard boat. It would be impossible to say that his presence was making a difference, but something was suddenly working. The crew, with yet another lineup change and the dean on their flanks, and Cosell calling it live and excitedly, pulled from behind to get the second place required to get into Saturday's finals.

Any relief at getting back in medal contention was short-lived. No sooner had Hoffman gotten out of the shell than Parker told him they'd been summoned to a meeting with the USOC. "When you get back to the dock," Parker told him, "leave the crew there and have a cab take you down. Dean Glimp will go with you." Hoffman was dumbstruck. Dean Glimp was not so reassuring, either. In the cab, he tried to make some awkward conversation with Hoffman. "So, Paul," he said, "I understand Harvard's going to be a target of the national SDS." Students for a Democratic Society? This was bizarre. "Dean," Hoffman tried to explain, "my father's a judge in the Virgin Islands. I don't belong to the SDS."

Parker had gotten there first and was proving to be even more irritating to the USOC's Doug Roby than Hoffman had ever been. Parker told the committee there, perhaps a dozen men, that he had no plans for removing Hoffman from the boat, as they were suggesting. "Don't kid yourselves," he told them. "Won't happen." He wasn't in the mood to be intimidated by "badgers," or what the *New Yorker* called "stiff-backed tutelaries." None of the crew ever knew exactly where Parker stood politically, but it probably didn't matter. When Parker told the committee that, whatever their disagreements with Harvard's politics, it could have been resolved weeks before, certainly before the eve of their finals, Roby blurted, "You're damn right that's when we should have taken care of it."

The hearing, if that's what it was, was one more affront to Hoffman's understanding of adulthood. This was how grown-ups behaved? "Don't you see what you're doing is disrupting the whole Olympics?" one of them asked him. *Bizarre*, he thought yet again. He thought it was clear they thought they were doing something organized, yet he couldn't detect any procedure at all. "Really, sir," he said, "what we're trying to do is to foster the spirit of brotherhood of the

Olympics." The meeting didn't wind down until ten that night, when the committee, having satisfied some sort of need to vent, just let it expire of its own pointlessness. Hoffman got back at eleven to the Village, where his teammates were waiting; they wouldn't have rowed without him, of course.

There were a lot of athletes in the same boat, figuratively. After all, the USOC had finally warned, a "repetition of such incidents would warrant the imposition of the severest penalties." How would the rest of the black athletes, or even some of the white ones, display solidarity without bringing the full force of the Olympic administration down on them. It was pretty clear it could and that it would.

The long jump was going to be one of those closely watched events, as much for the medal ceremony as the competition. The event should have been predictable, returning all three medalists from the 1964 Games, including the United States' Ralph Boston, who would be appearing in his third Olympics. None of the three were favored, not after the year Bob Beamon had been having. Beamon, a twenty-two-year-old from South Jamaica, Queens, had won all but one of his twenty-three meets in 1968 so far, and would have to be considered the best in the field.

However, he was inconsistent in all areas, from long jumping to politics. Nobody knew what to make of him. He could just sail away, off into the horizon on one jump, then foul the next three. Phil Shinnick, the 1964 Olympian who had failed to qualify in South Lake Tahoe, had studied him during the Trials and never did figure him out. He couldn't understand that accent, for one thing, and had no idea where his head was. "He was just out of it," thought Shinnick. None of his teammates really knew what to do with him, either. They were greatly disappointed when Beamon chose to compete at the New York Athletic Club, a boycott that had been about the only course of action the OPHR had unilaterally agreed upon. Beamon had his eye on the prize, but it was different from everybody else's. On the other hand, hadn't Beamon been suspended by the University of Texas at El Paso track team—and subsequently jumped uncoached for most of the year—for protesting the school's insistence on scheduling a meet with Brigham Young? And, whoa, wasn't he walking around the Olympic Village in a Nigerian tunic?

So on Friday nobody could be absolutely sure he'd win, or what he'd do if he did. Beamon didn't know either. He was "worried as the dickens" about his approach to the board when he nearly failed to qualify during Thursday's jumps. He had scratched on his first two attempts—alone among runners, Beamon did not put marks on the runway to help his takeoff—and only made a qualifying jump after Boston took him aside and told him to move it back three feet if he had to, but make a safe and legal jump. On his final jump, Beamon pitter-patted down the runway, half-jogging, taking choppy steps ahead of the board and made an uneventful, if relatively short, jump to qualify.

He had avoided the Olympic ruckus for the most part, staying forty minutes away from the Village in a villa provided by a U.S. track promoter. There were no distractions there. He was further pleased to see Gloria, his hometown sweetheart, show up, flown in several days before the Games. He was less thrilled, some time later, to hear that his wife, Melvina (from their frayed and perhaps forced marriage), was asking for him in the Village. So, some distractions, but nothing that couldn't be endured. And then Friday, still feeling "frightened" about all those scratches in qualifying, he learned about teammates Smith and Carlos being suspended. And, on top of all these growing concerns, he had committed the athletic sin of giving in to sex Thursday night. "I just left my gold medal on the sheets," he thought.

As the afternoon finals approached, all overcast in the Olympic Stadium, everyone was ready for a show. The field for the long jump might have been the strongest of any event. Besides Beamon, who loomed as the favorite after his startling season, there were Boston (a gold and silver medalist the last two Olympics), Great Britain's Lynn Davies (gold, 1964) and Igor Ter-Ovanesyan, the Soviet who had edged Boston by four centimeters in Tokyo. With two of the glamour races also scheduled for Friday—the women's 200 meters and men's 400 meters—it was going to be a good day to be watching track and field.

The air was fifteen degrees cooler than Thursday's qualifying and the Tartan runway felt a little harder to the jumpers. Beamon had already decided to go all out on his first try, never mind Boston's qualifying advice or even that the first three jumpers before him had all fouled. This was the finals. Somehow, no matter what had been swirling in his head minutes before, he was able to block everything as he stood at the runway. He didn't hear the crowd, didn't consider the possibility of scratching, didn't acknowledge the world-class competition around him. He took off, bounding down the runway, his knees high, and his sockless feet blurring until, finally, the right one stamped the white board, hard, and, by a hair, legally.

Boston watched all of Beamon's jumps with anticipation, knowing that one day he was going to put everything together and launch something majestic. As he stood there, it occurred to him that this just might be it. Beamon had unusual abdominal strength, which allowed him to keep his legs tucked longer than most jumpers. And, of course, he had spring. But this . . . seemed unusual. He was up there forever, his thin arms reaching out as if he meant to hang from the clouds. "That's over twenty-eight feet," Boston said to Davies. Davies doubted that very much. Nobody had ever jumped so far.

Beamon had no way of knowing if he'd made a good jump or not. The crowd had let out an enormous "oomph" but that didn't necessarily mean anything. He had landed with so much impact, landing almost on his rear and sand spraying everywhere, that he'd had to take three frog hops out of the pit to resume his balance. He thought he must have lost at least a foot by not landing on his feet. Well, he'd have more tries. He sauntered, all loose-limbed and casual, back to the top of the runway, where the Omega sign board would show his distance. Except that there seemed to be a delay.

Mexico City had arranged for a number of presumed technological advances for this Olympics, the Tartan track being one, the Cantabrian measuring device in the long-jump pit being another. It was a chest-high rail, with an optical reader that could slide its length for a more precise reading in the long jump. As Beamon continued to flap his arms and jog lightly, an official could be seen running the reader down to the end—8.60 meters, or 28'2", comfortably beyond any human's ability to travel, one jump at a time—until it fell off the rail. "Fantastic," said a judge. "Get a tape," some spectators shouted from the stands.

It took thirty minutes, an unbelievable delay, before anybody could be satisfied with a measurement and post it on the Omega board. It read 8.90, a legal jump with the assisting wind measuring the maximum allowable (suspiciously so, some thought) 2.0 mph. Beamon knew then he had set a world record and bounded straight up and down at the result. But he didn't know what that record was. Bouncing back up the runway to where teammates Boston and Charlie Mays were standing, Beamon asked what 8.90 converted to. "That's twenty-nine feet," Boston said. But that didn't seem right. Beamon had passed all of twenty-eight feet? "No, wait," said Boston, still calculating. "It's more than twenty-nine feet."

Beamon collapsed, not in mock faint, but in a near-complete neural shutdown—a "cataplectic seizure," doctors called it, defining it as an "atonic state of the somatic muscles on the heels of emotional excitement." He grasped Boston's legs as he sank, his face finally on the ground. He was now physically sick, as well. Boston and Mays helped him up and officials and trainers scurried around trying to attend to him. "I want to vomit," he told them. Then: "Tell me I'm not dreaming."

Beamon, on his very first jump, had advanced the world record from 27'4¾" to 29'2½"—nearly two feet. It had taken twenty-five years to move Jesse Owens's record just 8½" to Ter-Ovanesyan's record. To blast through that much distance on the way to a new record? It was incomprehensible. It was, to use those numbers, an eighty-four-year advance in one day. "A mutation performance," a statistician called it. The Portuguese Tables, a complicated system of comparing records from different events, put it another way. To make a similar advance in the mile, for example, would require a time of 3:43.3, an improvement of some seven seconds. An equivalent high jump mark would be 7'10½". Ridiculous.

The veteran long jumpers, still waiting their turn, did not need the Portuguese Tables to demonstrate their sudden irrelevance. Davies, for one, was disgusted. "We can't go on," he said to Boston. "We'll look silly." Boston seemed to be the clearinghouse for athlete reaction because next came Ter-Ovanesyan, a grudging pal after all these competitions. "Ralph," he said, with a thick accent, "compared to this jump, we are as children." When Beamon finally composed himself and rejoined them, Davies, grown even more disgusted, said, "You have destroyed this event."

In fact, he had. Nobody felt like jumping and it was up to Boston to rally them back into competition. "If you give him the gold," he said, "there's still two more medals." Boston was at least motivated by his mother's presence in the stadium; it was the only Olympics she saw her son compete in and he knew, "after fourteen years of jumping in sand," it would be his last.

With rain setting in, making the runway slick, the field was doubly depressed. Davies was stunned all the way back into ninth place, with jumps nearly a half-foot off his gold-medal-winning performance four years before. Ter-Ovanesyan at least bettered his bronze medal mark from Tokyo but still could not do better than fourth. Boston, who had jumped a whopping 27'1½" in qualifying, managed only 26'9½" for bronze, at least completing his Olympic set. East Germany's Klaus Beer, alone, seemed untroubled by Beamon's performance, jumping 3½" beyond his personal best for 26'10". As for

Beamon, he took one more jump, this time the Cantabrian device being up to the job, for 26'4½" and then, still delirious, passed on his last four runs.

There was still some drama remaining. The two U.S. medalists would be the first men to respond to the Smith-Carlos ouster. What would they do? What could they? Their gesture had been so powerful that there was really no way to improve upon it. Lee Evans had studied it and decided the only form of one-upmanship possible on a victory stand was to burn it down, "Jimi Hendrix style." When the time came, Boston, the reluctant radical, mounted the podium without his black Adidas (dyed specially by the company for some of the athletes) or socks. He was barefoot and he was defiant. "Send me home, too," he said, "because I protested on the victory stand."

The more shocking sight was Beamon, glum-faced now, who stepped up to the highest rank on the podium, his black sweats rolled up his shins to display long black socks. "Evidently," Boston thought to himself, "he had something on his mind after all."

Lee Evans was enjoying the kind of timing athletes only dream of. He couldn't have been better prepared. Everything was coming together at just the right moment. Just the day before, in Thursday's semifinal, he'd set a new Olympic record of 44.8. Two of his teammates finished well, too, giving the United States a great likelihood of a sweep in the 400 meters. (Actually, if there weren't Olympic limits, the whole field would have been American, never mind the medals stand. The top twelve 400-meter men in the world were all from the United States) So Evans was confident. Not even Larry James, dropping by his room Thursday night with the lane assignments, could shake him up. James, unable to mask his smile, told Evans he was in big trouble because he'd been assigned lane six—the staggered position that places the starting field in front of him—while Evans was going to be stuck in lane two, way out in front, unable to know what the crowd behind him was doing. Evans just laughed at the news. He'd run a 44.06 in Tahoe and was expecting to get into the 43s on Friday, and it didn't much matter where he started from. But James already knew that. Everybody knew that.

Friday morning brought more news, but this couldn't be laughed off. A gathering horde of reporters let him know that Smith and Carlos had been suspended from the team and were going to be kicked out of Mexico. What did he think of that? Evans ought to have considered the possibility—it was extremely naïve to expect these protests would be lodged without repercussions—but something that drastic just never occurred to him. He was shocked. He was furious. His initial reaction: he wasn't going to run, and in the meantime he was ready to fight anybody who got in his way.

By the time Bud Winter got to the Olympic Village—rushing there as soon as he heard about Smith and Carlos, sensing disaster—Evans was already in a bad way. In five hours, he was expected to run the race of his life but here he was in the lobby of the delegation office, "wild-eyed" and ready to come to blows with a U.S. team manager. Winter managed to collect his runner and walk him out of the office, but wherever they turned they were besieged by reporters. Some of them were alarmed that Evans seemed to have collapsed. "Why do you have to support him?" one of them asked. There was no getting away from them. Finally, Winter spotted the Japanese team bus parked near the warm-up field and hustled Evans into it. Winter told the driver he was a friend of Mikio Oda, the Japanese head coach—of course he was!—and that he'd need the use of his bus. "Big trouble here," he said, as the driver dutifully put the bus into gear.

Evans was thoroughly devoted to his coach, more amused than amazed at times, but devoted. When Winter told the team to hand in whatever shorts they planned to wear at the meet—and returned them with aerodynamic "speed holes" punched in, guaranteed hundredths of a second improvement—Evans would just laugh. The man was a complete eccentric, totally of another time. Once Winter had given him a ride to the track, about three miles from campus, and had never gotten the '52 Bug out of second gear. Moreover, Winter had pulled every knob on the car's control panel, as if he were readying a jet fighter for takeoff. When Evans finally disembarked he immediately sought out Smith. "Tommie," he said, "you wouldn't believe—" Smith held up his hands. "I know."

However, Evans had complete faith in Winter as a kind of mentalist, a soother. Not everybody bought into the coach's relaxation mantras, but those who did tended to win their races. Evans was one of those believers. It was Evans's understanding—what exactly had Winter told them of his wartime experiences, anyway?—that the old coach had been overseas, talking pilots from crashed planes back into the cockpit. So he was a man to be (mostly) listened to.

Winter had the bus driver circle the block to Evans's dorm and hustled him up to his room, where he just collapsed onto the bed. Five hours to go, and he was a complete mess! The old relaxer went about his business. Without telling him what to do—Winter seemed to be saying Evans could both run and protest—he proceeded to put his runner to sleep. It took him three minutes. Evans awoke from a trancelike state and experienced visions, so he thought, of both Tommie and John, encouraging him to run. In fact, Winter had produced both men in Evans's room and they explained, one at a time, that he had to race; they had their medals, now go get his. Together, they had freed him.

Evans had slept for two and a half hours and was refreshed. He met Winter at the warm-up field at 3:00 p.m., one hour before the race. Winter was relieved to see that Evans was completely relaxed. He ran his hand over Evans's forehead—a trademark caress of Winter's—to check for perspiration. None. A good sign. Winter then laid out the race strategy. He wanted Evans to run a 21.6 through the first 200 meters, so he'd have something to spare for the finish. Winter knew Evans would never run such a slow pace—he'd cheat on it—but put that number out there so he wouldn't cheat too much.

Relaxed or not, Evans still had a lot on his mind. Few took the OPHR movement more seriously than he. He resented the establishment's ability to squash it so easily, to co-opt so many of the other athletes, and to intimidate so many more. Jesse Owens! Sheesh! Owens had implored the Olympians to avoid embarrassing their country, promised them they'd all be taken care of. "Jesse," Evans said, to the man who came back from the 1936 Olympics and had to race against horses for money, "they didn't take care of you."

Evans had gone off to Europe earlier in the summer, with the promise of quick cash for easy races. A fellow athlete had taken him under his wing, showed him the ropes, where to stay, how to get around, how to bargain for that under-the-table money. Mostly it was three to four hundred dollars, sometimes a new suit for winning. Evans would walk a promoter down to a storefront and pick out his prize. The Italian promoters paid really well, one thousand dollars per race. This all was in direct violation of the amateur code and, for all the winking that was done in track and field, still cause for Olympic disqualification. His friend instructed Lee in the proper means of receipt—never sign your own name, but use a pseudonym. Evans always signed Jesse Owens. He didn't like Jesse Owens much, never did. Owens was just like his parents, "cowed" by white people, bent to their purpose.

Evans didn't make a lot of headlines away from the track, but that was because it was hard to get noticed in the company of wild orators like Harry Edwards and John Carlos. It would have been a mistake, in other words, to interpret his easygoing manner for a lack of resolve. The kind of mistake a "badger" or "stiff-backed tutelary" might make.

So, Doug Roby, still feeling the heat from Avery Brundage, was everywhere, reading everyone the USOC riot act. Hammer thrower Ed Burke had earlier stumbled upon a red-faced Roby giving coach Stan Wright "a lot of crap." And, now, Roby was here, intercepting Evans, Freeman, and James on their way to the 400-meter final. On their way to the final! "Now, boys," he began, not only stopping them in their tracks but interrupting their prerace reveries, "I don't want to upset you but . . ." Evans would have been furious to have this dream state broken in any case, but to hear Roby warning them of "the serious consequences that may befall you if there was any outward demonstration," well, it was just too much. Evans and Roby nearly came to blows. James pulled Evans away and they left Roby standing there, still fulminating. They proceeded into the stadium, nerves jangling.

As Evans prepared for his race inside the stadium he was dimly aware of activity all around him. He had reacquired his prerace zone ("Can beat 'em one more time," he sang to himself) and was checking his shoes when he looked up to see the high jumpers across the infield, their parabolas barely visible to him. As his name was announced, there was a tremendous cheer, which was very gratifying. Then he realized it was related to some commotion in the high-jump event and had nothing to do with him. He settled into his position in lane two and sang softly to himself.

The 400-meter race is called the longest dash, properly suggesting the difficulties of contradictory events. Yes, flat-out sprint speed is important. However, in a race that is just long enough to induce a near rigor mortis—bears are said to get on runners' backs at two hundred meters—strategy, and the ability to put the brakes on, is critical, too. Coach Winter sat in the stands, wondering if Evans would have the presence of mind, given everything he'd just been through, to adhere to any plan, or would he just fire out of the blocks in a fury and leave everything at the start.

And now they were delaying the start. Something happening over at the long jump. The interruptions, the delays, they were starting to add up. Winter heard the starter's instructions from his seat. *A sus marcos!* (Take your marks!), *Listo!* (Ready!), and then the gun. Winter could relax everybody, apparently, but himself. His runners could always gauge his state of mind by the condition of his face; if it was all nicked up, the coach was a nervous wreck. Now Winter was a nervous wreck. He shot straight up out of his seat, maybe a foot. Evans was equally quick off his mark, the best start of his life, anticipating the starter's pistol perfectly.

Evans was mindful of Winter's advice to proceed cautiously, but nearly everybody who was watching describes Evans the same way: possessed. Running blind, not knowing what James was planning behind him, Evans blew out the first 200 meters in a time of 21.4, a tenth of a second off his run in the Trials, and exactly where Winter wanted him, his fake advice notwithstanding. The thin air, punishing in the later stretches, seemed to give Evans a kind of lift, "sparks" under his feet.

James, meanwhile, was right behind him, running the same split as Evans. James had planned on running a 43.9, which would be a world record, and he'd trained all year for that time. He was on track here, right off Evans's shoulder. Evans didn't realize that, thinking he was at least five yards ahead, until the staggers evened out and he spotted James just to his left. He felt "faint" at the sight and returned attention to his technique: knees high, arms straight ahead. He was trying to picture Tommie Smith's elegant stride, to calm his struggling lunges. Winter, watching from the stands, grew comfortable as he recognized the "loose jaw, loose hands" stride developing in the last 80 meters. Still, there were no more than a few feet of separation between the two runners.

With three strides left, James, "the Mighty Burner," seemed to duck his head, Evans powering through to the finish, knees still high, running the full 400 meters. James had run his race, 43.97, but he had never passed Evans in his life and he didn't here. Evans finished with a time of 43.86, a world record.

By now, though, it was no longer enough to win, or even set a record. Athletes were now obliged to consider podium poses, ceremonial flourishes, the post-victory offering of signs and symbols. Even if

Smith and Carlos had rendered subsequent protests irrelevant, if not quite unnecessary, athletes still bore the burden of a response. Anticipation had to be satisfied. What, everyone wondered, would Evans do?

Evans, James, and bronze medalist Ron Freeman appeared on the same victory stand as the high jumpers had earlier, the one that Boston had mounted barefoot and Beamon with pant legs hiked up. But, for all the tension, the 400-meter men cut a curiously cautious pose—fists waving high, black berets they'd bought in Denver worn jauntily on their heads. They were careful to smile—"harder to shoot a guy who's smiling," Evans decided—and to doff their tams at the anthem. After the anthem, a grinning Evans shoved a fist into the air again, but the smile was sufficient to disarm his audience and, at the same time, puzzle and maybe even disappoint many of his black teammates; it appeared more a gesture of celebration, not protest.

Ambivalence was as unforgivable as indifference to fellow protesters in this time and place, but the risks were growing too great to continue a full-on assault against the establishment. Bets were hedged. Asked about the berets, Evans explained, as reasonably as he could, still smiling, "It was raining."

But, alas, there was no inevitability to these Olympics, no guarantee that personal conviction would be rewarded, that sacrifice would be repaid. Perhaps some could dull the blade of punishment by superior performance, maybe some could buy a small amount of reconsideration with a gold medal, a world record. But outrageousness of youth had no license without achievement. Which is to say, poor Harvard.

Saturday was the team's last chance, though not much of one, the way they'd been rowing. The eight-man crew, somewhat disorganized after all the changes, finished dead last in its race for a sixth-place finish in the standing, well away from the medals the "shaggies" had expected. It was disappointing, although at least somebody found the result satisfying. It was reported that Avery Brundage watched the team limp to the finish, without much support on his part. He held his hands clenched tight to his sides. There is nothing quite so vulnerable to retaliation, or some small amount of petulance, anyway, than a last-place boat.

Chapter 15

MONDAY

A Grunion Hunt, a Crying Tigerbelle, and a Jig for Joy

JIM RYUN WAS WARY OF Mexico City and its thin air. In 1967, he had run a 3:53 mile in a Los Angeles meet and then, to see what all the fuss was about, immediately traveled to Alamosa, New Mexico, where the air was just about as scarce as it would be for the next year's Olympics, where he hoped to run the 1500 meters, the metric mile. To his alarm, he was unable to even finish the mile on his first try. He just keeled over. Taking a more conservative approach to the distance the next day, he was timed at 4:30. Not even a good high school time. So, he thought, that's what the fuss was about.

From then on, his training regime was more or less informed by panic. Running across the plains of Kansas, where oxygen was as plentiful as the wheat it grew (didn't wheat actually produce even more oxygen?), was obviously going to be poor preparation. The only thing he knew to do was to do more. The spring of 1968 he was running an incredible 120 miles a week, trying to make up for the air's bounty with even more punishing workouts. That's when, completely washed out, he was felled by mononucleosis.

The comeback at high altitude—he returned to Flagstaff, Arizona, to complete his training in the fall of 1968—did not encourage him. He was so slow there at first he thought he'd contracted mono again. He improved enough to reestablish his supremacy as the country's best middle-distance runner but came to realize that no amount of high-altitude work was going to make him comfortable at a mile and a half above sea level. Maybe, it occurred to him, you just had to be born there.

This was on everyone's mind, though, not just his. His arrival in Mexico City touched off chaotic news conference, if you'd even want to call it that. He could hardly leave the plane for the scrum of reporters. Will Grimsley, the Associated Press lead writer at the Olympics, was gesturing wildly for Ryun's attention. "Grimsley here," he yelled out. Wade Bell, one of the 800-meter men leaving the plane, passed the writer and agreed. "It is grim here."

They were there mostly because Ryun was by far the most recognizable athlete to their U.S. readers. A lot of ink had been invested in his prospects. He was American, a world record holder, and a completely neutral figure when it came to the politics of the day. He didn't require a tremendous amount of explaining, just description. Nobody in amateur athletics had higher name recognition, thanks in part to his achievements but also to their own relentless coverage. It was no wonder that Grimsley expected to be recognized. He, and many of his colleagues, had been celebrating him for years now, visiting him in Kansas, calling him up whenever they could use a column. Ryun found this amusing, as he devised strategies to avoid them (at the University of Kansas he studied in empty rooms so he wouldn't be bothered by the more persistent among them, ringing the phone at the end of the hallway). But, now, the throng was nearly terrifying.

And what they most wanted to know, which he least wanted to tell, was how the high altitude was going to affect him. At a formally scheduled press conference, which was nevertheless heated enough that a writer compared it to "sharks at a grunion hunt," Ryun was asked again and again what would be a good winning time at this elevation. They'd heard that Kenya's Kip Keino, the up-and-coming distance runner, had run 3:39 over 1500 meters at altitude. Ryun said that sounded about right, pointing out that Keino, who had never beaten him in the mile, this time had the advantage of living at high altitude. So, they wondered, are you saying this is an unfair Olympics? Ryun backtracked at a world record pace, saying, not at all, everybody was dealing with the same thin air. Although, he thought to himself, some would deal differently.

Everywhere Ryun went in the Olympic Village, he was besieged. "Trials of an Unlonely Miler," according to a *Sports Illustrated* headline in that week's preview. He finally moved out of the Village, checking into the Villa Coapa apartments nearby. That's where his fiancée, Anne Snider, was staying with her family. He couldn't train unmolested, either. His first day at the Olympic Stadium, he was unable to run at all because of the photographers. He and George Young, a sometime miler who was in the steeplechase, had to mount fake charges at them just to get them to budge. Ryun began running the highways instead. One day, he was jogging from the Villa Coapa when he ran into a couple of writers from *Track & Field News*. They accompanied him on a thirty-minute run to the soccer stadium, where they all climbed over a spiked railing to get in and onto the track. At that point, they were relieved to see, Ryun left them in his dust.

Ryun had one night of relief. Roger Bannister, the first runner to break the four-minute barrier for the mile, was in Mexico City on behalf of the BBC. Bannister and his wife met Ryun and Anne (always referred to by the press as a "Kansas State cheerleader") for dinner one night. Though Ryun and Bannister talked about running, the two couples also discussed more mundane matters. Bannister shocked Ryun by telling him that he and his wife had removed the television from their house. That was something to think about!

It might have been better if Bannister had just reminded Ryun what a dogfight he would be in for. The mile is more like roller derby than a lot of the events, a lot of bumping and shoving going on. It's a contact sport and teams of runners tend to look out for each other, even as they try to lose the pack. Moreover, it is a race that lends itself to strategy. There is not much strategy in a 100-meter race compared to the 1500-meter event, where pacing is so critical. In the longer race, there is no opportunity to make up an oxygen debt rashly incurred on the first lap, short of collapsing in the infield.

Ryun was not a rookie. Even at the age of twenty-one, he had a lot of races under his belt. But, because of his talent, he was more often beyond the fray, unfamiliar with the jostle. He'd gotten an earful once when he moved out in a race and left George Young on his own behind him. "What were you thinking?" Young screamed at him after the race. "That was a half mile of me being poked in the kidney." Ryun was hard to poke in the kidney, unless you were carrying a long stick.

The Kenyans, who hadn't won a gold medal since joining the Olympics in 1956, had already won two by Sunday. Naftali Temu had won the 10K race a week earlier, Ron Clarke nearly expiring at the end, and teammate Amos Biwott, not once getting his feet wet, won the 3000-meter steeplechase, trimming another Kenyan and the previously undefeated Young, who finished third. Young told reporters afterward he'd never had a chance for anything but bronze. "I knew the Kenyans were going to be by any time."

"This feels just like Africa," Temu had explained. "We will be at home here." U.S. track coach Payton Jordan said, "They don't know the harmful effects of high altitude." He went on: "Four weeks of training at high altitude is fine but it still can't compare with living in rarefied atmosphere all your life."

Still, they were not invincible: Temu finished third in the 5000 meters and countryman Keino was second behind Tunisia's Mohamed Gammoudi. If anything should have given hope to Ryun for his own race, he had been matched against Keino in the semifinals and, just as he'd always done, beaten him.

However, something was afoot Sunday. Saturday night, a team

official pulled Ben Jipcho aside and explained his new Olympic duties. "Jipcho," he was told, "you have a bright future. Kip Keino is getting older and when he quits, it will be your turn." But just not yet. Jipcho was ordered to be the rabbit, set a killing pace that might lure Ryun into a fast start, and then give way for Keino, getting older at twenty-eight, and his more measured run. Jipcho was dubious. It didn't seem quite right, but he agreed to the plan.

Keino was keeping a murderous schedule anyway, having competed (and collapsed) in the 10K, won bronze in the 5K, and also run the prelims and semis of the 1500 meters, all in seven days. If that mileage weren't enough, he had to do three more miles just to get to the track on Sunday. His team might have been good at running conspiracies but it was lousy at bus schedules; both Keino and Jipcho had to abandon their bus, which was stuck in traffic, and run the remaining distance (three 1500-meter races) to the Olympic Stadium just to make their race. Explained a team official: "They had to warm up before the race anyway."

Ryun, such a favorite that one magazine said in its preview, "If he runs, he wins," recognized what was happening to him almost as soon as the gun went off. Jipcho, who didn't seem much worse for his recent wear, went out like a rocket. Ryun quickly understood that Jipcho was trying to tempt him into committing a kind of suicide. He just as quickly understood that Keino was the designated man to beat. Ryun's problem was, only Keino knew when the final surge was going to come. Ryun, who'd become almost paranoid about preserving his resources, might not have time to react.

Both Ryun and Keino hung back on the first lap as Jipcho finished off a 56-second quarter. Brutal. Then in the second lap, Keino began his charge and had completed two laps in an incredible time of 1:55.3. By the third lap the field had divided into two packs, Keino leading one group, Ryun another, but five meters back. By then, the race had gotten away from him. There was too much Tartan between him and Keino, too many other runners to fight past. Keino was not faltering and at the bell lap had a forty-meter lead. Ryun broke from his own pack and, accelerating through the backstretch, moved from tenth place to second, but it was a distant second. That much ground was simply impossible to recover and the greatest miler of his day finished in second, a full twenty meters behind Keino. It was the largest margin of victory, or rather defeat, ever.

Keino's time was an impressive 3:34.9, an Olympic record if still nearly two seconds off a world record pace. Ryun, meanwhile, had probably run the race of his life, given Mexico City's conditions, finishing in 3:37.8. As Keino and Jipcho roared around the track in a victory lap—could they run forever?—Ryun staggered to a bench. When somebody stopped by to console him, he looked up and said, "God, it hurts."

Back home in Topeka, his hometown newspaper was setting the news in large type: "Keino Whips Ryun." It would take a while to live that one down.

Sunday was track and field's final day, and if Ryun's event ended in disappointment, there was reason for hope in several others. In fact, any time the Tigerbelles were still on the schedule, there was something more substantial than hope.

The Tigerbelles, which is to say the U.S. women's track team, were getting scant attention throughout all of this, even though, out of their small number, they'd provided two of their country's eleven gold medals going into Sunday. Wyomia Tyus had gotten the Games off to a good start on Monday, winning her second gold in the 100-meter sprint. Nobody, man or woman, had ever repeated in that event.

Tyus was used to passing people. Growing up in rural Georgia, she had to ride a bus an hour to get to school, right past the all-white school that was within walking distance of her home. At Tennessee State, Tyus passed even the great Edith McGuire, coming from relative obscurity to easily outdistance her in the 1964 finals at Tokyo.

At Mexico City, now twenty-three, she was considered washed up, having lost most of her races that year. Although she qualified, she was additionally rattled by the disappearance of her fiancé, Art Simburg. Simburg, jailed by Mexican police for the crime of representing Puma at the Games, was sprung before the Games actually began, but Tyus had been nervous all the same.

The finals heat on Monday featured four of the five world record holders, including U.S. teammate Barbara Ferrell, the rare non-Tigerbelle. It figured to be a blazing race and it was, Tyus out front almost all the way, setting a new world record in 10.8 seconds, finishing well ahead of Ferrell.

The other Tigerbelle gold came from Madeline Manning, the shy little girl from Cleveland. Her mother had taken her to Tennessee State, traveling on a Greyhound, and dropped her off in the care of Coach Ed Temple. Manning cried, and then she cried some more when she was introduced to the team. She had no business in a room with Tyus and McGuire!

She more than held her own, though, and was the dominant distance runner for the U.S. by 1968. Women had only been running this far since the 1960 Olympics in Rome when the 800-meter race was put back on the program; it hadn't been contested since 1928, when several of the finishers had collapsed in exhaustion and doctors said the "endurance" race would make the women "old too soon." The bias applied even more strongly to black women, whose stamina beyond the sprints was suspect. Yet Manning had served notice to the rest of the world in a Canadian meet when, knocked into the infield by Yugoslavia's Vera Nikolic, the event's reigning champion, she somehow climbed back into contention and outleaned her at the tape. With that victory, Manning kept a two-year streak going and was headed to Mexico City.

Manning was "wide-eyed" at the excitement around her. The Czech gymnast Vera Caslavska had created a tremendous stir in the Games, not so much for winning the all-around competition as for her modest protest on the podium. Caslavska, who had become an enemy of the invading Soviet government, having signed the "Manifesto of 2000 Words" the spring before the Russians had rolled their tanks through Prague, had bowed her head during the playing of the Russian national anthem. Manning was innocent of international politics, but she understood the magic of matrimony. Manning leaned over the balcony of her apartment a day after the protest, Caslavska having married Josef Odlozil, the Czech 1500-meter champion. A VW carrying the newlyweds rolled through the Village streets and confetti rained upon them, and any sensible girl would have cried at the sight.

Manning's path to a gold medal of her own was not going to be so magical, as she was to be joined in the competition by Vera Nikolic, whose fierce intentions had already been expressed with a sharp elbow. Nikolic had established the world record of 2:00.5 at a meet in London earlier in the summer, and had additional motivation as one of Yugoslavia's few medal hopes; Manning knew her for a desperate player in the best of times.

The rematch, and whatever mayhem might have occurred, never took place. In one of the oddest moments of the Olympics, Nikolic dropped out of her semifinal heat 300 meters into her race and simply left the stadium. Reports swept through the Olympic Village that Nikolic had gone to a bridge and was about to commit suicide when her coach prevented her from jumping. Manning was dumbstruck. She knew that she now owned the event and would probably add to Tigerbelle lore with another gold medal, but this development seemed to complicate her mission more than simplify it.

Before leaving for her finals on Saturday, the troubled Manning roamed the Village looking for Nikolic. And she did find her. Manning hugged her and tried to talk to her. Nothing seemed to be getting through the language barrier. "I just want you to know," Manning told her anyway, "God created you; your life belongs to him." For whatever reason, independent of the words, they both began weeping, the girls now sobbing in each other's arms.

In the finals, shortly after, Manning, more relaxed than she'd ever been in her life, won the 800-meter gold in an Olympic record time of 2:00.9. Nobody was closer than 10 meters at the finish. It had been a breeze, and the Tigerbelles had done it again. Manning cried then, too.

Now, on Sunday, the Tigerbelles were back, running the sprint relay. Tyus anchored another gold medal performance, finishing five meters ahead of Cuba in a world record time of 42.87.

The men's relays were not without drama either. The U.S. sprint quartet was going to be running hurt. Could it win? The mile bunch probably couldn't be caught, but then what would they do on the podium?

Charlie Greene had pulled his hamstring in the 100-meter dash, pulling up at 70 meters and barely holding on to finish third behind U.S. teammates Jim Hines and Mel Pender. He was still limping around nearly a week later and, through two preliminary races, was not showing a tremendous recovery. Cuba edged the United States in the opening round and the semifinal, but there was no suitable alternate and it was determined that Greene, even at three-quarter speed, was the team's best bet. The team had grown close enough—when you saw one of them in the Village, you saw the other three—that it really wasn't a dilemma for them.

On Sunday, Greene, his leg bandaged, put the team in a hole, just as expected. Pender took the baton and began making up ground and by the time he passed it to Ronnie Ray Smith had narrowed the gap to three strides. Hines was two strides behind Cuba's Enrique Figuerola when he got the stick. Hines had told his teammates before the race that if they got him the baton just "close to the other guys" they wouldn't have to worry. This was close enough. Hines ran the final leg in 8.2 seconds, never been done, and won going away, another gold for the United States, another world record, 38.23 seconds.

The 4x400-meter relay didn't figure to be quite so scary for the United States. Lee Evans, Larry James, and Ronnie Freeman had already gone one–two–three in the 400 meters two days earlier. The fourth member of the team, Vince Matthews, had lost out in the only competition that really counted at that distance—the U.S. Olympic Trials. The United States had cornered the market for quarter milers.

Late Sunday afternoon, the team lined up with their usual brio. The emphasis was not so much on winning but on creating an unbreakable world record. No jive, they sang, we will run 2:55. That would have been a five-second improvement, Beamonesque, they might have said. That kind of time was feasible, only if it were simply a matter of adding personal bests, one on top of another. Of course, they were not exactly fresh at this point. All but Matthews had run five races in six days.

However, Matthews was the one who looked stale, falling behind his Kenyan competitor right before the handoff. Freeman got the team back on track with a 43.2 second leg, faster than anybody had ever run that distance. James kept it going on his leg and handed the baton off to Evans, giving him a 30-meter lead to go with it. Evans cruised to an easy gold, another world record, 2:56.16. Not Beamonesque, but out there.

By now, there was little hope of outdoing Tommie Smith and John Carlos when it came to a podium protest. The demonstration could not be improved upon nor, given the consequences, would it likely be repeated. Tyus, still indignant over being left out of the process, nevertheless dedicated the medals from the sprint relay to Smith and Carlos. The 4x400 men weren't even going that far. Evans was still fielding death threats—he'd gotten fifteen to twenty in his mailbox—but was past taking any of this all that seriously. On the podium, the four men pulled gloved hands from under their sweats but it was more in the spirit of a prank than revolt. All of them were laughing.

Still, it wasn't as if nothing had happened. When USOC president

Doug Roby tried to shake their hands, he got an emphatic snub from Evans. What was Roby thinking?

Ed Caruthers was nineteen years old for the 1964 Olympics, and he was without a coach or any friends and was pretty much on his own in Tokyo. About all he could do was rattle around the athletes' village. He played some Ping-Pong, but mostly he hung out in the dining room. He had three weeks before his event and, that far from home, it seemed forever. So what if he was going back and forth to the ice cream machine? What else did he have to do?

Anything, actually. If there was just one thing else, he should have done it. Caruthers gained ten pounds at that ice cream machine and, even if the weight was distributed invisibly along his 6'5" frame (he was not called Big Ed for nothing), he created quite a disadvantage for himself. Jumping 7'1" over a bar, which he had been doing that season, tops in the country, was never easy. Doing it with the equivalent of a Thanksgiving turkey tucked under his arm was probably going to be impossible. Despite a crash diet of breakfast cereal in the final days before his event, Caruthers could not return to form and he bombed out, jumping almost three inches beneath his personal best to finish eighth.

At least Caruthers had the luck of the quadrennial sweet spot, the fortune of his birth year, and could return for a second Olympics, still very much in his prime. Few Olympians are ever granted that second chance. Caruthers would not be that much older, at least in high jumper terms, and he would certainly be wiser. This time he would know better than to subsist entirely, or even partly, on soft-serve ice cream.

Resolve is a useful quality and it assures success in many walks of life, but the Olympics are organized by a terrible serendipity, above all else, and do not always yield to such trusted qualities as determination. Caruthers would find that self-sacrifice, at the dairy bar or anywhere else, would count for little, that his courage would not amount to enough, and that, at this Olympics anyway, even the jump of his life wasn't going to get him gold. It hadn't been much of a sweet spot, after all, coming in a year that honored idiosyncrasy above all else.

Who could have anticipated Dick Fosbury? Nobody, that's who. Caruthers had first seen him at the NCAA Championships in 1967, employing a "goofball kind of thing" to get over the bar and he was not impressed. Fosbury had jumped 6'10" in that meet, four inches below Caruthers's mark. To the extent that Caruthers thought about Fosbury at all, it was in terms of bemusement. Knowing that few facilities had the soft landing areas of the bigger track programs, Caruthers wondered how he even dared start to jump like that, crashing down on sawdust, right on his neck. "Maybe he should try to jump another way," Caruthers thought.

At the Los Angeles Trials the next year, when Fosbury won with a leap of 7'1", Caruthers was obliged to take notice. Fosbury, with his "goofball kind of thing," had joined that elite group of high jumpers and was now listed among the favorites in all the Olympic scouting reports. *Sport* magazine called Fosbury "our best bet." This guy had somehow changed the rules of engagement, recognizing a shortfall in natural ability, and cobbled together a technique to get over the bar at any cost. However, tradition prevails, it always has, and Caruthers liked his own chances. After all, he'd won the Olympic Trials in Tahoe, the ones that counted. And Fosbury, for all his improvement in the last year, had to struggle to make the team there.

Here in Mexico City, Caruthers was taking a much more disciplined approach, mindful of diet and nutrition. A gold medal would not be lost in the dining room this time. While he put his faith in athletic orthodoxy, Fosbury was conducting preparations that were almost daffy in comparison. He and Gary Stenlund were always tearing around the city, seeing what was up. They liked to rumble up to the Hotel Del Angel, off Paseo de la Reforma Boulevard, and they'd go up to the penthouse bar and hang out with the ABC crews. They'd sit at the feet of Howard Cosell and Jim McKay and just absorb their stories. And as far as training, well, Fosbury always had his own program.

The one thing Fosbury didn't like to do was jump in practice. He was a dedicated athlete, make no mistake, but he simply did not believe in jumping without proper incentive, or even atmosphere. It was a waste of time for him otherwise. The technique was all in his head and had been worked out through years of competition, evolving out of desperation, not practice. It was only in competition, with the adrenaline flowing and the excitement sparking all his neurons, that Fosbury could make a jump that mattered. And the crowd— he required attention to perform. With the crowd watching, he "behaved." In practice, with nobody watching him and nothing on the line, it was all he could do to make a few desultory repetitions. To watch him at practice was not to be impressed by his prospects. He would just stand there, looking around.

His Oregon State coach, Berny Wagner, had made the trip down to Mexico City and had insisted that Fosbury jump at least once. "Look," he told him, "you've got a month here, you're getting rusty, you need to jump. You gotta do something." So Fosbury put off his adventures with Stenlund for a day and went out to the practice field for a quick session. He was just going through the motions until another rainstorm rolled through, forcing everyone under cover. He crowded under a tarp and found himself shoulder to shoulder with Valentin Gavrilov, Russia's number one jumper. They sort of recognized each other, nodded, then engaged in a stumbling conversation about the issues of the day. Gavrilov was the enemy. Not only in sport, but in every way possible. Because of Gavrilov, Fosbury had had to duck under his school desk for air-raid drills. Because of Gavrilov and his people, he'd had to worry about nuclear clouds poisoning his family, about a space program that would subjugate his nation, about an education system that was leaving America in the dust. Yet here they were, chatting away in Gavrilov's halting English, about events in Mexico, conditions at the Village, just anything. The storm cleared out after an hour but Fosbury and Gavrilov, mortal enemies, remained under the tarp awhile longer, chewing the fat.

Saturday night, the eve of Sunday's high-jump finals, was not a restful one for Fosbury. Qualifying earlier that day—chopping the field down to a dozen finalists—had been reassuring on one count. The silver-dollar-size chunk of skin he'd torn off his heel when he missed a step in the village, his huarache flying off, was not going to be a problem after all. It hadn't been a deep wound but it had been tender, and Fosbury wondered if he couldn't use a shot of cortisone to numb it. But once qualifying had begun, he'd become worked up enough that he didn't feel a thing. So that would not be a problem. Now, however, that night had come, he discovered he couldn't sleep for more than a few hours at a time. He was still worked up. He was visualizing his jumps, over and over, and the nocturnal filmstrip playing across his eyelids was pretty much keeping him awake most of the night.

Sunday was one of those perfect days, a clear, crisp October day, temperatures in the mid-70s by one that afternoon, the high jumpers filing onto the infield. The Olympic Stadium was full, eighty thousand fans on hand for the Games' track-and-field windup. Besides the high jump, there were two men's relays, the 1500-meter race, a women's relay, and the marathon. It was going to be a wild day, though nobody could have guessed just how wild.

Among those in the dark was Caruthers. Poor Ed Caruthers. He had a plan for Sunday, which is a lot like having resolve—normally important, but likely irrelevant, perhaps laughable, in an Olympics. Caruthers figured on a jump of 7'3", maybe even 7'4", an Olympic record, by his fifth pass, by which time he'd have his gold. What he didn't calculate was the size of the field, which included many lesser jumpers, guys who had no shot but filled out the finals anyway. To accommodate their numbers, the competition was begun at a height of 6'6", a full four inches lower than Caruthers's planned entry point. It was taking forever to get even there.

Fosbury, on the other hand, had no grand plan, hoping to start at 6'8" and to increase his heights by two inches at a time until he got to 7'. It was slow going as the field remained intact, nearly at 7'. But at 6'11½", it started to thin, with five failing to clear. Everybody made the next height, 7'¼", but Caruthers needed all three tries while Fosbury made it on his first attempt. Caruthers, Fosbury, and the other American, seventeen-year-old Reynaldo Brown, passed at 7'1", while Italian and West German jumpers could not scrape over, and left the competition. It was now a Cold War showdown, just the United States and Russia, the way the Olympics were meant to be. The bar was set at just under 7'2", the sun was getting lower, and the fans were starting to get interested.

Fosbury had yet to miss an attempt and he made this one cleanly, too. Brown missed on all three, as did Russia's Valery Skvortsov. Gavrilov passed. Caruthers, having missed his first two tries, the day having gone much longer than he'd planned, stared at the bar on his third try and flew over it by a full two inches. With the field pared to a manageable spectacle, the crowd was paying more and more attention to the high jump. Fosbury, conducting his one-man anarchy in the event, kind of tickled them. They knew just enough about the high jump to understand how ridiculous he was. At every jump, they laughed.

Now it was growing more serious. Only the three medal winners, all having just tied Valery Brumel's Olympic record within minutes of each other, remained to sort out the podium order. The crowd was growing slightly frantic at the sight before them. They were not high-jump aficionados but they understood the drama unfolding. Also, the sight of Fosbury, rocking back and forth on his heels the entire two minutes allowed for his approach, then exploding over the bar upside down, was generating a lot of excitement. Those giggles, as they caught sight of the flop for their first time, were being replaced by something else. As Fosbury became to look more and more like a medalist and less and less like a circus clown, there were cheers. Few fan favorites have ever developed in less time.

All three made 7'2½" on their first try. Now at 7'3¼", the bronze medalist was determined. With the men's 4x100 relay team wandering through the jump area, Fosbury took his stance, rocked back and forth, and dove over, the crowd going wild. Caruthers made it on his second try, but Gavrilov, Fosbury's new buddy, could not clear and he was out.

It was nearly twilight, four hours into the competition. Shadows were touching the outside of the track and the air was cooling. Caruthers's strategy was now "out the door." He had seen how clean Fosbury had been in all his jumps—he had yet to miss in Mexico City, not in finals qualifying the day before and not yet on Sunday—and knew, having had to make ten jumps to Fosbury's six, he was fading. The crowd had swung entirely over to Fosbury. "This is like a home court advantage," Caruthers thought. Everybody had gone over to Fosbury's side. "The press," reported *Track & Field News*, "usually reserved even at these emotion-charged Olympics, cheered at his every jump." The *Los Angeles Times*'s Jim Murray was agape at the journalistic gift that was being handed to him. "Fosbury," he wrote, "goes over the bar like a guy being pushed out of a thirty-story window." A German writer exclaimed, "Only a triple somersault off a flying trapeze with no net below could be more thrilling." A Hungarian discus thrower who knew no English, nevertheless mustered an equally appropriate narration for Fosbury's flops. "Fantastic!"

The bar was set at 7'4¼", not a world record but both an American and Olympic record height, a touch more than either Fosbury or Caruthers had ever cleared. Fosbury's heels ticked the bar on his first attempt, his first miss of the competition. Caruthers missed. Fosbury missed again. Caruthers missed. The fans were on their feet.

For his third attempt, Fosbury went through his usual deliberations, that interminable rocking back and forth, the wriggling of his fingers, eating up the allowable two minutes in his strange deliberations. For Fosbury, this period of anticipation was partly to psych himself up, to capture positive beliefs and attitudes, but also to review the mechanics of the jump, which require untold adjustments as he converts horizontal force into vertical. He was always fighting his takeoff, which threatened to turn his pass into a long jump instead of a high jump. He rocked and the crowd counted with him: "One-two-three" and kept counting. "Forty," they counted, "forty-one." Fosbury thought just a little more and then, satisfied with his preparations, began his loping jog to the bar.

The moment he did so, the first marathoners entered the stadium. Normally, this is a moment of catharsis, a release of pent-up energy, as a long afternoon of plodding drudgery is suddenly celebrated. Their appearance, which is always a surprise, signals what is generally the biggest cheer of the Games. Not this time. They got just a smattering of applause. The crowd was devoted to this gangly guy with the upside-down floater. The rest of the Olympics was on hold, awaiting judgment on a somewhat personal, yet highly entertaining rebellion.

Fosbury veered off and threw his shoulder to the bar—it was shaping up as a perfect jump, after all—and lifted, peering sideways over his left shoulder. He was registering everything now. The eerie quiet of the stadium, the slight whoosh of his shorts, the clap-clap-clap of the marathoners as they worked their way to the finish (Mamo Wolde was reaching for the tape with both hands). The air really was thin up here, Fosbury at an altitude nobody had prepared for. He watched the bar "glide" under him, completed his ideal parabola and crashed backward onto the Port-a-Pit. From the foam landing he could look up and see it was clean but he hardly had to witness it for himself. Some eighty thousand people had already told him it was good: *Olé!*

Fosbury sprang out of the pit, flashing a victory sign and a wide grin. American marathoner Kenny Moore, entering the stadium on his way to a fourteenth-place finish, looked around, trying to understand the crowd's sudden reaction. What was going on? Seeing Fosbury loping around, his hands high, Moore instantly understood what had just happened. Not that many days before, Moore had been gathering the hate mail that had been stacking up for his two expelled teammates, resigned to two weeks of sustained ugliness. Now, this . . . just the kind of uplift—figuratively, literally—to transform the mood of the Games, to relieve the tension, to reinforce the parameters of play. Moore couldn't help himself and, continuing on down the straightaway, began dancing a jig.

Less happy was Ed Caruthers. His only chance at a gold medal was if Fosbury missed and he, jumping next, made the height. That couldn't happen now. Even if he made the height—he debated passing, moving the bar up a notch—it had been settled on misses. It felt pointless, anyway, as if the crowd had spoken on his behalf, rendering him an afterthought. There were strange forces at work at these Olympics, alternately punishing and rewarding convention, and it was impossible to know which side to choose. It didn't feel fair. He took his turn all the same. He brushed the bar on his way down, knocked it off, and lay in the pit for minutes, realizing he'd have an altogether different life than he imagined for himself, that difference made by half an inch.

Afterward Olympic officials told the press that Fosbury would not be available for interviews, as he "was too tired to come down and talk to you." The marathoners, having completed their twenty-six miles, were, however, on their way.

Chapter 16

WEEK TWO

A Cuddlesome Junior, a Ragtag Bunch,
and a Blonde in a Beehive

AT WEEK TWO, THEY HIT the reset button. Track and field was over and gone were all the angry black militants, the fierce young women, agitators, sympathizers, oddballs, profiteers, dopers, and malcontents. For all the confusion they had created, it had still been wonderful in its way, breathtaking, for sure, interesting, to say the least. There had never been a track meet like it, as far as performance. Of the twenty-four events, seventeen were finished in Olympic record time or distance. Only Mexico City's altitude, debilitating for all those lowlanders attempting the longer races, prevented a complete obliteration of the standing records. It had been a marvel, really. Forget Olympic records, track and field set or equaled fifteen world records. The U.S. men and women were responsible for ten of those, smashing some of them beyond all recognition.

Of course, there had been some attendant turmoil. This new generation of athletes, so full of themselves that their issues now must be your issues, had made an uncomfortable anxiety part of the ticket price. Maybe that's just the way it was going to be, the wised-up talent now wringing certain considerations out of their participation. What could you do but go along with such extortion? Had the black athletes boycotted, as was their original threat, the Olympics might have been considerably more peaceful, but also quite a bit slower. Of those ten world records, the potential boycotters had set nine.

However, they were home now. The Olympic spirit, as it was interpreted by white authorities, reasserted its soothing self. "Along came the second week," *Sports Illustrated* reported, "and sane and predictable things began to happen." That was more or less guaranteed by the Olympic calendar that, by either accident or design, saved the least threatening athletes and events for last. The schedule was now devoted to swimmers so young it was a wonder they were allowed in the deep end. Gymnasts and other assorted pixies. And basketball players, the only black athletes left in the Village ("Whatever happened to the integration of our pools?" the *New Yorker* wondered), screened for controversial leanings during the boycott threat. In other words, this was going to be more like it. It would be a show.

ABC had been getting bang for its four and a half million bucks, no question. The network's sports president, Roone Arledge, had made a number of big bets, aside from the astonishing rights fee, three times the amount that NBC paid for the Tokyo Games, and was raking in the chips. His decision to bring Howard Cosell along for the ride paid off for both men, the bombastic announcer adding to his reputation as somebody a step ahead of the times, Arledge getting access to a culture he didn't otherwise have. Their coverage of the black protest might not have been as complete as it could have been, but it *was* journalism, not just sports reporting.

Now, though, the network had a sane and predictable week ahead of it, full of wholesome and apolitical young athletes. Its 450-person crew, its 45 cameras, its "man in the sky," its helicopter, its Intelsat 3 satellite (NASA thoughtfully launched it in August to provide orbital coverage above Mexico, a global blind spot up to then), its somewhat bland announcing team (Cosell aside)—all were poised to capture a record haul for the most important demographic in the world, the U.S. audience. This, indeed, would be more like it.

The United States monopolized swimming, as it had since 1956, the last time Australia had beaten the Americans in the medal count. The steady addition of events to the swimming calendar each Olympics only served to inflate American dominance. It was a kind of gerrymandering of glory. In Rome in 1960, the United States led all countries with fifteen medals. In Tokyo, the United States had twenty-five medals to Australia's nine. With an even larger schedule at Mexico City, nine more medal opportunities having been added, it was only expected to be even more one-sided. Of the twenty-nine events, the U.S. swimmers had set twenty-one world records in their Trials.

Mark Spitz, an eighteen-year-old Californian, had held ten of them. He did not lack for confidence, and during the summer had predicted he would very likely win six gold medals at Mexico City. It was not unreasonable; he had won five gold at the Pan Am Games the year before. The boast was still unseemly, considering the tradition of humility within the swimming community. At the very least, it was an affront to Santa Clara teammate Don Schollander, who had won four gold medals at Tokyo and, though perhaps a little less dedicated to the sport, had not exactly retired.

Efforts to promote a rivalry between the two, which would likely provide the only drama in Mexico's swim tank (they were matched in the 200-meter freestyle, teamed on one of the relays), were half-hearted. Schollander was four years Spitz's senior and was doing adult things at Yale, like joining Skull and Bones, meeting future presidents. Spitz tried to needle Schollander, calling him "Joe College." But Schollander had little time for Spitz; nobody on the team did, except to pull a prank here and there. All he could manage, when pressed, was, "Mark is not very intelligent. His inane comments used to bother me, but now they make me laugh."

The women didn't even have that small kindling for a competitive fire. Their events were practically uncontested, with U.S. swimmers top-ranked by time in ten of their fourteen events. Debbie Meyer, alternately described as "pug-nosed" and "chubby-cheeked," had mastered the three freestyle events, 200 meters through 800, so thoroughly that her meets—her practices, even!—were essentially a succession of record-breaking times. She held world records in all three.

Meyer was the appointed darling of the Games, getting the *Life* magazine photo spread treatment, along with Bob Seagren and Charlie Greene. She complained she was "ugly," when in fact she was as cute as a button. She complained she was "dull," when really she was driven. She worried that she'd never find a boyfriend, when she was all the while beating the best prospects in the pool. Mike Burton, a fellow Olympian and the world record holder in the 1500-meter freestyle, found it "discouraging" when Meyer whipped him in pulling drills. "I pretend he is just another girl I have to beat," Meyer explained to *Life*.

She was the Peppermint Patty of her generation. She was desperate to play baseball with the boys and, careful to keep her short hair under her cap, managed to fool Little League coaches back in New Jersey for three games until she was found out and kicked off the team. There were very few activities for girls—ballet? no thanks!—and almost none that satisfied her competitive instincts. Maybe ice skating, if she could have tolerated the ridiculous getups. But, no, that was asking a lot. It wasn't until her parents took her to a local swim club that she began to think there might be something out there for her.

When her father was transferred to the West Coast, Meyer fell under the spell of Sherm Chavoor, the coach at Santa Clara. Chavoor, despite the fact that he couldn't swim himself, had somehow assembled the core of the Olympic team in his pool. Besides Meyer, he was training Spitz, Burton, and Schollander. Chavoor was a taskmaster and he burned out a lot of swimmers, but he knew how to make champions. All of his swimmers were in shape, for one thing.

Well, not in Mexico City they weren't. One by one, they were struck down by various ailments and injuries and no amount of overconditioning in Chavoor's pool was going to make a difference. Meyer was the first to go down. The night before the team departed from Denver, their jumping-off point from the States, she tripped walking across a motel parking lot to use a pay phone. The "queen," as she was called by some of the others, was now walking among her subjects on crutches.

The rest of the team was dealing with differing degrees of intestinal distress. Spitz got a case of it, Burton might have had a bad pizza (he lost fifteen pounds the day before the 400-meter qualifications)—everybody was, it seemed to Meyer, "gurgling and rumbling." As for Meyer, she got her ankle back in shape in time for the qualifying (at first she couldn't do flip turns, or even kick very well; thank goodness for that Olympic schedule), but then succumbed to the same malady as the rest. It was a mystery. She had been careful to drink only bottled water. She didn't even brush her teeth with tap water. Had she seen the worker methodically filling up twenty-gallon bottles with tap water in week one, instead of week two, things might have been different. But here she was, losing five pounds in a single day, and not just any day either. It was the day of the 800-meter qualifying and the 200-meter final later that night.

These little girls, with their cute bangs, their dimples, their pug noses and chubby cheeks—easy to misread. She had already won the 400-meter freestyle Sunday night, beating U.S. teammate Linda Gustavson by nearly four seconds. The pool in Mexico City, with its high gutters, was considered slow, nothing like the one in Long Beach where the United States had set all those world records during the Trials. The water here was far from smooth, "enough to make you seasick," one of the men complained. But not even whitecaps were going to slow down Meyer.

Now with more than choppy water to roil her stomach, it might be another story. At eight hundred meters above sea level, the effects of altitude start to come into play, as well. The week before, Burton had wandered over to the stadium and had watched the 10K run in horror. He'd be racing the chlorinated equivalent—the 1500-meter freestyle—and was frightened by what he saw: guys dropping out just laps into the race. But Meyer, who had asthma on top of everything else, refused to acknowledge the altitude. *I've got a job to do*, she thought.

She chugged out, knowing she didn't have to win, but still had to swim well. She qualified easily, fastest of the bunch. After an afternoon's rest, during which the *turista*, as everybody so delicately described it, subsided, she returned to the pool and swam what was always her toughest event: the 200-meter sprint. It was another Olympic record and more gold for her, though the margin of victory over teammate Jan Henne was just a half-second.

The 800-meter freestyle Thursday night was anticlimactic and Meyer won it easily, waiting nearly 14 seconds for teammate Pam Kruse to come in after her. It was the third and final gold for *Life*'s "cuddlesome high school junior."

The "Gidget Goes Olympian" quality that *Sports Illustrated* found so welcome in week two suffered some interruptions, though none like occurred in week one. Although Meyer was leaving everyone in her wake, just as expected, there were still some surprises. The happiest was provided by Mexico's Felipe Muñoz, who won the 200-meter breaststroke, beating the Russian world-record holder, giving his country the first gold medal of their own Games (Mexican boxers would win two more golds before it was over). Mexico did not fancy itself an international sporting power but, nevertheless, was anxious to make a good showing in its own country. It had already been disappointed on the soccer field, where its favored team was forced to settle for bronze (their fans were upset enough to throw seat cushions onto the field in disgust) and embarrassment loomed.

So the seventeen-year-old Muñoz's victory was somewhat of a relief. Afterward, his new fans began throwing their hats into the pool. One thing you could get from these Games was that Mexican fans sure liked to throw things.

The U.S. men's team might have outclassed the world, as far as talent, but their share of the program was turning out to be something less than its intended intramural when it came to the actual competition. For one thing, Spitz was not winning the six gold medals he predicted. There was not a little smirking among his teammates, but the rest of the world was definitely puzzled. When he won only silver in the 100-meter butterfly (and was consequently dropped from the medley relay), *Sports Illustrated* identified him as an "overscheduled, haunted, upset young man." And it just got worse for him. He finished last in the 200-meter butterfly and then, defending another of his world record events, couldn't even beat Joe College in the 200-meter freestyle.

Spitz did compete on the gold-medal-winning relays but it was far short of the achievements he had predicted for himself. For that matter, Schollander, who had only qualified in one individual event, was not having the time of his life either. Schollander, in anchoring the gold-medal-winning 4x200-meter relay, had been surprised by Australian Mike Wenden, who had cut a body-length's lead in half. So what was supposed to be a Spitz-Hollander duel instead turned into a Schollander-Wenden shootout. Wenden won, in agonizing style; he was taking two short strokes for every one of Schollander's and he nearly passed out at the end, slipping from the ropes, requiring rescue. Spitz, meanwhile, was completely out of the running and might have required the Coast Guard himself. It appeared that Schollander, the hero of Tokyo, was now four years too late while Spitz, who had merely been the hero of Long Beach, might be four years too early.

Still, with Burton winning both the 400-meter and 1500-meter events, Charles Hickox winning two individual medleys, it was a U.S. rout. Including diving, the U.S. took 57 medals, about two-thirds of the prizes. Second-place Australia had 3 gold medals to the Americans' 21. Not close.

Much more dramatic, considering Olympic history, was basketball. The United States, which, after all, had invented the sport, had never lost a game in Olympic competition. The Americans were 45–0 since basketball was introduced in 1936, the rest of the world going for silver. Nineteen sixty-eight figured to be different. In fact, not only was the United States expected to lose a game, but it probably wouldn't win gold.

Of all the sports, basketball was the most affected by Harry Edwards's proposed boycott, although nobody was admitting as much. Nearly two dozen of the country's top collegiate players, including three from NCAA champion UCLA, refused to try out for the Olympic team. There were a variety of reasons to shun the process, among them the poor timing of both the Trials and the Olympics, each coming during the academic year. One of them, Houston's Elvin Hayes, had signed with the San Diego Rockets of the upstart American Basketball Association and was thus ineligible.

It seemed just as likely that there was something else going on. Lew Alcindor, named player of the year (this after he'd matched up with Hayes in the "game of the century"), had made his sympathies known when he'd gone head to head with announcer Joe Garagiola on the *Today* show. He was clearly intrigued with the boycott but he refused to commit and, even when he was a no-show at the Trials, would not give any reason beyond academic demands. Of course, Alcindor, along with UCLA teammates Lucius Allen and Mike Warren and other collegiate stars like Wes Unseld (who said he was too "tired" to try out), sacrificed little in their abstention. They'd all go on to the NBA (or ABA) and enjoy rich careers, Olympic participation or not.

That left a comparative ragtag team for Henry Iba, the legendary Oklahoma State coach, to mold. Iba bristled at the inevitable characterization, but there was no getting around the fact that his tallest player, the man who would supposedly supplant Lew Alcindor in his lineup, was 6'9" Ken Spain. Ragtag or not, his team was not shaping up as an international world-beater, having won only one of three games each against Yugoslavia and Russia during a summer trip to Europe. "The U.S. team, on paper at least, will be weak at all positions," according to ABC's own guidebook. It was no wonder that Olympic previews were predicting bronze for the United States. Of course, neither Iba nor guard Jo Jo White was attached to the squad at the time, and who knew how good some of these kids were.

Come Olympics, though, it became another story. Led by nineteen-year-old Spencer Haywood, the youngest ever to make a U.S. basketball team, and White, the U.S. swept through the Games without incident, defeating Yugoslavia, 65–50, in the gold medal game. Again, not close.

This was making for wonderful television back home in the States. ABC was dazzling its critics and its viewers with technology—split screens, slow motion, instant replay (giving "the viewer the advantage of seeing deserving performances twice and perhaps three times," ABC bragged), but it had more going for it than that. Nobody had ever broadcast so much of an Olympics or done it with such immediacy; at Tokyo, NBC was hamstrung by the time difference and delivered its news in fifteen-minute blocks, late at night. Here in the western hemisphere, ABC was able to present much of the forty-four hours it had blocked out in prime time, a lot of it live.

Some critics were appalled at the number of commercials that were interrupting the events. "Commercials were moving in faster than sprint races," complained a critic at the *Los Angeles Times*. And some viewers wondered whether ABC's obsessive interest in all things American was really true to the Olympic spirit. Not that ABC required defense (most critics were too overwhelmed by this new "saturation coverage" anyway), but nobody believed ABC was doing this for any reason but to gather the most viewers possible and to make as much of its investment back as it could. As for the idea that

ABC was somehow overlooking the rest of the world in its determination to bring back a U.S. narrative, well, weren't the Americans winning all the medals?

They were winning most of them, for sure, but not all. The second week of Olympic competition featured the more internationally flavored gymnastics. Gymnastics, women's in particular, was more artistry than athletics and it was extremely television-friendly. The girls (and they definitely were girls) wore colorful costumes and pranced gracefully across a small space, producing a spectacle, a stage show, terrific television. It just happened that it wasn't very United States-friendly. The United States, men or women, had not medaled in this sport since 1932 and, as long as Russia and other eastern European nations were still willing to do so much as a cartwheel, weren't going to here either.

ABC was learning that drama translated perfectly well on the small screen—it required no subtitles—and that a rooting interest wasn't always essential. Story lines might develop independent of desired demographics. ABC, for all its interest in American viewership, was not going to ignore potential commotion, which perks up any broadcast. Commotion, it had learned well in week one, could easily compound into something else altogether. Ratings, even.

So it was following the women's gymnastics quite closely. There was zero possibility of some kind of U.S. story here, but there was something else that was quite interesting, and it involved a slight Czech woman in a tall blond beehive, Vera Caslavska. Caslavska was a gymnastic story anyway, competing in her second Olympics (at twenty-six, not a girl at all), after beating Russia's legendary Larissa Latynina for the all-around title in Tokyo four years before. However, she wasn't returning as the reigning gymnast so much as she was a political refugee.

It was barely two months to the day since Russian tanks had stormed into Prague, effectively ending her career. Caslavska had taken a stance—she signed the "Manifesto of 2000 Words" protesting Soviet occupation—that guaranteed real consequences, that took genuine bravery. She fled the city and trained in the country until, with five weeks before the Olympics, she was given the government's go-ahead to safely compete.

The five weeks in the wilderness—reportedly she trained on tree limbs and did floor exercises across a meadow—did not hurt her gymnastics. She won gold on the vault, on floor, and the uneven bars, her only failure being silver on the beam. ABC announcers, well-schooled by now in podium nuances, noticed something odd during one of Caslavska's many award ceremonies. During the presentation of her gold for floor, which she shared with a Russian gymnast, Caslavska appeared to be doing something strange, something small, but something strange, during the Soviet national anthem.

When Caslavska was later presented gold in the all-around, sharing space on the podium with two Soviet gymnasts, ABC was prepared. "And now," said ABC's Jim McKay, "the Soviet anthem." The screen showed Caslavska dipping that blond beehive, just as she had at the earlier presentation. "She has turned her head to the right and down, just as she had at the last ceremony. This does not appear to be an accident."

It was a slight gesture, but as remarkable as a fist in the sky. A modest bow, but as furious as a punch in the face. It was just a quiet glance downward, but also, thanks to this new and lively medium, a wild and desperate shout, bouncing off Intelsat, heard loud and clear in 400 million homes.

Chapter 17

PAPPY'S BOYS

Rateros, Various Sarges, and a Lucky Picture of a Pretty Girl

EORGE FOREMAN HAD BEEN ready to go home for some time, ever since Tommie Smith and John Carlos had been ushered from the Olympic Village. He had regained his footing and was presenting a better picture of himself in the ring, but that first flush of enthusiasm for this project was gone. "We'll never be boys again," he thought. Also, he had to face this big Russian.

It seemed to him he had done plenty already, more than enough. The Russian, Ionas Chepulis, was obviously more experienced. Not that anybody knew a thing about him, the idea of scouting opponents not having arrived in amateur boxing. But he was old, old as the hills. And bald. Foreman knew this about Russians, in general. They were very tough, and they did pushups in snow and ice. That was what he was up against. He thought, "I have a bronze medal, even if I don't win another fight. If I could just come up with an excuse to get out of this fight, go on with my life, I'd be a happy boy."

After his fight with Lucjan Trela, in the first week of the Games, Foreman had made some necessary adjustments. For one thing, he had come across a better boxing shoe. Somebody just showed up in the Village one day and presented him with a pair of Adidas. Foreman didn't grasp the angle, and didn't even know there was a name written on the shoes, but these new shoes gripped the canvas, and he was no longer slipping and falling in the ring. "Turned into a knockout artist then and there."

While the altitude remained a problem in the third round on—he was huffing and puffing if it went past two—he persuaded himself that the thin air was less of a drag on his big fists. One more thing to hasten the instant of contact. "Just before I throw," he thought, "I've hit him." A knockout artist, indeed.

On Tuesday, in the Olympics second week, Foreman scored a technical knockout over Romania's Ion Alexe. Then on Thursday, Foreman became one of three U.S. boxers to advance to the finals, when he flattened Italy's Giorgio Bambini in the second round. Knockouts were the way to go because the scoring was becoming increasingly iffy. When U.S. teammate Al Jones failed to stop Britain's Christopher Finnegan in their middleweight semifinal, even though he chased him for all three rounds and knocked him down twice, he left himself open to the rules of interpretation, not to mention international aspirations, and lost a 4–1 decision. The crowd, which had no particular rooting interest in the bout, went wild, screaming, "*Rateros!*" and throwing everything at hand into the ring: papers, coins, and even shoes. When Pappy Gault saw some fans trying to wrench their chairs from the floor, he mounted the ring and motioned for peace. It wasn't until Foreman had knocked Bambini out in the next bout that the crowd settled down.

The other two boxers from the U.S. team to reach the finals were Ronnie Harris, the lightweight, and Albert Robinson, the featherweight. Although, by the time their bouts would be fought Saturday night, the last competition of the Olympics, it would be difficult to tell who was actually the featherweight.

Harris, like most of the other athletes visiting Mexico for the first time, had been careful not to drink anything but bottled water. Montezuma's revenge was about all that some of the athletes knew of their host country and few were taking chances. And yet Harris, like scores of his fellow Americans, got dysentery all the same. If this was a mystery that Debbie Meyer had solved, catching the Village help refilling the bottles with pure Mexican tap water, the news had yet to get around to her U.S. teammates. When Saturday's fight came around, Harris had no trouble making the 132-pound limit. He weighed in at 127.

The night of the fight, the three U.S. boxers shared a dressing room and two of them were more or less sharing a toilet stall as well. Foreman, nervous beyond belief, kept going to the toilet, but nothing would come out. Harris, nervous for different reasons, kept going to the toilet, and everything came out. "What if I loose my bowels on national television?" he thought. This was if he could get to the ring in the first place. He was so weak he needed help from his teammates to stand up.

Harris had plenty to think about, in any case. His opponent, Josef Grudzien, had been one of Poland's gold medal winners from 1964, having handily beaten a U.S. boxer in Tokyo who was also named Ronald Harris. Grudzien, perhaps thinking this was a rematch, was understandably confident. And then, on the off-chance Harris might win, there was this: would he accept his gold medal from Avery Brundage?

Unlike his fellow boxers, Harris had given this some serious thought. Perhaps because he was one of those "college kids" Foreman had previously dismissed, the idea of a gesture appealed to him. Kent State, where he was a junior, was becoming a highly politicized campus and Harris, a young black man himself, was sympathetic to civil rights causes. Maybe he wasn't wearing an OPHR button, maybe he hadn't been to any meetings, and maybe he hadn't threatened a boycott, but he felt every bit as strongly as his more vocal brethren. "I know what it is to be a black man in America," he thought. "Do I break down what John Carlos and the rest stood for, do I wipe that out? Because I'll go back home to America with my gold medal and I'll still be a second-class citizen."

His conflict was all the more deeply felt for being unsupported. Who could he talk to about this? Coach Gault? Big George? Any of the various Sarges he shared the gym with? He called home. His mother said, "Ronnie, do it for me. Work within the system. People will try to take away the good you've done and it will always overshadow your victory." It wasn't what he wanted to hear, but it was what he expected to hear.

Of the three of them in that dressing room Saturday night, though, it was Robinson who should have been the most concerned. He was about to enter one of those international frays that seem to enliven nearly every Olympics, and hardly ever to the benefit of their reputation. Robinson, the twenty-one-year-old Navy man, was, as *Sports Illustrated* put it, "walloping the frijoles out of Mexico's Antonio Roldan" in their featherweight final, when a spout of blood issued from Roldan's forehead. Robinson indeed was winning easily when the wound occurred, Robinson hitting him cleanly with his right late in the second round, well at arm's length. Most of the sixteen thousand in the Mexico City Arena saw it that way. Harris, between his trips to the bathroom stall, was able to see it clearly from the passage to the arena. "So obvious he used a punch to cut him." Perfectly within the rules.

The referee, a Russian official, ruled it a butt, never mind the distance between the two fighters, and disqualified Robinson. Not even the largely Mexican crowd, which did have a rooting interest in the bout, could get behind that decision and the boos rained down on the ring. Robinson at first slumped against the ropes in disgust. He rallied for a brief show of sportsmanship, shaking his foe's hand and telling reporters nearby, "I have nothing to say, the referee said it all." Back in the dressing room, where Foreman and Harris were still waiting, he lost it, crying, shouting, and pounding walls.

So Foreman lost it. Foreman was proving to be nothing if not impressionable and volatile and he was now once more in a fragile condition, railing at the unfairness, the injustice of the decision. Robinson, the little guy, was his roommate! This wasn't right! It was up to Harris, who was next on the card, and with plenty of his own troubles, to calm Foreman down. And then Harris asked for help getting to the ring.

"I'm sick," he thought to himself on the way to the ring apron, "but I'm not dead." When the bell finally rang to start the fight, a clarity was restored, his focus regained. He forgot he'd ever been sick and realized almost immediately that he could easily pepper his more experienced opponent. Every time Grudzien swung, Harris unleashed a flurry of punches. Not even the referee, who warned Harris repeatedly for using an open glove to hit Grudzien, could distract him. Harris subtracted that punch from his repertoire, and continued to overwhelm Grudzien with his speed. When it was over, Harris was awarded a rare unanimous decision from the judges. Back in the dressing room, he told Foreman, still agitated, "George, there's nothing to it. Go on out there and do it."

Foreman had been entertaining the writers with bits of poetry and his own homespun logic—"If the Lord is willing and the creek don't rise, I'll get him," he had promised for his fight—but hardly felt confident now that the moment had come. In fact, he would have preferred if the moment had not arrived at all. But Harris's calm had a tremendous effect on him. "I've never seen anything like it." He marched out to the ring and administered one of the most savage beatings in Olympic history.

He bloodied Chepulis's nose almost immediately and shook him repeatedly with left hooks to the body and head. The Soviet fighter, who'd been a last-minute substitute on the team, wouldn't go down and, instead, absorbed a continuing barrage of jarring punches until the referee stopped it, according to a wire service report, "to save the balding twenty-nine-year-old Chepulis from needless punishment" in the second round. Nobody was more grateful than Foreman. *If the fight goes another two minutes,* he was thinking, *I faint.*

Foreman was given the winner's bouquet of roses, which he presented to Chepulis. And then, he did something even stranger. Now wearing his robe, he reached into his pockets where he had placed a lucky penny, lucky beads, and a lucky picture of a pretty girl, Sandy, from Walnut Creek, California. Also, a lucky flag, a tiny American flag. It was the flag he chose to produce, holding it aloft as he descended the stairs. He did not wave it out of a specific patriotism, certainly not in reaction to the protest of the week before, and definitely not as a reproach to those who would use this stage to demonstrate their disagreements. He was thinking of Albert Robinson. "I was thinking, *Gotcha,* to those judges. That's all. The international rules of boxing were, cheat America. I wanted to show those judges, make sure they knew who I was, what colors I was wearing. So I waved that flag. 'Gotcha.'"

International interpretation put Foreman's flag-waving in the redemptive category and much of America in particular, especially the part that was white, found it a reassuring corrective to the disruptions that had otherwise characterized these Games. That is, to the point that it was noticed. By then, the Games were winding down, bags packed, tents folded. There was far more interest in Foreman's next career move—who would guide him in an eventual professional career was an important question even as he was conducting his amateur career—than whatever meaning he attached to his postfight flag-waving.

Even less noticed were the awards ceremonies for the boxers later that night. Brundage had made himself scarce around the podium whenever black athletes happened to be on them. He had abstained. He felt safer among the U.S. boxers, though, and used the occasion, as he put it in his diary, "to erase the bad impression left by track-and-field athletes." And so, grabbing for his first black hand since that initial "bad impression," he reached up to Ronnie Harris. Harris gritted his teeth. *Do I fail my mom and do it for my people?* he wondered. "Everybody else was so full of joy, but I had that complexity of spirit." He wondered, further, what he would sacrifice by taking Brundage's hand. "Could I be the black leader, the one that stops racism?" It seemed that some kind of opportunity was there, but not really. "In the end, there is no cause greater than a mother's request." Reports of the day say Brundage shook his hand "enthusiastically." Harris knew he'd be haunted by this decision for the rest of his life. As Brundage pumped away, Harris was thinking, *I'll never do one of these again.*

Chapter 18

GOING HOME

Boy Scouts, Psychedelic Mileage, and a Black Bra

BEFORE THE ATHLETES could be scattered to history, discharged into destiny, or more likely returned to their previous anonymity, there was the strange Olympic debriefing known as the Closing Ceremony. Organizers had never known exactly what to do with this part of their ritual. It was, from a competitive perspective, entirely pointless. The medals had been counted; there would be no style points. It was difficult to sustain interest in one more set piece of their amateur sacrament.

They had tried something new in 1964 when, hoping to keep it relevant, organizers had allowed the athletes to enter the stadium for the Closing Ceremony in relative informality. No more nation marches, lock-stepping behind a flag, just a bunch of kids flooding the field. There was a reluctant acknowledgment that this might be fun for them. It seemed to work too well, however, as the athletes pranced merrily around the track, totally unrestrained, the New Zealanders blowing kisses to the Japanese emperor. (Good Lord!) The emperor, apparently, was the only one amused. He laughed and waved back. Olympic organizers were outraged at this breach of etiquette and vowed not to allow that ever again.

Obviously, there was now the potential for something beyond even fun. If there was one thing they had learned at the 1968 Games, it was that today's youth had become highly unpredictable, vulnerable to outside rhetoric, and capable of outlandish and embarrassing behavior. And this was during the competition, when organizers could still mete out punishment and hold medals over their heads. Now, when there was no longer anything to be gained or even preserved by obedience, control might simply be out of the question. Their little sendoff, which had merely collapsed into rowdiness in Tokyo, could very well explode into an international situation.

The problem, USOC president Doug Roby explained, was freedom, too much of it. "We recognize that these incidents may be the result of granting athletes what might be considered excessive freedoms in the cause of human rights." Olympic organizers had long since decided to limit the number of on-field athletes to seven per team, but they were never more confident of their decision than now. All those troublemakers could now watch from the stands. There would be decorum, order, and sanity at last. This was not going to be New Year's Eve in Times Square.

Arthur Daley of the *New York Times* explained this for his readers: "Spontaneity appalls the stuffed-shirted elders of the International Olympic Committee. They prefer regimentation and they obviously were outraged by the spirit of hijinks that swept over the athletes during the Closing Ceremonies at the Tokyo Olympics."

The athletes were not happy at this news, sprung on them at the last minute. But then, a lot of them were no longer there. Many of the track-and-field athletes, having concluded their competitions a week before the Closing Ceremony, had skedaddled. Two of those, of course, had been sent packing. For quite a few of them, the final rendezvous had been the *Track & Field News* banquet earlier that week. This was the closing ceremonies for their tour group, the

TAFNOTers, and featured Hugh O'Brian, television's Wyatt Earp, and as many Olympians as could be gathered there. This last cohort was lured by the promise of drawings for new televisions, a promise more or less kept as the lottery was weighted in their favor. About one in two walked out with a new set.

Dick Fosbury and his buddy Gary Stenlund had stuck around but, just as they had managed to miss the Opening Ceremony, so did they miss the Closing. The two of them, along with the two U.S. swimmers they'd camped out with weeks earlier, set off in Stenlund's VW camper for a resort in the mountains. Fosbury was tired of the attention, weary of controversy, exhausted from people asking his opinion, his reaction, how he named his jump. He was glad to be away, somewhere with a pool and a few beers, and some pals to enjoy them with. His Olympics had ended awhile back, anyway.

These Games would take time to digest, for anybody. There had never been a competition like it, Mexico City's thin air contributing to world records in every race shorter than 400 meters and in almost all of the field events, too (but sabotaging efforts just about everywhere else). There were eighteen world records in track and field alone, making this a team for the ages. It was, as U.S. track coach Payton Jordan crowed, "the greatest competitive Olympics in history." For the United States it amounted to a reemergence as an athletic power as it regained its former Olympic supremacy, again taking the lead in the medal count: 107 to 91 for the Soviets.

The performances were all the more impressive when the circumstances of conflict were considered. Hardly one of those world record setters competed without some kind of compromise, having to find the middle ground between national duty and individual ideals. Many of them had been determined to use these Games as a platform for protest, even knowing there could be consequences. It had been important, in a year like 1968, to be true to their race and their culture. Yet it was just as important to run as fast as they could, jump higher and longer than anybody had before them. Had there ever been such ambition, arrogance, or presumption? Such accomplishment?

What happened in the 1968 Olympics was happening everywhere, as the aggrieved reached out to their presumed oppressors. Kids were marching in streets, questioning their leaders' ability to speak for them. Just as black athletes had begun to agitate for better representation in sports, which they were increasingly dominating, so too did all youth, all over the world, wondering why they didn't have more say in the wars that were killing them.

The 1968 Olympics was just one more example of this crumbling control. The whole notion of amateurism, a hypocrisy that is more easily maintained when millionaire authorities can threaten their unpaid "workers" with a kind of unemployment, was being undermined. Sports was becoming a big business, and it was not likely that the athletes were willing to continue to support everyone else's profits on their backs. Athletes could now expect to discover money in their shoes, if not elsewhere. And the Games' purity was getting harder to protect in other areas, as well. This was the first Olympics to have drug testing but, if the only athlete disqualified were a Swedish pentathlete (too much booze), authorities were probably behind this curve, too.

Olympic officials could no longer count on excluding politics, on tolerating racism, or even abetting gender inequality. The world was changing and if they hoped to remain relevant to this Olympic movement, so should they. The top-down system, where authority actually meant something, was no longer surefire, for one thing. A charismatic speaker or an especially fast runner could rise up to challenge the old order, rules be damned. There was no longer such a thing as blind obedience. All sorts of agendas had to be accounted for. Free expression suddenly ruled the day.

Take the Closing Ceremony. Olympic organizers already had reason to guess that their authority was no longer absolute, having endured the threat of boycotts and actual demonstrations. But they never dreamed their ability to dictate order had become this fragile. On Sunday, with all the events completed, there was nothing left to do but put on a modest pageant; then everybody could pack their bags and go home. There would have been at least some small victory over this new inclination toward chaos, a reassuring reset of tradition. Instead, all hell broke loose. Or as Arthur Daley put in the *New York Times*, "It was a scene of magnificent disorder."

It began in dignified fashion, the trimmed delegations marching in behind their flags. Al Oerter, who'd won a fourth gold medal in as many Olympics, carried the American flag; Russian weightlifter Leonid Zhabotinsky, who had carried the Hammer and Sickle one-handed during the Opening Ceremony ("straight out as if it were a matchstick," wrote one observer), was apparently depleted by his own gold medal effort and was seen to switch hands on the final turn. One more win in this Cold War. IOC president Avery Brundage said a few words, an eight-hundred-piece mariachi band played, and fireworks rocketed into even thinner air. The scoreboard suddenly flashed MUNICH 72, making the handover official. It was a wonderful display, all according to plan.

And then, to the delight of all but a very few (stiff-backed tutelaries, badgers, and stuffed-shirted elders), a lone American athlete left his dedicated place in the stands, leapt over the wall and crossed the dry moat of Tartan track. There he was confronted by Boy Scouts, waving sticks, "using the technique of a bullfighter with a bull," according to Daley. Others followed the bull's example, and quickly overwhelmed the young security force, although marathoner Kenny Moore was actually captured by some Scouts, and was being carried back to his proper seat when he broke free, losing a shoe in the scuffle. By now the infield was full of athletes with insufficient credentials, who were completely out of control, two weeks' worth of performance anxiety, or rather a young lifetime's worth of preparation, boiling off in unscripted relief. Daley believed he saw some athletes doing a "tribal dance that looked suspiciously like a discotheque frug." It's not likely that Daley could have recognized the difference between the two, but we can be fairly sure from his account that it wasn't a march.

The president of Mexico Gustavo Díaz Ordaz smiled happily. He had even greater reason for relief, his country having pulled off what everybody else felt was impossible: a safe, if not quite sane, Olympics. Beside him Brundage "looked grim," although reports besides Daley's say he did relax into a smile of his own. There was nothing to be done for the moment anyway, and the revelry continued for a half hour, the infield full of thousands of athletes now, some on shoulders, some snatching flags, others wearing sombreros. It was horrible, frightening, exciting. It was wonderful.

"Curtain Drops on Spicy Olympics," a headline back in the States read. As if it were over, or ever would be. First of all, there would be hell to pay. It would take a long time to sort the righteous from the reckless. And even at that, justice would be grudging. It would takes years, decades, before a consensus could be reached on those Olympics, on whether the modest revolt was necessary, on whether it accomplished anything, and whether those rebels acted heroically or just foolishly. In the meantime, as we say, hell to pay.

Everybody got caught up in it, even those who believed they were playing by the rules. Sprinter Mel Pender had been shot full of regret, wishing he had done more, not just stood quietly on the stand with the other relay runners. He was a strong force within the OPHR, but was muted in public by his submission to national security. As an Army man, he had no alternative to martial obedience. He was loyal to his country in ways most of his teammates could not understand. And, having already denied everything that was human to serve his country in Vietnam, he could tamp down any impulse to protest if so ordered.

Yet, within a week of returning home to Georgia, expecting a transfer to flight school where he would learn to fly helicopters, he discovered that the promise had been voided. He'd been ordered to behave at the Olympics on pain of a Vietnam assignment. And he had, hating himself for it. All the same, he was ordered back to Vietnam.

Fellow sprinter Jim Hines, who "does not buy all that the militants try to sell," according to *Sports Illustrated*, was not rewarded either for his refusal to protest. Whatever his true beliefs—he did snub Brundage, didn't he?—there was no question about his ambition, which was to glide from the Olympics into the NFL, with as little racial baggage as possible. But that didn't really happen. Hines, who was Miami's sixth-round draft pick and who did not even make the team at first, blamed the "glove situation" for his failure in the league and estimated it cost him $2 million.

George Foreman's flag-waving after his gold-medal bout, whether it was in the spirit of patriotism or just team pride, would earn those millions and many more once he turned pro. There is nothing as agnostic as boxing. But, he too, was disappointed upon his return home. His promenades in Houston's Fifth Ward were now a form of community service instead of predation. He offered himself as an example of greatness fulfilled, the heavy swing of his gold medal, wearing the nap of a favorite turtleneck sweater smooth, proof of opportunity.

He had a confounding confrontation, though, when an old friend popped from the shadows, not offering congratulations but contempt. "How could you do what you did?" he asked Foreman. "How could you wave that flag when our brothers were protesting? How could you?" Foreman was at first confused, then beyond remorse, as he began to understand his role in these Olympics. He had nothing to be proud of, after all. He took that gold medal, an everlasting source of shame, at least in the Fifth Ward, and put it in a drawer and didn't take it out again for many, many years.

There was retribution all around. Small-time punishments, a pettiness that was incredible to behold. Brundage, the man who inflated

Smith's and Carlos's gesture into everlasting iconography, wanted to undo the whole thing, insisting that the Mexican organizing committee "erase" images of the famous ceremony from its official documentary (they didn't). He did manage to exclude mention of the demonstration from USOC's official report, although he couldn't quite contain it from history.

Brundage presided over one more summer Olympics, creating yet more controversy when he refused to suspend the Munich Games after the Black September Palestinian attack that killed eleven Israeli athletes. He retired that year.

USOC president Doug Roby, in an amazing show of petulance, wrote Harvard coach Harry Parker, "At one time I, personally, was in favor of disqualifying you and your crew for acts grossly unbecoming to members of our Olympic Team. I am now glad that I did not encourage such a harsh action for I feel that miserable performance of you and your crew at Mexico City will stand as a permanent record against you and the athletes which you led." The Harvard athletes managed, all the same, all becoming either doctors or lawyers.

Of course, Tommie Smith and John Carlos were in for the worst of it. They came home as outcasts, terrorists, when they might have been welcomed as heroes. The Los Angeles Rams withdrew an earlier offer to Smith and even the Army refused him, his ROTC experience notwithstanding. Football legend Jim Brown, who had lent Smith two thousand dollars against an NFL contract, asked for his money back. His marriage came to an end.

Carlos's marriage also came to an end, his wife, Kim (she had "the most beautifully coiffed Afro you've ever seen," Ralph Boston used to say), killing herself in 1977. There was no NFL career for him either, no jobs for a while. A decade later he, like Smith, began working with youth. Smith eventually found a career at Santa Monica College, a junior college, coaching track. Carlos wound up at a Palm Springs high school after working with underprivileged youth in Los Angeles. Lifetime awards and giant statues on the San Jose State campus were so far in the future that, for most of their adult lives, it was just point-less to speculate on redemption.

A surprising number of the athletes from those Games did end up working with youth. Bob Beamon became a parks director in Florida and ran a foundation. Lee Evans got involved in coaching athletes in Africa, coming home between stints to coach at the University of South Alabama. None of them became famous, none rich. However they all behaved, they behaved consistently.

Harry Edwards, who was the most famous figure from the 1968 Olympics who was not actually at the 1968 Olympics, became a pro-fessor of sociology at the University of California, Berkeley, where his overflow classes contained an indefinite number of FBI agents. Edwards remained the go-to guy among journalists for any public explanation of race and its relationship to sports, but by then he was choosing scholarship over rabble-rousing. As years went by, and he entered the mainstream (he joined the San Francisco 49ers, hired by fellow San Jose State alumnus Bill Walsh as a sort of consultant), his natural personality—to the surprise of most who meet him he is both thoughtful and funny—began to betray his menacing bulk and dan-gerous rhetoric. Jay Silvester, who wanted to fight him on the spot at the Los Angeles Trials, eventually met him and liked him. In later years, Edwards and the FBI agent who shadowed him enjoyed regular lunch dates. That's how it was with Harry.

The Olympics are tough, even without the burden of proving one's case over a lifetime of good works. There is so little innocence available, and it is nearly impossible to do the right thing. By cruel design, they take the very best from around the world and transform all but a very few of them into losers. It is the comeuppance of all time, a vicious leveling. Jim Ryun, who thought he had run the race of his life, returned home to find his country felt left down. He appre-ciated it when Kenya's Kip Keino asked his forgiveness for his part in Ryun's national shame, but soon realized that nothing could ever make up for failure, not in this country.

So many of them would be haunted by second place, or running out of the medals, or just not qualifying. Phil Shinnick, who felt he was cheated out of an Olympic comeback at the South Lake Tahoe Trials, would have nightmares for the rest of his life, showing up at the stadium without shoes, without credentials, or just too late for the long jump. It doesn't seem anything should be that important but it is, every four years.

For Dick Fosbury, at least, it wasn't. His status as champion, coupled with his determined idiosyncrasy, made him a national hero of sorts. When he went home to Medford, they held a ticker-tape parade for him, but because there were no buildings over two stories tall, kids had to run alongside his car showering him with confetti. To his astonishment, there was demand for all things Fosbury, even beyond Oregon. He went on *The Tonight Show* and tried to teach Johnny Carson and fellow guest Bill Cosby how to do the flop (performing in dress shoes, he memorably slipped on his own try). He went on the *Dating Game*. But his heart wasn't in it. It wasn't even in the high jump anymore. He competed at Oregon State one more season, but it was a forced march, a satisfying of an obligation to his school. As soon as he completed the season, finally finding enough fire to win the NCAAs, he quit the sport and petitioned the engineering school for readmission. All he'd wanted in the first place was a degree in engineering.

Meanwhile, his buddy Gary Stenlund was still a long way from changing his life, literally cruising through the sixties in his VW camper, high as could be. He went seven years without cutting his hair, taking the camper on cross-country trips, Ken Kesey style, the van showing its psychedelic mileage in spray paint. One night in the seventies, "stoned and tripping," he rolled that van into an Ohio cornfield. There was nothing he could say to the cops that night, especially as he was nude, except for some black sheepskin. In later years, it must be reported, Stenlund sobered up, stayed sober, and returned to sports, but that was it for the camper.

There are enough images to remember the 1968 Olympics by, but let's not let it be a rolled VW camper, an upside-down and backward flop, or even gloved fists punching holes in Mexico City's twilight. How about this:

The day after the Closing Ceremony, as everybody gathered their belongings and wits, Harvard coxswain Paul Hoffman (yes, him!) was lounging in the lobby of the Hotel Reforma, waiting for his parents. It was all over, nothing to do but go home, await history's sentencing, but, in the meantime, here was Wilma Rudolph, the great Tigerbelle, coming at him. Rudolph hadn't competed since the 1960 Olympics, but she was still a force of nature, as much a personality now as performer before.

"Hey, Hoff," she said. "You speak Spanish, right?" Hoffman said he did (of course!), and Rudolph explained the situation. She was attending a party given by the Tobago-Jamaica track team and she needed a black bra that fastened in front. See, she was going to wear a black sleeveless dress. Hoffman stared at her, dumbfounded. He was a hard man to dumbfound, but she had done it. She needed him to translate for her as she shopped the boulevard's intimate-apparel departments. He stared at her a little more.

But Wilma Rudolph was no less persuasive since she'd hung up her spikes. She had no trouble dismissing a young Cassius Clay in Rome, way back in 1960, putting him in his place when he tried to woo her. She wasn't going to have much trouble with Hoffman, Harvard man or not. Like everybody else, Hoffman was going to do whatever she wanted.

And so the two of them—Hoffman, 5'7" tall and Rudolph, 5'11" plus 3 inches of Afro—went out on the Paseo de la Reforma, black bra shopping, ducking in and out of stores, giggling, covering their faces in mutual embarrassment, shaking their heads. Up and down they went, looking for that perfect bra, laughing now. It must have been a sight, two kids like that.

ACKNOWLEDGMENTS

Thanks to Mark Reiter, a full-service agent if there ever was one, for his ideas and enthusiasm. Thanks to Marty Beiser, my editor, who understood what I was trying to do, maybe even before I did.

And thanks to all the research librarians—at San Jose State, at the LA84 Foundation Sports Library, and at Topeka, too—who sprang into action on my behalf. Theirs was a constant reminder to dig just a little deeper.

Notes on Sources

Chapter 1: Roads to Glory

All the material came directly from interviews with George Foreman, Dick Fosbury, Madeline Manning, and John Carlos. Fosbury's high school classmate, Bill Enyart, was also interviewed.

Chapter 2: 1968

The year 1968 is one of the most thoroughly documented in U.S. and world history. Besides a number of 1968 retrospectives, including single-subject issues from both *Time* and *Newsweek*, several books were extremely helpful. Mark Kurlansky's *1968: The Year That Rocked the World* and Charles Kaiser's *1968 in America* were excellent resources.

Chapter 3: Speed City

Interviews with Bert Bonanno, Ed Burke, Lee Evans, and Art Simburg were helpful in fleshing out the eccentric Bud Winter and his Speed City track program. Tommie Smith's autobiography, *Silent Gesture*, contained some material on his time at San Jose State. Winter's several books were also useful, particularly *Relax and Win*. And *Sports Illustrated* ran several stories on Winter's program in the pre-Olympic years. Harry Edwards was also interviewed about his time as an undergraduate there. Details from his youth in East St. Louis came from various profiles of him, as well as an autobiography, *Revolt of the Black Athlete*. Urla Hill, who mounted an exhibit of photos and artifacts on Speed City, was also helpful.

Chapter 4: Countdown to Mexico

Jim Ryun was interviewed for this chapter, but his account was supplemented by a number of lengthy profiles from 1968, including pieces in the *New Yorker, Sports Illustrated, Life,* and *Sport*. Details on Bob Beamon's youth came from his autobiography, *The Man Who Could Fly*. Art Simburg was interviewed on the subjects of Tommie Smith and Wyomia Tyus. Smith's autobiography was again helpful.

Chapter 5: A Boycott

Harry Edwards was interviewed on the birth of the Olympic protest and his struggles through the Olympic year. There was, in addition, a lot of coverage of his movement in particular and the black athlete in general: Pete Axthelm, writing first in *Sports Illustrated*, then *Newsweek*, reported the subject vigorously in news stories throughout the summer, as well as in a *Newsweek* cover story, "The Angry Black Athlete." Jack Olsen's multipart series on the black athlete that appeared in *Sports Illustrated* in July was thought to be so inflammatory at the time that editors scheduled vacations the week of its publication. Amy Bass's book, *Not the Triumph But the Struggle,* was an enormous resource, for this chapter and several others. It is an exhaustively researched book on the 1968 Olympics and the transformation of the black athlete during that time. Accounts of the Harvard crew's involvement with OPHR were drawn from interviews with Paul Hoffman, Cleve Livingston, and their coach, Harry Parker. There was also a long story on the team that appeared in the *New Yorker* before the Olympics. HBO's 1999 documentary, *Fists of Freedom,* was an excellent resource as well.

Chapter 6: A Desperate Innovation

Dick Fosbury was interviewed for his role in the development of the flop. Berny Wagner, his coach at Oregon State, was interviewed. Bruce Quande, who stumbled upon a kind of flop before Fosbury, was also interviewed. Dr. Jesus Dapena, a professor of kinesiology at Indiana University (and a one-time high jumper), provided much of the event's history and its science.

Chapter 7: The Trials

Interviews with Jim Ryun, Dick Fosbury, Bob Seagren, Phil Shinnick, George Foreman, Mel Pender, and Madeline Manning set the stage for the Olympic Trials, in their various venues. HBO's *Fists of Freedom* contains footage of the South Lake Tahoe site and really does show runners disappearing behind trees. Payton Jordan, the men's Olympic track-and-field coach, was interviewed on the site selection. Accounts of Bill Bowerman's involvement at South Lake Tahoe are drawn from Kenny Moore's book, *Bowerman and the Men of Oregon.* Gary Stenlund provided the account of his run-in with Bowerman. Bob Beamon's gambling escapade came from his autobiography.

Chapter 8: Denver

Lee Evans and Mel Pender provided accounts of the athletes' final meeting to decide on a form of Olympic protest. Paul Hoffman described his meeting with Olympic officials. George Foreman described his meeting with Nixon officials.

Chapter 9: Mexico City

TAFNOT 68, a small pamphlet put out by *Track & Field News* for its tour members, detailed living conditions at Villa Coapa. There was scant coverage of the massive student movement in Mexico at the time, the exception being the *New York Times* accounts that summer. The paper's bureau chief in Mexico City, Henry Giniger, proved to be a reliable source, keeping abreast of the riots. As for the massacre of students at the Tlatelolco housing project, there was very little original reporting. Research over the years has filled in many gaps; it can be found in such books as Mark Kurlansky's *1968*, Kevin B. Witherspoon's *Before the Eyes of the World*, and Amy Bass's *Not the Triumph But the Struggle*. All cables from the CIA and the State Department were made available by the National Security Archive, a nongovernmental research institute that publishes and catalogues declassified documents it acquires through the Freedom of Information Act.

Chapter 10: Opening Ceremony

Gary Stenlund and Dick Fosbury were interviewed for their accounts of the Opening Ceremony, Hal Connolly for his. Art Simburg was interviewed about his time in a Mexican jail. Background on the Dassler family feud comes from Barbara Smit's book, *Sneaker Wars*.

Chapter 11: And They're Off

Jay Silvester and Ed Burke were interviewed for their remembrances of Al Oerter. Mel Pender provided the account of the 100-meter race.

Chapter 12: Protest

John Carlos was interviewed on his experiences at East Texas State and his eventual transfer to San Jose State. Tommie Smith's account of his 200-meter race was drawn from his autobiography, *Silent Gesture*, and many other accounts, including a BBC documentary done in 2008 and HBO's *Fists of Freedom*. Carlos and Smith have given different accounts over the years explaining the selection of tokens, and which man provided them. This is the more-accepted version. Paul Hoffman's firsthand account of Peter Norman's involvement, which also is subject to different versions, is the most reliable.

Chapter 13: Harder and Higher

George Foreman and Bob Seagren were interviewed. Seagren's gold-medal-winning vault was well-chronicled in the press.

Chapter 14: Aftershocks

John Carlos was interviewed on the protest aftermath. Tommie Smith's account of phone calls from Olympic officials came from his autobiography, *Silent Gesture*. Harold Connolly was interviewed on the white athletes' reaction to Smith's and Carlos's ouster. Lee Evans, Bert Bonanno and Art Simburg were interviewed on Evans's prerace distractions. Evans provided the account of USOC president Doug Roby's warning on the way to the race. He also provided the anecdote about racing in Europe, where he cashed checks under the name Jesse Owens. Paul Hoffman and his coach, Harry Parker, were interviewed about their "hearing" on the eve of the rowing finals. Phil Shinnick and Ralph Boston were interviewed on Bob Beamon's world-record long jump. Some details of Beamon's preparations were drawn from his autobiography, *The Man Who Could Fly*.

Chapter 15: Monday

Jim Ryun was interviewed on his Olympic preparation, but extensive accounts of his comeback from mononucleosis appeared in the *New Yorker, Sports Illustrated,* and *Life* magazine. Rich Clarkson, a journalist who became Ryun's friend, provided accounts of the media mob in Mexico City. Madeline Manning was interviewed on her race and Tigerbelle lore. Mel Pender provided background on the relays. Ed Caruthers, Dick Fosbury, and his coach, Berny Wagner, were interviewed on the high jump event.

Chapter 16: Week Two

Debbie Meyer was interviewed on her Olympic experiences. Accounts of Vera Caslavska's snub on the podium come from many sources but snippets of video from ABC's coverage can be easily found; her reaction to the Russian national anthem after winning gold in the all-around is one of them.

Chapter 17: Pappy's Boys

George Foreman and Ronnie Harris were interviewed on the boxing finals. Foreman's insistence that his postfight flag-waving was meant as a jab at international judging, and not John Carlos's and Tommie Smith's protest, flies in the face of Olympic lore. Yet, while Foreman was indeed conservative and by then extremely patriotic, he was more tightly bound to his teammates, not just the fellow boxers he felt had been robbed of decisions but Smith and Carlos as well, than his country.

Chapter 18: Going Home

Ed Fox of *Track & Field News* described the tour group's final banquet. Others interviewed: Dick Fosbury, Gary Stenlund, Mel Pender, George Foreman, John Carlos, Ralph Boston, Lee Evans, Harry Edwards, Jim Ryun, and Phil Shinnick. Paul Hoffman provided a copy of the letter Doug Roby sent to Harry Parker. Marathoner Kenny Moore, who went on to a writing career, did an excellent series of stories on Tommie Smith and John Carlos, detailing their post-Olympic travails.

INDEX

ABC, 161, 176, 177, 208, 216, 223–25
Adidas, 92, 125–28, 188, 228
African Americans:
  as athletes, *see specific athletes*
  discrimination and racism against,
    17–18, 26, 28, 162
  housing for, 24, 87
  income of, 17, 93
  Olympic boycott of, 51–68, 85, 87,
    99–101, 149, 153–62, 222, 229
  Olympic protests of, 153–62, 175,
    188, 216
  in war, 17
Agee, Philip, 111
Alcindor, Lew, 55, 61, 164, 222–23
Alexe, Ion, 228
Ali, Muhammad (Cassius Clay), 17,
  56–57, 96, 177, 245
Allen, Lucius, 222
American Basketball Association (ABA),
  222
Arizon, Paul, 71
Arledge, Roone, 177, 216
Army, U.S., 79–80, 150, 166, 242
Axthelm, Pete, 59–60, 67, 160

Babka, Rink, 87, 143, 144
Baden-Baden, 104
Bailes, Margaret, 92
Bambini, Giorgio, 228
Bannister, Roger, 39, 199
Barbour, Ralph Henry, 40, 93
Basilio, Norma Enriqueta, 120, 136
basketball, 71, 222–23
BBC, 177, 199
Beamon, Bob, 42–45, 58–59, 61, 88,
  167, 183–88, 243
  BYU incident and, 45
  childhood of, 42–44
  inconsistency of, 45
  protest of, 194
  revoked school scholarship of, 61
  world record set by, 185–86
Beamon, Melvina, 184

Beconta, 127
Beer, Klaus, 188
Bell, Wade, 198
Benson, Dean, 73
Berlin Olympic Games (1936), 57, 125,
  191
Big Lois, 6
Biwott, Amos, 200
Black Panthers, 53–54
Bonanno, Bert, 106–7, 110, 116, 160, 161
  as spy for CIA, 110–11
Bonanno, Betty, 24
Boston, Ralph, 45, 57, 60, 61, 92, 128,
  183, 185–88, 194, 242
Boulter, John, 142
Bowerman, Bill, 83, 84, 85, 86
boxing, 92–97, 163–69, 227–33
boycotts:
  of 1968 Olympic Games, 51–68, 85,
    99–101, 151, 153, 156, 163–64,
    222, 229, 238
  of NY Athletic Club meet, 56, 58,
    149, 184
  see also Olympic Project for Human
    Rights
Brando, Marlon, 15
Brigham Young University (BYU), 45,
  61, 184
Brill, Debbie, 75
Brill bend, 75
Broadus, Charles "Doc," 94–97, 168–69
Brooklyn Dodgers, 71
Brown, Jim, 93, 242
Brown, Reynaldo, 90–91, 211
Brumel, Valery, 77, 211
Brundage, Avery, 60, 62, 81, 108, 109,
  111, 149, 153, 159, 192, 195, 229,
  232–33, 240, 241–42
  as head of IOC, 57, 104, 130, 178,
    239
Burghley, Lord David, 151
Burke, Ed, 83, 106, 145–46, 192
Burton, Mike, 218–20, 221
Bush, Jim, 46

Cal Poly Pomona, 131
Carlos, John, *iv*, 9–10, 34–35, 55, 102,
    127, 135–36, 153–54, 155–57,
    158–62, 192, 241
  gambling schemes of, 84
  as known wild man, 48, 155
  post-Olympics life of, 242
  protest of, 153, 161–62, 168, 176–77,
    194, 206, 229
  suspension from Olympics of, 175,
    179–80, 185, 189, 227
  world record set by, 89
Carlos, Kim, 160, 242
Carson, Johnny, 244
Caruthers, Ed, 57, 90–91, 207–8,
    210–12, 214
Caslavska, Vera, 136, 203–4, 224–25
Castro, Fidel, 111
Chavoor, Sherm, 218–19
Chepulis, Ionas, 227, 231–32
Chevalier, Maurice, 108
Chicago American, 179
Chicago Tribune, 56, 176, 179
CIA, 110–11, 113–14, 115
Civil Rights Act (1964), 16
Clark, Henry, 96
Clark, Robert, 53–54
Clarke, Ron, 139–40, 141–42, 200
Clay, Cassius (Muhammad Ali), 17,
    56–57, 96, 177, 245
Cleveland Division of Recreation Track
    Club, 8
coaches, suspicious activities of, 110–11
Columbia University, 15
Comité Anti-Olímpico de Subversión, 113
Connolly, Harold, 122–24, 131, 143,
    178–79, 181
Connolly, Olga Fikotova, 122, 124
Cornell University, 28, 53
Cosby, Bill, 244
Cosell, Howard, 161, 176–77, 182, 209,
    216
Council on Youth Fitness, 8
Cultural Olympiad, 108
Cummings, Candy, 71
Cunningham, Glenn, 39

Daily Mirror, 44
Daley, Arthur, 60, 135, 136, 161, 236,
    239–40
Danek, Ludvik, 144

Dassler, Adolf, 124–26, 130
Dassler, Armin, 128, 129, 173–74
Dassler, Horst, 126, 127, 128, 129
Dassler, Rudolf, 124–26, 130
Dating Game, 244
Davies, Lynn, 185–88
Davis, Iris, 167
Davis, Steve, 4–5, 6, 72, 74
Deford, Frank, 48
de Gaulle, Charles, 16, 113
Denver, Colo., 99–102
de Varona, Donna, 45
Dianabol, 131, 132, 135
Díaz Ordaz, Gustavo, 112–15, 240
  "Strategy Committee" of, 114
Dooley, H. Kay, 131–32
Dow Chemical Company, 56
draft notices, 32–33, 34
drugs, 130–32
drug testing, 132, 238
Dylan, Bob, 164

East Texas State University, 34, 155,
    156, 175
Ebony, 58
Echeverria, Luis, 114
Echo Summit, 81–82, 86
Edwards, Harry, 25–29, 30, 48, 67–68,
    113, 154, 160, 164, 192
  academics of, 27–28
  Olympic boycott and, 53–62, 67, 85,
    99–100, 149, 151, 222
  post-Olympics life of, 243
  rhetoric of, 55, 156, 243
  Winter and, 28–29
Edward VII, King of England, 123
Eldorado National forest, 81–82
Elliott, Herb, 39
El Sol de México, 115
Enyart, Bill, 4–6
European Track and Field
    Championships, 130
Evans, Art, 181
Evans, Lee, 33–34, 46–47, 55, 59, 67–
    68, 85, 160, 161, 188–94, 243
  death threats received by, 206
  draft notice received by, 34
  Olympic boycott and, 67, 100, 154
  protest of, 206–7
  in races with Smith, 46, 47–48
  technique used by, 193
  world record set by, 89

Family Weekly, 109
Ferenczy, Alex, 8, 9
Ferrell, Barbara, 92, 128, 203
Figuerola, Enrique, 205
Finnegan, Christopher, 228
Flagstaff, Ariz., 41–42, 197–98
Flores, Jose, 106–7
Foreman, George, 93–97
   aggressive manner of, 2, 3, 94–95
   boxing education of, 95
   childhood of, 1–4
   in Nixon campaign, 101
   on Olympic boycott, 101, 164
   Olympic protest and, 101, 164, 241
   Olympics and, 166–68, 227–28, 229,
     230–32
   at Olympic Trials, 97
Fosbury, Dick, 70, 72–80
   changing style of, 7
   first competition of, 6
   jumping technique of, 73, 176
   at Olympic Games, 208–14
   Olympic Trials and, 82, 90–91
   post-Olympics life of, 244
   practice jumps avoided by, 209
   scholarship of, 76
   Stenlund's friendship with, 119,
     120–21, 137, 208, 209, 237
   teenage years of, 4–7, 70, 72
   on *Track & Field News* cover, 78–79
Fosbury flop, 70, 74, 75–78, 211, 212
Fox, Ed, 107–8, 133
Frazier, Joe, 165
Freeman, Ron, 180, 192, 194, 206
Fresno City College, 26

Gammoudi, Mohamed, 141, 200
Garagiola, Joe, 61, 164, 222
Gault, Henry "Pappy," 163, 164–65,
   166, 167, 228, 230
Gavrilov, Valentin, 209–10, 211
gender testing, 130
Germany, 16
Glimp, Fred, 182
Gordien, Fortune, 144
Grants Pass, Oreg., 6–7, 73, 93
Greene, Charlie, 57, 85, 148, 149,
   150–51, 205, 218
Gregory, Dick, 51
Grimsley, Will, 198
Grudzien, Josef, 229, 231

Gustavson, Linda, 219
gymnastics, 224–25

Harris, Ronnie, 166, 228–31, 233
Hartfield, John, 90–91
Harvard crew, 62–67, 92, 181–82, 195,
   242
   Olympic suits of, 101
   personalized letters of, 67
Hary, Armin, 126–27
Hawthorne, Jesse, 175
Hayes, Bob, 46, 57, 127, 149, 151
Hayes, Elvin, 222
Hayes, Lester, 2
Haywood, Spencer, 223
Hells Angels, 53–54
Hemery, Dave, 142
Hempe, Carl, 94
Hendrix, Jimi, 188
Henne, Jan, 220
Hester House gang, 2, 3
Hickox, Charles, 221
high jump, 71
   at 1968 Olympics, 207–14
   Olympic Trials and, 82
   styles of, 6, 70–79
Hines, Jim, 58, 85, 148, 149, 150–51,
   205, 241
Hitler, Adolf, 57
Hoffman, Paul, 101–2, 160, 165, 181–
   83, 245
Horine, George, 72
Hotel El Diplomático, 175, 177, 179
housing:
   discrimination in, 24, 87
   at 1968 Olympics, 103, 117, 145,
     199
   at San Jose State, 24, 53–54, 68
Houston, Tex., 1–2, 93, 95, 222, 241
   Fifth Ward of, 1, 2, 4, 93, 95, 97, 241

Iba, Henry, 222–23
Inman, Stu, 26
International Olympic Committee
   (IOC), 18, 57, 59–60, 104, 130,
   132, 178–80, 236, 239, 242

Jamaica High School, 44–45
James, Larry, 100, 189, 192, 193–94,
   206
Jet Start (Winter), 32

Jipcho, Ben, 201
Job Corps, 93–96, 164
Johnson, Dennis, 30
Johnson, Lyndon B., 14
Johnson, Owen, 40
Johnson, Rafer, 57
Jones, Al, 228
Jordan, Payton, 83, 85, 88–89, 145, 200, 237
Junior Olympics, 44

Kansas, University of, 40–41, 198
Keino, Kip, 140, 199, 201–2, 243
Kennedy, Jackie, 173, 180
Kennedy, John F., 8, 15
Kennedy, Robert, 16
King, Martin Luther, Jr., 16, 17, 55, 56, 60–61, 149, 156
Kruse, Pam, 220

Labadie, Enrique, 116
Latynina, Larissa, 224
Leave It to Beaver, 43
Lemoore High School, 31
Life, 40, 49, 126, 169, 173, 218, 220
Lipsyte, Robert, 106, 175
Liston, Sonny, 96–97
Little Olympics, 81
London Olympic Games:
    of 1908, 123
    of 1948, 141
long jump, 44–45, 87–88, 182–88
Look, 40
Los Alamos Olympic Trials, 91–92
Los Angeles Olympic Trials, 42, 82, 85–86, 88, 90, 208, 243
Los Angeles Times, 78, 82–83, 139, 161, 173, 176, 212, 223

McGuire, Edith, 202, 203
McKay, Jim, 88, 108, 225
Macombs Dam Park, 10
Major League Baseball, 71
Malcolm X, 53
"Manifesto of 2000 Words," 204, 224–25
Manning, Madeline, 8–9, 92, 133, 203–5
Marbley, Harlan, 165–66
Matthews, Vince, 206
Mays, Charlie, 88–89, 186–87
Medford, Oreg., 4–5, 244

Medford Mail-Tribune, 74
Melbourne Olympic Games (1956), 122, 143–44, 200, 217
Mexico City:
    1968 Olympics awarded to, 104, 109
    student demonstrations in, 111–17, 133
Mexico City Olympic Games (1968), *see* Olympic Games of 1968, Mexico City
Meyer, Debbie, 49, 218–20, 229
Miller, Lennox, 151
Mills, Billy, 87
Missoulian, 7
Modesto Relays, 34, 87
mononucleosis, 41–42
Montecito Country Club, 57
Moore, Kenny, 84, 213–14, 239
Morley, Jefferson, 114
Mormon Tabernacle Choir, 108
Morrow, Bobby, 126
Munich Olympic Games (1972), 242
Muniz, Armando, 166
Muñoz, Felipe, 220
Murphy, Audie, 19
Murray, Jim, 139–40, 141, 146, 147, 176, 212
Musburger, Brent, 179

National AAU Tournament, 96, 97
National Conference of the Associated Student Government, 56
National Conference on Black Power, 67
National Junior Championships, 76
National Mobilization Committee to End the War in Vietnam (Mobe), 15
NBC, 216, 223
NCAA, 55, 79, 222, 244
    Championships of, 33, 80, 208
New Oakland Boxing Club, 96
New Republic, 112
Newsweek, 40, 49, 67, 160
New York Athletic Club (NYAC), 56, 57, 58, 149, 184
New Yorker, 40, 41, 92, 105, 108, 136, 182, 216
New York Pioneer Club, 10
New York Times, 60, 92, 105, 106, 116, 135, 161, 164, 175, 176, 236, 239

New York Times Sunday Magazine, 54
Nikolic, Vera, 203, 204
Nixon, Richard, 101
Noel, Ken, 53, 59
Nordwig, Wolfgang, 172–73
Norman, Peter, *iv*, 157, 159, 160
North Carolina Agricultural and
    Technical College, 45
Norton, Ray, 23–24, 30
Notre Dame University, 71
Nurmi, Paavo, 39

Oakland, Calif., 32, 94, 95, 168
Oakland Indoor Games, 78
Oakland Tribune, 96, 97
O'Brian, Hugh, 237
O'Brien, Parry, 123, 124
Oda, Mikio, 190
Odlozil, Josef, 204
Oerter, Al, 85, 87, 143–47, 239
Olympic Coordination Authority, 107
Olympic Games, 55, 62
    Adidas-Puma wars in, 126–30
    Closing Ceremony of, 235–40, 245
    feel-good stories of, 37
    of 1908, London, 123
    of 1924, Paris, 140
    of 1936, Berlin, 57, 125, 191
    of 1948, London, 141
    of 1956, Melbourne, 122, 143–44,
        200, 217
    of 1960, Rome, 30, 49, 72, 122, 126,
        144, 203, 217, 245
    of 1964, Tokyo, 19, 40, 51, 72, 86,
        87, 88, 104, 110, 122, 123, 127,
        131, 142, 143, 144, 145, 149, 165,
        183–84, 185, 202, 207, 216, 217,
        224, 235–36
    of 1972, 242
    Opening Ceremony of, 13, 107–8,
        113, 119–37, 139, 165, 180, 237
    as star-making machine, 38–39
    steroid use in, 130–32
    VIP treatment of athletes of, 121
    see also International Olympic
        Committee; United States
        Olympic Committee
Olympic Games of 1968, Mexico City,
    14, 18, 37–38, 39, 67, 103–17,
    122, 124, 160, 198–214
    Adidas-Puma war in, 127–30

basketball in, 222–23
boxing in, 227–33
boycott and, 51–68, 85, 99–101, 153
Closing Ceremony in, 235–40, 245
collapsed runners in, 139–40, 141,
    142
gymnastics in, 224–25
high altitude as issue in, 81, 82, 86,
    109, 139–41, 197, 200, 213, 215,
    228, 237
high jump in, 207–14
housing issues at, 103, 117, 145, 199
long jump in, 183–88
nations' parade in, 134–35
Olympic Stadium of, 120, 133–34,
    150, 185, 199, 201, 210, 235
Olympic torch ceremony in, 120, 136
Olympic Village of, *see* Olympic
    Village, Mexico City
Opening Ceremony in, 107–8, 113,
    119–37, 139, 165, 237
Organizing Committee of, 106, 109
preparation for, 104–6, 132–33
protest during, 153–62, 175, 188,
    206, 216
security at, 133
steroid use in, 131–32
swimming in, 217–21
track and field in, 79, 139–51, 197–
    214, 215, 236–37
unfinished construction for, 106, 117
VIP treatment of athletes at, 121
Olympic Project for Human Rights
    (OPHR), 56–57, 59, 60, 91, 140,
    149–50, 163, 184, 191
    buttons of, 101–2, 159, 160, 229
    see also boycotts
Olympic Trials, 97, 144, 145, 217, 219,
    222
    Los Alamos, 91–92
    Los Angeles, 42, 82, 85–86, 88, 90,
        150, 208, 243
    South Lake Tahoe, 42, 61, 81–91,
        119, 131–32, 150, 157, 172, 184,
        189, 193, 206, 208, 244
    urine testing at, 84
Olympic Village, Mexico City, 106, 108,
    111, 115, 120, 129, 130, 133, 140,
    142, 167, 168–69, 173–74, 177,
    178, 180, 183, 184, 189, 199, 204,
    205, 210, 216, 227, 229

Onassis, Aristotle, 173, 180
Oregon State University (OSU), 76, 77, 91, 209, 244
Owens, Jesse, 57, 62, 125, 178–79, 180, 187, 191
Ozzie & Harriet, 43

Papanicolaou, Christos, 172
Parker, Harry, 181, 182, 242
Patrick, David, 83, 86, 90
Paul, Robert, 101–2
Paul VI, Pope, 14
Pender, Mel, 18–19, 92, 100, 102, 148, 149–50, 151, 160, 161, 205, 240
Plaza de Las Tres Culturas, 114–15
Pleasanton, Calif., 94, 95
pole vault, 170–73, 176
Police Athletic League, 44
Portuguese Tables, 187
Press, Irina, 130–31
Press, Tamara, 130–31
P.S. 622 (New York, N.Y.), 43–44
"Psychology for Aviators and Athletes," 22
Puma, 89, 92, 125–30, 161, 169, 173, 203
Pyramid of the Moon, 120

Quande, Bruce, 75

race relations, 16–19, 24, 243
racism, 26, 28, 149, 155, 162, 233, 238
Reagan, Ronald, 53–54, 56, 58
Redden, Arthur, 166
relaxation, 22, 24, 28, 32, 89, 147, 158, 190, 191, 193
riots, 16–17
   in Detroit, 16
   in France, 15–16, 113
   in Los Angeles, 16
   in Mexico City, 111–16, 133
   in Newark, 16
Robinson, Albert, 165–66, 167, 228, 230–31, 232
Robinson, Jackie, 71
Roby, Douglas, 62, 178, 180, 181–82, 192, 207, 236, 242
Rogers, Ray, 163
Roldan, Antonio, 230
Romary, Janice, 124, 135
Rome Olympic Games (1960), 30, 49, 72, 122, 126, 144, 203, 217, 245

Rose, Ralph, 123
ROTC, 33, 47, 149, 154, 242
Route of Friendship, 108
rowing, 62–63, 181, 195
Rudolph, Wilma, 45, 48–49, 245
Ryun, Jim, 39–42, 43, 49, 197–202, 243
   background of, 40
   mononucleosis of, 41–42, 198
   as Olympics poster boy, 39
   at Olympic Trials, 89–90
   training of, 197–98
   USOC dispensation for, 42

Sadler, Dick, 96
St. Olaf College, 75–76
San Francisco All-American Games, 78
San Francisco Golden Gloves tournament, 95
San Jose City College, 33
San Jose Mercury News, 176
San Jose State College, 21–24, 25, 27, 30–31, 34, 46, 47, 56, 89, 106, 110, 127–28, 153–58, 172, 242, 243
   segregation at, 24, 26–27, 53–54
Saturday Evening Post, 54
Schiprowski, Claus, 171, 172–73
Schollander, Don, 217, 218, 221
Schul, Bob, 86
scissors jump, 6, 71, 72, 75
Scott, Jarvis, 128
Scott, Winston, 114, 115–16
Seagren, Bob, 83–84, 86–87, 89, 169–74, 176, 218
Shinnick, Phil, 87–89, 184, 243–44
Silvester, Jay, 131, 142–43, 145–47, 243
Simburg, Art, 30, 31, 34–35, 49, 92, 124, 155
   Puma and, 128, 129, 203
   Smith's friendship with, 32–33, 157
   as unofficial recruiter, 33
Simpson, O. J., 34
Skvortsov, Valery, 211
Smit, Barbara, 126
Smith, Denise, 159, 160
Smith, Red, 179, 180
Smith, Ronnie Ray, 148, 205
Smith, Tommie, *iv*, 30–33, 34, 46–48, 59, 153–57, 158–62, 241
   increasing activism of, 48
   injury of, 157–58

Olympic boycott and, 51–52, 55, 56, 100, 153–54
post-Olympics life of, 242
protest of, 153, 161–62, 168, 176–77, 194, 206
racing Lee, 46, 47–48
Simburg's friendship with, 32–33, 157
sunglasses of, 32
suspension from Olympics of, 175, 179–80, 185, 189, 227
threats received by, 157
trademark acceleration of, 46
as Winter's favorite, 47
world records held by, 46, 89
Sneaker Wars (Smit), 126
Snider, Anne, 41, 199
South Africa, 56, 59–60
South Lake Tahoe Olympic Trials, 42, 61, 81–91, 119, 131–32, 184, 189, 208, 244
Southern Rhodesia, 56
Spain, Ken, 223
Speed City, *see* San Jose State College
spinal meningitis, 8
Spitz, Mark, 217, 218–19, 221
spondylolisthesis, 86
Sport, 42, 208
Sports Illustrated, 40, 42, 47, 49, 59, 67, 86, 87, 89, 92, 97, 105, 116, 132, 150, 160, 179, 199, 216, 220, 221, 230, 241
Sputnik, 38
State Department, U.S., 110, 113–14, 129
Stenlund, Gary, 84–85, 119–21, 136–37, 208, 209, 237, 244
steroids, 130–32
straddle jump, 72, 76–77
student demonstrations, 15, 154–55, 238
in France, 15–16, 113
in Mexico City, 111–17, 133
Student Nonviolent Coordinating Committee (SNCC), 15
Students for a Democratic Society (SDS), 15, 182
swimming, 217–21

TAFNOT (*Track & Field News* Olympic Tour), 107, 108, 117, 236–37

Tartan track, 81–82, 185, 186, 239
Temple, Ed, 49, 203
Temu, Naftali, 141, 200
Tennessee State University, 48–49, 128, 202, 203
Teotihuacán, Mexico, 120
Ter-Ovanesyan, Igor, 87–88, 185, 187, 188
Tet Offensive, 15
Texas, University of, at El Paso (UTEP), 45, 53, 59, 60–61, 184
Texas Relays, 60–61
Thomas, John, 58
Thorpe, Jim, 96
Tigerbelles, 32, 48–49, 91–92, 101, 102, 128, 133, 202–5, 245
Time, 179
Timmons, Bob, 40, 41
Today, 61, 222
Tokyo Olympic Games (1964), 19, 40, 51, 72, 86, 87, 88, 104, 110, 122, 123, 127, 131, 142, 143, 144, 145, 149, 165, 183–84, 185, 202, 207, 216, 217, 224, 235–36
Tonight Show, 244
Topeka Capital-Journal, 41
Toronto Maple Leaf Games, 8
Track & Field News, 57–58, 78–79, 82, 84, 87, 133, 150, 156, 199, 212, 236
Track & Field News Olympic Tour (TAFNOT), 107, 108, 117, 236–37
Trela, Lucjan, 167–68, 227
Tribune of Honor, 135
Trinidad, 10
triple jump, 77
"Triumph and Tragedy at Tahoe," 87
Trusenov, Vladimir, 144
Tyus, Wyomia, 32, 48–49, 91–92, 101, 124, 128, 129, 202–3, 205, 206

Unitas, Johnny, 93
United States, 14–15
defense spending of, 17
Mexican embassy of, 111
Olympic coaches from, 110, 200
Olympic flag dipping refusal of, 123–24, 180
race relations in, 16–19, 24

United States Olympic Committee
    (USOC), 42, 56, 57, 61–62, 67,
    81–87, 101, 111, 122, 160, 177–
    83, 192, 206–7, 236, 242
Unseld, Wes, 222

Vanderstock, Jeff, 169–70, 173
Vaslov, Yuri, 123
Vaughn, Jon, 83
Vietnam War, 14–15, 16, 17, 19, 79–80,
    88, 149, 240–41
Villa Coapa, 103, 117, 199
Voting Rights Act (1965), 16

Waddell, Tom, 181
Wagner, Berny, 76–78, 91, 209
Walker, Art, 57, 180
Wallington, James, 166
Walsh, Bill, 243
Warren, Mike, 222
Washington, University of, 87
Washington Post, 114, 176, 181
Wenden, Mike, 221
Western Region Black Youth
    Conference, 55–56
Western roll, 6, 72

Westmoreland, William, 15
White, JoJo, 223
Wind, Herbert Warren, 42
Winter, Helen, 24, 35, 47
Winter, Lloyd "Bud," 21–24, 25, 26,
    31–32, 33–35, 47, 89, 154, 172
    Bonanno as disciple of, 106, 110
    books on running of, 23
    coaching techniques of, 22–24
    deferment letters written by, 33
    as eccentric, 190
    Edwards and, 28–29
    at 1968 Olympic Games, 158, 160,
        161, 189–91, 192–93
    scholarship splitting by, 29, 30
    Smith as favorite of, 47
Wolde, Mamo, 141, 213
Wolfe, Vern, 170
World University Games, 51
Wright, Stan, 62, 67, 157–58, 192

Yates, Dorothy Hazeltine, 22
Young, George, 199, 200

Zhabotinsky, Leonid, 123, 135, 239
Zolov, Eric, 104

Breinigsville, PA USA
17 February 2011
255807BV00002B/2/P

9 780803 236295